# The
# Grail Seeker's
# Companion

# The Grail Seeker's Companion

## A Guide to the Grail Quest
## in the
## Aquarian Age

John Matthews & Marian Green

Illustrations by Chesca Potter

THOTH PUBLICATIONS
Loughborough, Leicestershire

A CIP catalogue record for this book is available from the
British Library.

Cover design by Bob Eames

Printed and bound in Great Britain

Published by Thoth Publications
64, Leopold Street, Loughborough, LE11 5DN

ISBN 1 870450 49 3
web address: www.thoth.co.uk
email: enquiries@thoth.co.uk

# Dedication

This book is dedicated to all the Seekers of the
Aquarian Grail,
to all the Companions on the Inner Quest,
to all the Sustainers of the Sacred Mythology,
in word and deed.
May they accomplish their True Will.

For the Helpers, Inner and Outer


'Let not him who seeks cease until he finds,
and when he finds he shall be astonished'.

*Gospel of Thomas*

# Acknowledgements

We should like to thank all the friends and colleagues who aided and abetted us in various ways throughout the writing of this book, and before that over a number of years of conversation and exploration. In particular thanks go to Caitlin Matthews for helpful suggestions on Qabalistic topics, for allowing us to quote liberally from her work on the *Preiddeu Annwn*, and for her part in the meditation entitled *To the Castle of the Grail* and *The Procession of the Grail*. Jerry Ozaniec came to our aid at a late date regarding matters of gematria, and placed his formidable knowledge at our disposal. Murray Hawtin gave valuable pointers about Arthurian heraldry, and others helped us test-drive the various exercises with scarcely a blink. To Peter Lamborne Wilson for so much encouragement. To all of those named, and to Bob Stewart, Basil and Roma Wilby, the late, great Dick Swettenham, and all the gang, we send a big thank you. Not forgetting Chesca Potter, who rose to the occasion with a will and produced inspired illustrations from our own inadequate thoughts and actually seemed to enjoy it all! Thanks also to Tom Clarke for giving this one a new lease of life.

J.M. & M.G.
Oxford and Bristol, 2003

# Contents

# Preface 2003 Edition

Since we wrote this book in 1988 much has been written about the Grail, though no new theories of any great importance have been set forward. What is true, however, is the continued interest in the concept and symbolism of the sacred vessel, which continues to be sought by countless people who set out on their own personal quest.

Over the years both authors have taught the mysteries of the Grail to many hundreds of students, and we have been consistently astonished by the depth of insight and perception possessed by these dedicated people. It is thus a great pleasure that we see this new, fully revised and updated edition of the Grail Seekers Companion once again made available to the public. We have had many requests for this book over the years, and are grateful to Thoth Publications for giving us the opportunity to bring this about. We would like to dedicate it to all those students, now and in the future, who continue to share the path of the Grail with us.

J.M. & M.G.
Oxford and Bristol, 2003

# Introduction

The origin of any symbol is not something which can be traced to a given point in time or space. This is no less true where the Grail is concerned, and despite many attempts to fasten such a label upon it, it has resisted them all.

There are those who subscribe to the belief in a Celtic Grail, a Cauldron which holds the secrets of life and death and promises food for all comers. Others prefer the Christian interpretation which identifies the Grail with the chalice of the Eucharist or the vessel in which some of Christ's blood was collected. Still others seek an emerald from the crown of Lucifer, the Light-Bringer, which fell to earth during the war in Heaven that ended with the rebel angel's descent into our own sphere.

Whatever one's personal choice the goal is consistent: the Grail is a life-enhancer, bringing change and enlightenment to those who seek it, offering gifts sometimes greater than those sought, sometimes lesser. And, as with all such more-than-ordinary objects, the search is often long and hard, taking in many by-ways of human experience.

Let us suppose, then, that you, the reader, are about to set out upon such a quest. What would you need to know that might improve your chances of success? How would you start, and who, or what, would you be likely to meet along the way? In this book we have tried to supply at least some answers to these questions - only some because no one can give them all - and to suggest some practical ways in which the knowledge gained thereby can be applied to daily life, thus indicating what, in fact, the relevance of the Grail search might be for us now.

We have tried to make this a guide-book not just to places, but also to people, stories, theories - a reference book of Grail-ology, including history, ritual, meditation, advice and instruction. In short, it considers everything you are likely to need before you set out on the most important adventure of your life - an adventure requiring dedication, determination, a good deal of common sense, and an ability to delve deeply into strange and arcane mysteries. It will not be easy.

To every journey there must be a purpose, and this is true also of the Grail Quest, but because this venture can take you through many worlds and different levels of experience, what is brought back may not be physical in substance. In many ways, this is the key to the whole matter. In modern times there has been much thought, writing and television exposure about a physical treasure with holy or antique value. We are, sadly, living in a materialist society where people are judged by the size of their house, car and bank balance, not their spiritual worth. The inner values, which cannot be counted on computers or classified in their files, defy this kind of thinking and so are seemingly worthless.

The Grail Quest is an attempt to rebalance this. Certainly it is possible that the quest might lead to wealth, to fame, to material success, but these will be side-effects, the shadow of the real quest. If you look only for material riches that is all you can possibly gain, and it will cost you just as much effort, patience and dedication, whereas if you seek the inner reality of the spiritual quest you will win the spiritual prize which 'moth and rust cannot corrupt, nor thieves steal'. There is no easy way to explain the value or even the concept of gifts of the spirit, except to say that they are the hardest to obtain, and cannot be bought - love, honour, peace, healing, joy and inspiration. Some of them might appear to be for sale, but those which can be bought are shells of the real thing, for true love, honour and so on are all gifts of the spirit.

We met someone recently who had joined a course of instruction in America, and as a sort of graduation ceremony all participants who chose to do so were able to walk along a twelve-foot fire pit. They had overcome their fears in life and transformed them into a different mode, and it was intended that they should then go away and be better car salesmen or clerks or accountants! What a waste of spiritual experience! What a limitation of a life-changing experience which could turn ordinary folk into saviours of the world, healers of the Waste Land - but in that materialistic set-up the only

Fig. 1: The Shapes of the Grail

goal was to achieve a larger bank balance! Everyone has vast potential to succeed at the seemingly impossible, to draw on strengths both physical and mental. We have all seen the newspaper reports of mothers who have lifted cars off their injured or trapped children, or of people who have swum great distances or endured enormous hardship in war, famine and disaster - that potential can be used to bring us greater results not merely in the material world but on the true quest.

Suppose, then, that someone asked you to draw a picture of the Grail. What would you put in? What leave out? Can it be drawn at all? Does it have a single form, or many? If you were able to decide on any one image, it would probably end up by dissatisfying you, as though this were only half an answer. In fact, you might well end up with something like a constellation of objects, each one related to the other in some way, but above all related to something else, a central something which is the real Grail. But none of this really answers the question: what is the Grail? To answer that we have to make our own journey into the Grail lands, meet and talk with those who are its guardians, experience for ourselves something of its magical power. And in so doing, learn something about ourselves.

That wise commentator Jessie L. Weston long ago concluded that we should rid our minds of the idea that the Grail story is simply that of a quest. It is, rather, of initiation that the texts and stories treat. The seeker certainly undergoes many adventures on the way to the Castle of the Grail, but it is the tests he undergoes on reaching it that decide both his fate and that of the Waste Land through which he has come. The significance of the ritual Question and Answer, the Broken Sword which must be restored, the Cup, the Lance which drips blood, the trance or sleep of the initiate, are all familiar from other sources, in the ancient mystery schools and their latterday followers in the modern occult orders.

All this is in line with the constant references in the texts to the secret nature of the Grail - as something which should not be spoken of openly to those ignorant of its true meaning and purpose. That these were at one time bound up with a life-giving ritual is beyond doubt - hence the concept of the Vessel of Plenty, a valid and recognizable mystery-school theme, which was easily translated into Christian terminology as the 'Cup of Life' when the Grail legends underwent metamorphosis during the Middle Ages, becoming at first identified with the vessel in which Joseph of Arimathea caught some of Christ's blood, and later with that used to celebrate the first Eucharist.

Similar stories, told of Nicodemus and associated with relics of the Holy Blood at Fecamp, Bruges and Valencia, may have given the necessary inspiration to transform the vessel of the mysteries into the vessel of Christ's Passion. Thereafter it became the symbol of a quest for purity and self-sacrifice which lay at the heart of the mystical spirituality of the Middle Ages, though it never lost the underlying theme of oneness with Godhead which also permeated the mystery-school teaching of the Classical and pre-Classical world.

The end result was still similar - a desire to reach out beyond the confines of everyday life to discover the meaning lying outside the worlds of sense and form. The vessel of the mysteries, the Grail, formed a point of contact between two modes of being: the everyday and the numinous. Those who drank from it left behind the one and entered the other. That there are still a great number of people in the world seeking the same thing is testified by the continued interest in the mysteries themselves and in the Grail in particular. It is to those seekers, first and foremost, that this book is directed. Both the authors, after a number of years spent teaching and discussing these matters, felt there was a need for a book which begins at the beginning and leads the way through the often tortuous maze of texts, characters and theories which revolve around the symbol of the Grail. This done, we shall proceed to offer our own interpretation of how the Grail functions in the world today. Finally, we will suggest some of the ways in which the mysteries can be practically applied to take us further on the quest and to help us consolidate what we have already learned.

Whether you seek the Grail as an inner goal, a kind of mystical experience, or as a treasure-hunt, or simply out of curiosity, it is hoped you will find all you need to begin the journey. Certainly, you should find no shortage of companions along the way - and you will encounter an endlessly rich storehouse of symbolism, mystery and experience destined to change your life forever. As a contemporary seeker, Abhisiktananda, puts it,

> At bottom, the quest for the Grail is nothing else but the quest for the Self. A unique quest signified in all the myths and symbols. It is one's own self that one is seeking through all. And in this quest one runs in every direction, whereas the Grail is here, nearby, one has only to open one's eyes. And it is the discovery of the Grail in its last truth, Galahad's direct look inside the vessel instead of being merely nourished by the Grail, or drinking from the Grail, which mysteriously traverses the hall.

# PART ONE: BACKGROUNDS

# Chapter One

## Of Texts and Pretexts:
### The Stories of the Grail

The myth was to each according to his need:
This and his powers determined what he heard.

Anne Ridler: *Taliesin Reborn*

The immediate way into the enchanted realm of the Grail is through the texts. Most of these were written during the Middle Ages, between the beginning of the eleventh and the end of the thirteenth centuries and include a wide range of material, styles and interpretations, some being little more than straightforward adventure tales while others aim at the heights of mystical spirituality. All, however, are alike in a feeling of mystery and dreamlike strangeness which sets them apart from the rest of the Arthurian literature to which they belong and reflects the powerful inner-plane impulse which gave them birth. Apart from one or two minor works, the main texts with which we shall be dealing, are as follows:

1.      *Le Conte del Graal* by Chrétien de Troyes;
2-4.    *The Continuations of Gautier de Danans* by Menassier and Gerbert de Monteille;
5.      *The Elucidation;*
6.      *Peredur* (included in the Welsh *Mabinogion* cycle);
7.      *Parzival* by Wolfram von Eschenbach;
8.      *Diu Crône* by Heinrich von dem Tulin;
9.      *The 'Didot' Perceval* (or *Prose Perceval*);
10.     *Joseph d'Arimathea* by Robert de Borron;
11.     *Le Grand Saint Graal;*
12.     *The Queste del Saint Graal* by Walter Map;
13.     *The Morte dArthur* by Sir Thomas Malory;
14.     *Sone de Nansai;*
15.     *Perlesvaus*;
16.     *The Spoils of Annwn.*

Together these tell us all we can know about the Grail outside of our own realisations, which may one day be added to that list. We shall look at each of the texts in turn, outlining their history and including a brief synopsis. This should serve as a beginning for the Grail seeker, who should then go on to read as many of the texts as possible in full, making them a part of his or her own inner landscape in which to journey and participate until the mysteries of the Grail begin, one by one, to give up their secrets.

**Perceval** or **Le Conte del Graal**, composed by the poet Chrétien de Troyes in 1185, was left unfinished by him at his death. It contains what may be called the 'basic' story - with one or two exceptions all those written subsequently draw upon Chrétien's version, either elaborating on or adding to it according to their own understanding. Debate still rages over Chrétien's own sources, but it is certain that he drew upon a story already ancient and widely known. He may indeed not have been the first to write down the events of the quest, but for good or ill he left his mark upon all that followed.

Perceval is brought up by his mother in the forest, where in ignorance of the ways of the world he happily hunts game with roughly made throwing spears. Then one day he meets three knights in the wood. Thinking them angels because of the brilliance of their armour, he questions them concerning their origin. Learning from them of Arthur's court and the institution of knighthood he vows to go there in search of adventure, and ignoring his mother's anguished request that he should remain with her he rides off on an ancient nag to find his way in the world of chivalry. Before he departs his mother gives him certain advice: always to give help to any women in distress, but take no more from them by way of reward than a kiss - though if one should also wish to give him a ring let him take that also. Also if he meets with anyone on the road he should not part from them without knowing their name, for those who conceal such things are of no good to anyone.

Armed with this advice, the first person Perceval encounters along the way is a beautiful woman in a scarlet pavilion, whose ring he takes and whom he kisses. He then proceeds to Arthur's court where he enters in time to witness the arrival of a red knight who spills wine in the queen's lap and carries off her golden cup. Still mindful of his mother's instructions Perceval pursues the knight, kills him and returns the cup to the queen - acquiring the red knight's armour on the way by the simple expedient of cooking the body over a slow fire!

At the court he seeks training in knightly pursuits and then sets out on further adventures. The most important of these is when he arrives at the castle of the Fisher King, whom he finds presiding over a hall in which are 400 men sitting round a fire while an old man lies upon a couch close by. The Fisher King presents Perceval with a Sword which he accepts unthinkingly. A procession passes through the hall, led by a squire carrying a Spear from which blood drips upon the ground, followed by two squires each carrying a ten-branched candlestick. After this comes a damsel carrying a 'Grail' which blazes with a light so bright that it puts out the light of the candles and of the stars. Following her is another maiden carrying a Talleors (variously translated as meaning a dish, a bowl, a casket or a tabernacle). Perceval watches all this but fails to ask its meaning. He retires for the night and on waking finds the castle deserted. He sets out in search of the Fisher King and his people, but no sooner has he crossed the drawbridge than the whole castle vanishes. Perceval then encounters a damsel cradling the body of a knight in her arms and lamenting bitterly. She tells him that the Fisher King has long since received a wound in the thighs, which has never healed, though it might well have done so had Perceval asked about the procession of the Grail. She also informs him that the sword which he was given at the castle will break if he is not careful, but that in such a case he can restore it by dipping it in a lake near which its maker, the smith Trebuchet, dwells.

Returning to Arthur's court Perceval is upbraided by a hideous damsel who appears from nowhere to mock him for so foolishly failing to ask the Question which would have healed the king and make his country prosperous again. Determined to right this wrong, and to learn more of the mysterious Grail, Perceval sets forth again and after many adventures meets with a band of pilgrims who reproach him for bearing arms on Good Friday. Five years have passed since he left Arthur's court and in his eagerness to discover more about the Grail he has forgotten God. Perceval confesses his sins to a forest hermit and learns from him that his mother died of grief after he left her. He feels great remorse but has still not rediscovered the Castle of the Grail.

Here the story changes course to deal with the adventures of Gawain, whose quest is to free an imprisoned damsel. By way of reward, she shows him an underground crypt where the Sword of Judas Maccabeus is kept. It is now called the Sword of the Strange Girdle and we shall encounter it again in other of our texts. Continuing his adventures, which at this point have nothing to do with the Grail, Gawain is ferried over a rise to a magical Castle of Ladies where many damsels are held prisoner awaiting the one who will deliver or marry them, thus putting an end to the enchantments of the place. Gawain undergoes many trials and tests in this place, including the adventure of the Perilous Bed, which is so designed that anyone who sets foot upon it or attempts to lie down, is at once assailed by invisible opponents, who fling spears and fire arrows at him, and is then attacked by a lion. But Gawain overcomes them all and is proclaimed lord of the castle.

Here Chrétien's narrative breaks off, in mid-sentence, and there perhaps the story might have ended, but it exerted such a powerful hold over the imagination of mediaeval Europe that others felt drawn to try to solve the problems left by the unfinished poem. There are three surviving attempts to 'finish' what Chrétien began. The first is by a poet calling himself Gautier de Danans.

**The First Continuation** by Gautier de Danans takes up where Chrétien left off by following the further adventures of Gawain, bringing him at last to the mysterious castle where Perceval had seen the Grail. On his way Gawain stops to pray in a chapel and sees the altar light quenched by a black hand. In the Grail Castle he sees a room wherein lies the body of a knight holding a Cross and a Broken Sword. That evening, while at table with the Fisher King and his court, he witnesses the Grail procession and is presented with the Broken Sword which he is asked to restore (here we seem to have the fragments of a lost tale, in which Perceval is given a sword which will break and then Gawain is asked to restore it without knowledge of the smith, Trebuchet, and the magic lake which will enable him to re-forge the sword anew). Gawain duly fails to do what is required and is declared unfit to achieve the mystery of the Grail. He does, however, ask concerning the Lance, the Sword and the Bier. He only gets to hear about the first of these things because he then falls asleep, having heard that the Spear was that which had pierced the side of Christ on the Cross. When Gawain wakes he finds himself by the sea-shore, and the country around him, which has hitherto been waste, has burst into flower because of his question concerning the Lance. Had he asked of the Grail also, matters would have been even better.

Gautier's story now returns to Perceval, and there follows the episode of the Chessboard Castle, in which Perceval arrives at a deserted castle and discovers a chessboard set out for a game. He plays against an invisible opponent and is defeated. Furiously he is about to fling the board and pieces out of the window when a beautiful woman rises from the moat and begs him not to. He falls instantly in love with her, but she refuses to grant him her favours unless he brings her the head of a certain stag, for which purpose she gives her hound into his keeping.

Perceval rides off and fights with a fearsome apparition called the Knight of the Tomb, whom he defeats. He encounters another damsel and asks about a great light he has seen shining far off in the forest. The damsel vanishes, however, without answering him, only to reappear next day and tell him that the light came from the Grail, which was given to the world as Christ hung on the Cross. Perceval asks to know more of this but is told that only a holy man may speak of such things. Soon after he sees a beautiful child sitting in a tree. This is the prelude to further adventures during which he sees a tree with many lights upon it, yet when he draws near finds a chapel. Here he shelters when a terrible storm overtakes him. On the altar within lies the body of a dead knight. A great light shines out suddenly and is extinguished by a black hand. Perceval is afraid, but on the morrow again meets the damsel who told him of the Grail. She now informs him that the child he saw in the tree, the mysterious chapel and the black hand are all connected with the mysteries of the Grail. After further adventures Perceval finds his way back to the castle of the Fisher King and again witnesses the procession. This time he asks concerning them, but before he can be answered is told that he must mend the Broken Sword. This he does, but Gautier's continuation breaks off before we can learn any more.

**The Second Continuation** is attributed to Menassier, who is believed by some to have been of Jewish descent. He describes the Grail procession again, after which the Fisher King tells Perceval that the Lance belonged to the centurion Longinus, who had pierced the body of Christ on the Cross. The Vessel is that which was used by Joseph of Arimathea to collect blood from the wound. He goes on to tell something of Joseph's history: how he had been imprisoned by the Romans but set free by Vespasian, after which he brought the Lance and the Cup to Britain, travelling by way of Sarras (here called the City of the Saracens) where he finds the King, Evelach, in the Temple of the Sun and helps him to defeat his enemy King Ptolemy of Egypt.

Perceval then hears how the tree of lights in the forest is a fairy tree, the lights of which would deceive him but that he is destined to achieve the wonders of the Grail. He learns that the broken sword is the same weapon which caused the wound of the Fisher King and that it will only be restored when the evil knight responsible for the murder of the king's brother is brought to justice and his head displayed from the tallest tower of the Grail Castle.

Perceval sets forth again and after a great struggle defeats the Demon of the Black Hand in the Perilous Chapel, fighting his way to the altar on which is a golden cup covered by a veil. Using this, dipped in holy water, to cleanse the chapel, Perceval is triumphant when he sees the altar-light mysteriously relit. He then goes on to avenge the king's murdered brother and in due time himself succeeds to the Kingdom of the Grail. He reigns for seven years, at which point he meets a hermit who leads him back into the forest, taking the Cup, the Lance and the Dish with him. He lives as a hermit for ten years and when he dies it is believed that the Holy Relics are carried to Heaven, since when no man has dared say that he has seen them.

**The Third Continuation.** We might consider that Menassier had done a good job in tidying up the loose ends left by Chrétien and Gautier, but there is at least one more continuation, by an author simply named Gerbert, which takes the form of an epilogue. In it Perceval is given a wife - Blanchfleur, the damsel of the crimson tent from whom he stole a ring and a kiss at the beginning of his career - and a son: Lohengrin, the Swan Knight, who founds a whole dynasty of Grail Knights of whom other tales tell. In addition to this we hear further of Perceval's attempts to re-forge the Broken Sword. Here he takes it to a forge guarded by twin serpents, on which lies a sword which had taken a year to forge and which can only be restored in the same place. Perceval slays the serpents and the smith restores his broken blade, which he explains he had forged long since and broken at the gates of Paradise. He is obviously an example of the Otherworldly Smith, who forges weapons for the gods and keeps the secrets of the mounds in Celtic mythology. This reconciliation of the Broken Sword theme which has run throughout the Grail texts to this time is of some significance. Further account is then given of Joseph of Arimathea's wanderings, including the setting up of the first Table of the Grail, from which the heathen Evelach, coming too close, was held back by an angel bearing a fiery sword.

**The Elucidation.** Apart from these three Continuations of Perceval, there also exists a short text known as The Elucidation, which takes the form of a prologue to Chrétien's poem and sets out to explain the meaning of later events. In this it is only partially successful, since the story it tells, though fascinating, seems little related to what is to come.

The story of the Grail (we are told) falls into seven parts, in which Master Bleheris relates how the rich land of Logres came to be destroyed. Attendant upon the wells and springs of the land were damsels whose task it was to entertain all wayfarers and see them fed with rich fare, but King Amangons and his men raped the Maidens of the Wells and carried off their golden cups so that thereafter their wells dried up and the land became waste. No longer could the court of the Fisher King be found. Many years later the Round Table Knights, hearing of this evil deed, set out in search of the damsels and found many wandering in the woods, each protected by a knight. These they overthrew and sent to Arthur. One, Blihos Bleheris, knew the whole story and told Arthur that the maidens now wandering the woods were the offspring of the original Well Guardians and that they would wander so until they found again the court of the Rich Fisher.

Arthur's knights determined to go in search of the court, and of its master who knew much of the arts of magic and could change his semblance at will. Gawain was to find the court and have much joy there, but before that Perceval found it - that same Perceval who asked about whom the Grail served and also about the Cross of silver, but not why the Spear dripped with blood. And the story will tell how the Grail served all with rich food, but this is Perceval's story and should await its turn, for when the Good Knight shall come that has found the court of Rich Fisher three times, then shall the full story of the Grail be told. Indeed the court was found seven times in all, and of each discovery there is a tale (the text lists these stories but none appear to have a direct connection with the Grail and are anyway lost). After this the land was restored, the streams ran again and the forests were thicker than ever. And in the land the descendants of the Well Maidens built the Castle of Maidens, the Perilous Bridge and the Orgellus Castle.

There follows an account of Perceval's parents, but this reads as though attached to the preceding matter, which will be seen to have little or nothing to do with Chrétien. It seems, rather, to be a much earlier story which the author (who also makes himself one of the characters) had heard and decided to add to the literature of the Grail. It does, however, offer several clues to the later material. The whole episode of the well-maidens - obviously otherworld characters - their rape and the subsequent drying up of the land, offers a convincing explanation of the Waste Land; while the character of the Fisher King here plays a more important role - seeming more like a positive version of the enchanters Garlon or Klingsor, whose acquaintance we shall make in later texts but who oppose the Grail rather than becoming its guardians. There is, too, the suggestion of a cult of sacred wells, of an otherworld being who rules over them, and of the intermingling of human and fairy blood. As always in Arthurian matter the Kingdom of Logres is an inner realm of Britain within Britain, a shadowy place whose borders overlap those of Arthur.[1]

**Peredur.** We must look next at the story of Peredur Son of Evrawc, as told in the collection of stories known as the *Mabinogion* (Tales of Youth) which, though it has only come down to us in mediaeval versions, portrays far earlier aspects of the Grail and its attendant symbols than do the typically mediaeval romances, and this opens the way to older, pagan aspects of the sacred vessel which we shall be dealing with later...

Peredur is the seventh son of Evrawc, Earl of the North, who falls, together with his six other offspring, in a series of battles and single combats. The surviving son Peredur is, like Chrétien's hero, carried off by his mother, this time into the desert, to be brought up in ignorance of his station and of the world of men. Once again he meets three of Arthur's knights, though this time it is his mother who tells him they are angels, presumably to discourage him from following them. In this she is unsuccessful, and the story follows the series of events set out by Chrétien until Peredur's arrival at a castle by a lake, where he sees two people, an old lame man and his attendant, sitting fishing. This is not, however, the Castle of the Grail: it belongs to Peredur's uncle, who teaches him something of the arts of war. After this he journeys on and reaches the castle of another uncle, where his strength is tested by being asked to cut through an iron staple with his sword. He does so twice, but twice the pieces magically reunite. The third time they remain severed (here it seems that the theme of the Broken Sword has been transferred to the staple - it should really be the blade which breaks

---

[1] This important text will be dealt with more fully than present space permits in a work by John Matthews, *The Grailless Lands*, published in 1988.

thrice and is finally reunited by Peredur). However, there then come into the hall of the castle two youths bearing a huge spear from which flow three streams of blood. All present begin loudly lamenting, but Peredur fails to ask concerning the Spear, having been told by his other uncle to forbear asking questions to which he is unlikely to receive an answer. Two maidens now enter, carrying between them a Salver containing a man's head in a pool of blood. The lamenting is redoubled, but Peredur falls asleep. Next morning he rides forth, and finds a beautiful woman by the roadside lamenting over the body of a dead knight. She reveals that she is Peredur's foster-sister, and accuses him of causing his mother's death by deserting her. She then demands that he avenge the death of her husband, the dead knight, who was slain by the Knight of the Glade. This he does, subduing the man and (rather strangely) forcing him to marry his widowed sister.

Peredur then embarks on a series of new adventures, including one where he is instructed by one of the Nine Witches of Gloucester, and another where he is entranced by the sight of three drops of blood in the snow, which remind him of the colour of the cheeks and lips of the lady he loves best in all the world.

Subsequently he slays a serpent coiled on a golden ring, which he takes. He then returns to Arthur's court where he is unrecognized. Kay insults him and wounds him in the thigh, but he overcomes all obstacles and wins the love of a lady. More adventures follow, in the course of which Peredur comes to the castle of a huge, black, one-eyed man whose daughter takes a liking to him and warns him against her father. But Peredur overcomes him and learns that he lost his eye while trying to steal a magic Stone from the tail of a serpent on the Mound of Mourning. Peredur sets out to slay the serpent and is aided by a lady he finds sitting on a mound and a youth named Etlym. He slays the serpent, gives the magic stone to Etlym and sends him home to marry his sweetheart. Peredur returns to Arthur's court and there follows the episode of the Hideous Damsel, who after reproaching Peredur for having failed to ask concerning what he saw at the Castle of the Lame King, tells of various adventures where fame can be won. Peredur is joined by Gwalchmai (Gawain), and the two set forth on different quests. The story follows the adventures of the latter for a time. Peredur, meanwhile, arrives at the Castle of

Wonders and there follows the episode of the Chessboard Castle - however it is the 'black' maiden, who came to chide him for not asking the question, who appears and tells him that he will find the chessboard again (he has succeeded in throwing it away) in the castle of Ysbidinogyl. He overcomes a black giant at this castle and is then sent forth on quest for the stag (here described as having one horn in the centre of its head, so that it may well have been a unicorn). With the help of the hunting dog, Peredur catches and slays the stag, but another lady accuses him of an evil deed and takes the dog. He may only retrieve it, and his honour, by going to a certain cromlech and fighting three times with a black man. He does so, but the man disappears and Peredur finds himself near a castle where sits an old lame man. Gwalchmai is with him, and a youth enters who says that he was the black maiden, both at Arthur's court and later at the Chessboard Castle, and that he is one of the same maidens who carried the head on the salver. This head, it now transpires, belonged to Peredur's cousin, murdered by the Nine Witches of Gloucester who also caused his uncle to be lamed. Peredur now seeks the aid of Arthur and his men, and a great battle ensues in which the Witches are all slain as was predicted long ago.

Thus ends the story of Peredur, which we can see reflects the version as told by Chrétien but also contains earlier elements. It is a confused tale with several repetitive episodes, such as the slaying of the two serpents. Here the only trace of the magical objects in the Grail Castle are the Spear which runs with blood and the head on the Salver (here given a prosaic interpretation). There are also the magic Stone and the ring guarded by the serpent, which seem to reflect an earlier aspect of the sacred treasures in Chrétien's poem. The various black giants who appear throughout, as well as the black maiden who turns out to be a boy, are all obvious otherworldly figures, and there are elements of borrowing from early Irish myth throughout - as in the episode in which Peredur is taught by one of the Nine Witches, a parallel with the training of Cuchlain (the Irish Gawain) by the female warrior Scathach. Overall the story of Peredur is far more savage and unpredictable than that of his later aspect Perceval; but there is no lack of subtlety about it, and beneath the surface gleams the complex and colourful world of the older Celtic heroes who stand behind so many of the characters and stories of the Arthurian cycle. In the final episode, where Peredur enlists the aid of Arthur, there are echoes both of the Culhwch and Olwen story, also from the Mabinogion, and the ancient Preiddeu Annwn, in which Arthur raids the Otherworld in search of the Cauldron of Immortality. It has been described as a later copy of Chrétien's poem, but while the text may date from a different period, the actual content of the work is far older, and in all probability contains the earliest Grail material of any of the texts under review here.

**Parzival.** Wolfram von Eschenbach's poem, which follows Chrétien's chronologically, has been written about and studied at great length because of its extremely complex symbol system which has made it a favourite with esoteric interpreters such as Walter Stein and his disciple Trevor Ravenscroft (see Chapter 4). Certainly there is much within it that repays study: the colour symbolism and the names of the characters alone warrant a book to themselves. But beneath the layers, and despite the fact that Wolfram continually attacks Chrétien for not telling the story as it should really be told, it differs hardly at all in its basic plot and characterization. Where it does so is in describing the Grail as a Stone rather than a Vessel, which has lead various commentators to connect it with alchemical mysteries. In effect, however, its general attributes remain the same: it grants extended life, well-being and spiritual food to those who serve it.

Another point of difference from Chrétien - indeed from all other versions - is the provision of Parzival with a half-brother (who is also pied: one half black, the other white), the offspring of an earlier liaison between Parzival's father and an eastern princess. In fact, Wolfram displays throughout the text a marked awareness of eastern, particularly Arabic, traditions, which helps bear out his claim to have received the story from a Provençal singer named Kyot, who in turn had it from an Arab poet in Toledo named Flegitanis.

Wolfram also describes at some length the establishment of the Grail Castle on the sacred mountain, Muntsalvach, and of the select order of knights whom he called 'Templiessen' (Templars) who are vowed to celibacy and good deeds. Their king, Amfortas, is wounded because he took up the cause of carnal love. Far more is made of the Broken Sword episode, connected with a spell which Parzival must master before he can become lord of the Grail Castle. In the same way, the role of Kundry, the Loathly Damsel, is much emphasized.

Wolfram departs most directly from the Chrétien version in the provision of an adversary to the whole family of Grail initiates - the evil magician Klingsor, who has castrated himself and in thus mocking the affliction of the wounded king represents the negative forces opposing those of the Grail. To Gawain is given the task of overcoming him, and as always he has many adventures which contrast those of the Grail Knight himself. Parzival, at the end of the story, fights with his parti-coloured half-brother Feirefitz, but they are reconciled and Parzival asks the Question which frees Amfortas from the torment of his wound. Parzival now becomes King of the Grail Castle and Feirefitz marries the Grail Maiden, Repanse de Schoy. Of their union is born Prester John, the great Christian king in the East who is the inner guardian of the Grail in our own time. Parzival's own son is Lohengrin, the Swan Knight, whose adventures have little or nothing to do with the Grail.

**Diu Crône** (The Crown) This version by Heinrich von dem Tulin, borrows substantially from Chrétien but differs markedly in its treatment of the central episodes. Though as yet untranslated from the German, and described by at least one commentator as 'a confused tissue of nonsense', Diu Crône contains some of the richest symbolic material to be found in the literature of the Grail - while in making Gawain its hero it is consistent with what are probably the earliest traditions of the quest.

The early parts of the story have nothing to do with the Grail, though they do include some strange episodes. Suffice it to say that by verse 19,000 of the poem Gawain is in search of the Grail, accompanied by Lancelot, Kay and a knight called Colgrevance (interestingly, this same grouping of characters reappears later in Malory and in another of Chrétien's Arthurian poems unconnected with the Grail). They part at a crossroads and each undergoes a series of adventures. Gawain arrives at the Castle of Wonders, where he meets with the sister of the magician who owns it - here called Gansgutor but fulfilling a similar role to that of Klingsor.

She warns him to take care not to fall asleep if he wishes to learn of the Grail. Eventually, after several further adventures, Gawain makes his rendezvous with Lancelot and Colgrevance (Kay has been imprisoned elsewhere) and the three enter the Grail Castle. Here they are led into a hall of surpassing splendour, where the floor is strewn with roses and an ancient man lies on a bed watching two youths playing chess. As evening approaches the hall fills with youths and maidens, and a single youth enters with a sword which he lays before the old man. Gawain is offered a drink, which he refuses. His comrades, however, accept and fall instantly asleep. Then two damsels enter carrying lights, followed by two knights with a Spear and two more women with a Toblier (possibly tailleor, a dish or plate) on which are three drops of blood. They are followed by the most beautiful woman ever created, carrying a box and accompanied by a weeping maiden.

The Spear is laid on the table and next to it the Toblier. In the box carried by the beautiful woman is a piece of bread which she breaks into three, giving one piece to the old man. Gawain now recognizes her as the magician's sister and at once asks concerning the events he has witnessed. The people in the hall leap up with cries of joy. The old man tells Gawain that these are the mysteries of the Grail which none have seen save Parzival who failed to ask about them. Through his question Gawain has freed both the living and the dead, for though they seem real enough the old man and his companions are really ghosts - only the fair lady and the weeping maiden are living beings, who because of their purity are allowed to possess the Grail and feed him from it once a year. All Gawain's adventures have come from the Grail, and now that he has succeeded where all others have failed he must accept as a reward the Sword, which will help him in every danger he encounters from now onwards. After this no one will see the Grail again and he must ask no more concerning it. As daybreak falls the old man finishes his story and at once he and the court vanish away, leaving only the magician's sister and her attendant.

There are several points worthy of notice in this version. The scene in the hall where Gawain enters is interesting because it recalls specifically Celtic tradition with the chess-players and the mysterious old man in the rose-strewn hall. There are echoes here also, one feels, of the game played by Gawain against invisible opponents - however, it is not referred to again. And there are echoes too of the broken sword theme in the weapon presented to Gawain - though in this instance he does not have to effect a repair. And what are we to make of the Toblier, which in this version stands for the Grail? The wooden box containing bread and the dish with the three drops of blood take the place of the usual talismans. Their effect, however, is similar: giving pseudo-life to the ancient man and his followers just as the more usual form of the Grail give spiritual life to those who serve it. There is an echo also of Eastern Orthodox ritual in the dividing of the bread into several pieces - this is done prior to the celebration of Holy Eucharist, when the priest also stabs the bread with a small spear in token of the wounding of Christ.

More than anything in this text, one is left with a feeling of otherworldliness. Whatever source - if any - its author was following it must have been one which preserved an older stratum of tradition - as witness also the part played by the magician's sister, who is able to inhabit both the world of her brother (the Klingsor figure) and the Grail. It is as though Kundry, the Loathly Damsel, were to be found officiating at the Grail Castle with the holy vessel in her hands!

**The Prose Perceval.** This romance, more commonly known, after its discoverer, as the *Didot Perceval*, has been described as controversial because it takes a line so independent from the rest of the Grail stories that it seems to have been influenced by no other. Its author may have been Robert de Borron, who also composed three other Arthurian romances, but this is not certain. It was written between 1190 and 1225 and thus follows closely on Chrétien's version, but it clearly comes from an entirely different source.

Beginning with a brief prologue outlining the history of Arthur's crowning and the coming of Merlin to court, the story then tells how the great magician gave the Round Table to Arthur. It has been made by him after the pattern of one constructed by Joseph of Arimathea which was in turn modelled on the Table of the Last Supper. Here only the best men and women may sit, and if any who are false attempt to they are at once swallowed up. One place is always left empty in token of Judas, and only the Best Knight, true son of the Church and of chivalry the finest, may sit there at the appointed time (presumably redeeming the actions of Judas).

Merlin speaks of the Grail, which was given into the hands of the Fisher King to guard. But he is now old and sick and will only regain his health when the best knight in the world comes to sit at the Table of the Grail and ask the Question: what use is the Grail? At this time 'the Enchantments of Britain' will end and a new time of prosperity begin. Merlin departs to Blaise his master to tell all of this and to have it set down in writing.

The story now turns to Alain le Gros, grandson of Joseph of Arimathea and thus of the Grail lineage. His son is named Perceval and as Alain lies near to death he is instructed by the Holy Spirit to send Perceval to Arthur, who will ensure that he is trained in chivalry until he can journey to Ireland where Alain's father Brons has the Grail. Brons cannot die or be cured of his infirmities until he is able to pass on the secret words taught him by Joseph concerning the Grail.

At court Perceval outshines all others in knightly pursuits. In a tournament he is sent a suit of red armour by Gawain's niece, and overcomes all his opponents. All say that he should claim the empty place at the Round Table. But when he seats himself the earth groans and cracks open. A voice reproaches Arthur for disobeying Merlin's advice and adds that only by the goodness of Alain le Gros is Perceval spared. Now the Best Knight in the World must go further in search of the Rich Fisher who is old and infirm. Perceval and several other knights vow to set forth immediately. They separate, and the story follows Perceval who first encounters a maiden weeping over the body of a knight - one of the Round Table fellowship who had already been in search of the Grail. Perceval avenges him against a red knight and proceeds to the Chessboard Castle, where the episodes of the white stag and the hunting dog follow. These vary from Chrétien only in that it is an old woman who takes the little dog, promising to return it to Perceval only if he goes to the grave of a dead knight and says, aloud: 'May the felon who put you there, appear'. This Perceval does and a black knight appears whom he defeats. After further adventures he meets with his sister, who tells him that he is of the Grail lineage and advises him to visit their uncle, a wise hermit.

They do so together and Perceval learns much of the history of the Grail, which he is destined to find - only his sinful nature having kept him from the house of his grandfather, Brons.

Vowing repentance Perceval sets out again, encountering various other adventures and finally coming to a river where he sees three men fishing from a boat. One bids him follow the river downstream until he comes to a house where he will find lodging and shelter. Perceval takes all day to get there, but is welcomed as though expected and given a scarlet robe to wear. The Fisher King is carried into the hall on a litter: he wishes to do Perceval every honour as his grandson. A squire comes out of a chamber bearing a Spear that drips blood, followed by two damsels bearing silver Plates covered in white cloths, then a squire with a Vessel in which is Our Lord's Blood. Perceval wonders about this but fails to ask. Next morning he finds himself alone. He proceeds on his way and meets a damsel who rails at him for his failure, which might have ended the Enchantments of Britain. He meets again the woman who stole the stag's head and the dog, and retrieves them. More adventures follow as Perceval seeks everywhere for his grandfather's house. At length he is found wandering on Good Friday and is sent back to his uncle the hermit, who tells him that his sister is now dead. Perceval does penance and then wanders again until found by Merlin, who reminds him that he is still in search of the Grail. Perceval asks when he will find it. 'Before a year'. 'A long time', 'Not so'. In fact Perceval finds himself back at the Castle of the Fisher King in only a day. The Grail appears, together with the other Relics, and this time Perceval asks to what use the Vessel is put. Instantly the Fisher King is restored. He asks who Perceval is and on being told he is his own grandson instructs him in the secret words entrusted to him by Joseph of Arimathea from Christ himself. Brons then dies and Perceval remains at the castle. The Enchantments of Britain are ended and at Arthur's court the seat which cracked when Perceval sat there is restored. Merlin tells Blaise what has happened and takes him to Perceval before continuing to Arthur to tell all that has occurred.

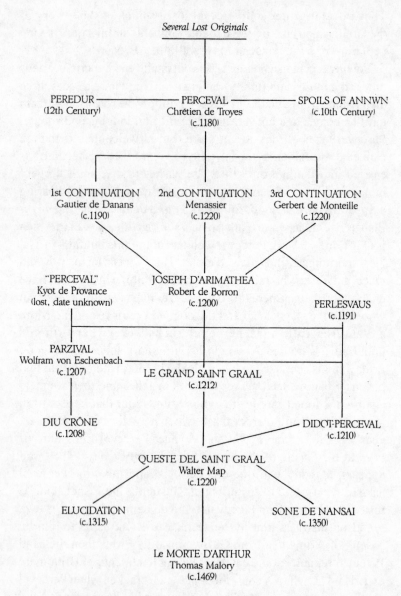

Fig. 2: *The Tree of the Grail Texts*
(Dates are approximate, as are relationships of the texts to each other.)

The *Didot* is one of the shortest and most clearly structured of all the Grail stories, and it is singular in the extent of the part played by Merlin. The Grail and the accompanying talismans take on their most Christian aspect, and there is an emphasis on the necessity of the colour red as worn by the Grail knight, perhaps signifying the Holy Blood. Galahad, in the later and most Christian version, also comes to Camelot in red armour, and though it is said to be an aged hermit who brings him in that version it is easy to believe that this is in fact Merlin in one of his many guises.

Of interest also is the shadowy figure of Blaise, described as Merlin's 'master'. He appears as an almost monkish or hermit-like figure, yet is obviously held in high regard by the magician, from which one may infer that he is of an older and more powerful order, though this is not made clear in the text.

The significance of Perceval's uncle Brons, who is to be found in Ireland, is not to be overlooked. Brons is a variant of the name Bran, and in Welsh legend this figure appears as a giant god-like character who possesses a Cauldron of inexhaustible supply - an early archetype of the Grail.

Perceval's own character is perhaps here more clearly delineated than in any of the texts. Endlessly striving, he fails continually, only to try yet again. He is prey to human weakness, yet is unbeatable in feats of arms and chivalry. Of all the Grail heroes, in all of the versions, he seems nearest to our own endeavours in his quest for the Grail.

**Joseph of Arimathea.** We must now look briefly at a text which, though written after Chrétien and his continuators, narrates the prehistory of the Grail, filling in background information not found, or only hinted at, in the earlier texts. This text is *Joseph of Arimathea* by Robert de Borron. It was part of a trilogy by this author, of which only the Joseph and a fragmentary Merlin now exist.

Robert tells the story of the Last Supper and the betrayal and Crucifixion of Christ and, drawing largely on the apocryphal Gospel of Pilate, adds the story of Joseph of Arimathea who together with Nicodemus acquires Christ's body and the Cup with which He celebrated the first Eucharist. While they are preparing the body for burial, some blood flows afresh from the wounds and is caught in the Cup by Joseph. After the Resurrection Joseph is thrown into prison, where he is visited by the risen Christ who gives him the Cup (previously hidden in Joseph's house) and instructs him in the mystery of the Sacraments: the bread and wine are His body, the tomb is the altar, the platter its sealing stone, the grave cloths the corporeal, and the Vessel in which the blood was caught shall henceforth be called a Chalice. All who behold it shall be of Christ's company, have fulfilment of their heart's desire and eternal joy. Joseph remains in prison, kept alive miraculously by the Grail, until years later the Emperor Vespasian, having been healed of leprosy by the Veil of Veronica, becomes a Christian and frees him - justifiably amazed to find the old Jew still alive.

Joseph now gathers various of his kin around him, including his sister Erygius and her husband Brons, and with their followers departs for far-off lands. All goes well for a time, but in one place where they stay the host's family are dying of hunger. Joseph kneels before the Grail and is instructed to build a table in memory of that at which the Last Supper was held and to send his brother-in-law Brons into the water to catch a fish. This is then to be placed on the table opposite the Grail, which must be covered. Joseph is to sit in the place of Christ, with Brons on his right and next to him an empty place to signify the seat occupied by Judas.

The people come and all are fed by the fish. Some sit down and are gratified with food and sweetness; others are judged to be sinners when one of their number, Moyes, attempts to sit in the place left vacant and is swallowed up. A voice tells Joseph that only the prophesied person will be able to sit there; he will be a great-nephew of Joseph, the grandson of Brons and Erygius. In due time the couple do indeed produce twelve children, of which eleven marry, but one, Alain, remains single. Of him will one day issue an heir who will fulfil the purpose of the Grail. Meanwhile he is to take charge of his brothers and sisters and journey westward.

Another of Joseph's followers, named Petrus, will be brought a letter by an angel, telling him to go where he wills. He will say 'The Vale of Avaron' (Avalon?), and there he will go and remain until the coming of the Grail winner, whom he is to instruct in the mysteries of the Sacraments.

All falls out as the voice foretold, while another angel relates that Brons shall henceforth be called the Rich Fisher because he fed the company from a single fish. He is to go westward with Petrus and there await the coming of his grandson, to whom he shall entrust the Vessel at last - at which time the meaning of the Trinity will be made known to all. Next day Brons receives the Vessel and is initiated into the secret words which Joseph received from Christ himself while in prison.

Such is the essential narrative of the Joseph, which is at times a confused and garbled story, possibly put together from several disparate sources. At times, however, it is illumined by passages of great beauty and mystery - particularly in the parts relating to Brons, the Rich Fisher, who in later versions becomes the Fisher King, a most significant character in the romances. Here also we first hear of the mysterious 'Secret Teachings' given by Christ directly to Joseph and which are clearly the inner mystery of the Grail. The implication is that this is more than the symbolic explanation of the meaning of the Tomb, the Stone, the Platter and the Cloth, which are also explained to Joseph. These were, anyway, hardly secret, being openly taught by mediaeval theologians.

There are other confusions, such as the apparent doubling of the character of Brons (sometimes called Hebron) and Petrus, who is clearly intended to recall St Peter, the Rock upon which the Christian church is built. Also notable are the references to the Vale of Avaron, which may well be Avalon, to which Brons and Petrus, but apparently not Joseph, proceed. Later traditions which have Joseph coming to Avalon (or Glastonbury) seem to stem from another source or possibly from a misreading of this admittedly confusing text.

**Le Grand Saint Graal.** We now come to the three texts which are probably the most important of the various versions because they represent the fullest and most consistent account we possess, and because of the numerous clues which the modern Grail seeker can follow up in his or her own quest. The first of these texts is the anonymous *Grand Saint Graal*. It begins with a mysterious prelude, omitted from most modern editions, but which is nonetheless worth seeking out for its unique account of the origin of the Grail story in written form.

In the year 717 after the Passion of Christ as the writer of the text lies in his hut in one of the wildest areas of White Britain feeling doubts about his faith, Christ appears to him in a vision and gives him a book no bigger than a man's palm. It is written by the Saviour Himself and will resolve all doubts. Next morning the writer finds that the book is real, and on opening it finds it divided into four parts headed as follows: 'This is the Book of thy lineage'; 'Here begins the Book of the Holy Grail'; 'Here begin the terrors'; 'Here begin the marvels'. As he reads these words thunder and lightning and other wonders occur.

On Good Friday following, as he is celebrating Mass, an angel lifts him to the Third Heaven and his doubts are set at rest. He locks away the book, but on Easter Sunday, when he would read further, it is gone. A voice tells him he must go to the planes of Walescog (Wales?) and follow a wonderous beast to Norway where he will find what he seeks. The beast leads him to a hermit's cell, then past the Pine of Adventures to the castle of a knight. On the third day he comes to the Lake of the Queen and to a nunnery. He exorcizes a possessed hermit and recovers the book. Christ commands him to make a copy of it before Ascension Day and he begins at once. The text of the *Grand Saint Graal* which follows is that of the little book, written by Christ himself and therefore doubly authentic.

The story of Joseph, more or less as related by Robert de Borron, is told first, though with much added detail. We follow especially the adventures of Joseph and his companions in the wilderness. Here Joseph is instructed to build a wooden ark, rather than a table, to contain the Grail. Only Joseph and his son Josephus may touch it, and through it they may speak with Christ.

Continuing their wanderings the company arrive at the city of Sarras, midway between Babilon and Salavandre. Joseph and his seventy-five companions enter the city and visit the Temple of the Sun, where is the seat of judgement. There they find Evelach, Lord of the Saracens, whose armies have just suffered a crushing defeat at the hands of the Egyptian King Tholomes (Ptolemy). Joseph explains Christian doctrine at some length and promises Evelach victory over his enemies if he becomes a follower of Christ. Evelach is unsure but gives the company lodging.

Next day, in the place that had been called the Spiritual Palace by Daniel, they celebrate before the Ark of the Grail. Josephus opens the doors of the ark and sees a man all in red and with him five angels, each with six wings, also in red. Each carries in their left hand a bloody Sword, and in their right, variously, a cross, nails, lance, sponge and scourge. He then sees Christ nailed to the Cross, with blood running down from hands and feet and side into the Grail. He is so overcome with the sight that he strives to enter the ark but is restrained by the angels. Joseph, in some wonder, also looks in the ark and sees an altar covered with white cloths, under which is a red samite pall covering three Nails, a bloody Lance-head and a Dish. In the centre is an exceedingly rich Vessel of gold and silver and precious stones. Seven angels then issue forth carrying water and watering pot, gold basins and towels and gold censers. An eighth issues forth carrying the Holy Dish and a ninth with a head more beautiful than anything ever seen by mortal eye. A tenth angel appears carrying a Sword, followed by three more with tapers. Last of all comes Christ himself.

Joseph receives the Sacraments and is made bishop of the company. He is seated in a chair, dressed in robes brought from out of the ark, and consecrated. An angel keeps the oil with which he is anointed and it is used thereafter by all the kings of Britain up until the time of Uther Pendragon. Joseph then enters the ark alone and celebrates the Sacrament using the words taught him by Christ. The wine and bread become flesh and blood, but the bread is also a Child which though divided into three parts is also eaten whole. Christ then bids Joseph celebrate the mysteries daily.

Evelach now sends for Joseph and agrees to be baptized, receiving the name Mordrains (slow-of-belief). His brother Seraphe is also baptized and takes the name Nasciens. Joseph paints a red cross on a white shield and bids Evelach carry it before him in battle. Evelach is later captured, but on praying to Christ a white knight appears and defeats Tholomes. Evelach is victorious and insists that all his people be baptized or suffer banishment. Many choose to go and are attacked by demons outside the walls. Out of pity Josephus goes to help them, but is stopped by an angel who wounds him in the thigh for leaving off his baptismal work to go to the aid of unbelievers. The wound will always trouble him and the Spear-head remains in his thigh.

The work of conversion continues until all in Sarras are Christian. Joseph then brings Nasciens, Mordrains and Saracinte, Mordrain's wife, to the shrine and shows them the wonders. Nasciens remembers a dream in which he heard a voice telling him that his life would only be complete when the mysteries of the Grail were revealed - though he concludes that this must be the Grail since he feels totally at peace and fully achieved. In his ecstasy he then attempts to look within the vessel and is at once blinded. He tells Josephus that his own wound and his blindness will never be cured until Josephus can draw forth the iron from his thigh. As they stand lost in thought a voice announces: 'After my vengeance, my healing', and an angel touches Josephus' thigh with the shaft of the Spear, whereat the head comes out of the wound and with it three great drops of blood which the angel catches in a Vessel and with them anoints Nasciens' eyes. His sight is restored and the angel relates that the Spear will henceforward become a part of the mysteries and that it signifies the beginning of great and marvellous adventures in lands where God would lead them all, and in which earthly knighthood would become spiritual knighthood. Wonders will happen wherever the Lance is found, great and terrible wonders in token of the Grail. But the true marvels are to be seen by one other man only, and he will be the last of Nasciens' line; while the Spear will wound but one other, of Josephus' line, who will be struck through both thighs and not be healed until the coming of the Good Knight of Nasciens' kin. So saith the true crucified one, adding: 'Upon the first and last of My mysteries will I spend the vengeance of the adventurous Lance in token of Myself, having received the lance-stroke while on the Cross'.

Joseph, Josephus and the company set forth again, but the text turns to Mordrains and Nasciens, of whom it relates a long series of miraculous adventures designed to test their faith (and presumably that of their readers) in which many wonders occur, including a visit to the Turning Island which seems reminiscent of various Celtic wonder-tales, and the first appearance of the Ship of Solomon, of which we shall hear much more in a later text. Eventually the story does return to Joseph and his followers, who have been wandering from place to place, guarded by the Grail, until they finally arrive in Britain, then still containing many pagans. They cross the water by means of Joseph's shirt, which miraculously bears them all from shore to shore. Joseph feeds 500 people with twelve loaves. Many adventures befall them and they are finally rejoined by Mordrains, who on approaching too near the Grail is blinded as was Nasciens. He is, however, promised that he shall not die until the coming of the Good Knight.

The story now follows events more or less as described by Robert de Borron, with the adventure of the Perilous Seat and the episode of the Rich Fisher (here attributed to Bron's youngest son Alain le Gros). In the Forest of Broceliande Joseph is wounded in the thigh and on being healed leaves behind the sword which wounded him and a piece of steel which had broken off and remained in the wound. The parts will only be restored by Galahad, the one appointed to win the Grail.

Returning to his company Joseph finds them wondering how to cross a great lake of water. They all pray for guidance, and a hart followed by four stags (Christ and the four Evangelists, we are later informed) appear and lead them all across.

Years pass and Josephus dies. His body is taken to Scotland where it wonderously causes a famine to cease and is at length laid to rest at the Abbey of Glays. Before his death he entrusts the Grail to Alain, who after further wanderings comes to the Terre Foraine where he builds a castle to house the Grail. This is named, in Chaldee, Corbenic (which can mean either Holy Vessel or Blessed Body), but is sometimes also called the Palace Adventurous. None may sleep there in the presence of the Grail, as the king of that land (who marries Alain's daughter) finds when he attempts to do so and is wounded through both thighs by a man all in flames. Alain dies and others of his line are named as Kings of the Grail: Alfasein, Aminadep, Catheloys, Manaal and Lambor. The latter, fighting with an enemy called Bruillant, flees to the shore where he finds the Ship of Solomon and goes aboard. Bruillant catches up with him and Lambor slays him with the Sword which he finds on board. This is said to be the first blow struck with that Sword in Britain, and from it come many woes, for the land is laid waste because of it. Lambor falls dead from drawing the Sword, and Pelleans becomes the new Grail King. He is subsequently wounded through both thighs while fighting a battle against Rome and is henceforth called the Maimed King, for he may not be healed until Galahad, the Good Knight, comes. From

Pelleans' line descends Pelles, on whose daughter Lancelot is to beget Galahad in future times.

Thus at great length is the vast tapestry of the Grail's early history and wanderings unfolded. *Le Grand Saint Graal* is rich in allegory, miracle and mystery. The symbolism of the Grail Ark alone will repay many hours of study and meditation. The number symbolism of the thirteen six-winged angels and the strange variations on the Grail procession are also not without their significance.

The Ark of the Grail, which seems able to contain far more than its size would give one to suppose, relates both to the earlier Ark of the Covenant and to Pandora's box. Much comes from it that is wondrous, and would-be Grail seekers might certainly do worse than to attempt a drawing or painting of the scene described, thus giving themselves something to meditate upon for many hours.

The strange prelude, with its voyage into otherworldly realms - the Pine of Adventure, the Queen's Lake and so on - is unique among the Grail texts in that it actually ascribes the writing of the story to Christ - authorship which, one assumes, would scarcely be challenged in the Middle Ages! It is, above all, a moral tale, embellished throughout with the matter of theology and the wonders of Christian miracle and dream. Much of it, indeed, reads like a dream, events piled one upon the other in often bewildering succession. It is at times fairly hard going, so much richness is there, but if persevered with can yield much that is of value.

A great deal of the text is taken up with preparing the way for events that are to follow: the adventures involving Arthur and his knights. There is much talk of lineage: Lancelot is descended from the line of Nasciens and Gawain from Joseph of Arimathea (see p.214-5). The rest of the cycle to which this text belonged has been lost, but we can supply the next section from another work of the same kind, generally known as the 'Vulgate' cycle, composed, according to some, by one Walter Map, and by others by one or even several Cistercian monks. It contains the whole story of the Round Table, from the birth of Arthur to his death, and includes the *Queste del Saint Graal*, our next text for consideration, which can be seen as a natural working out of much that was hinted at in the *Grand Saint Graal*.

**Queste del Saint Graal.** On Whitsun Eve the company of the Round Table are assembled at Camelot. A youth enters to summon Lancelot in the name of King Pelles. He is taken to a convent where he finds the young Galahad whom he knights. In Camelot the chair of each knight bears his name - all except one, the Siege Perilous, which bears the legend that 450 years have passed since the Passion of Christ, but on this Whitsun the seat shall find an occupant.

In the river a block of red marble is sighted floating, with a sword stuck into it, on which is written that only the best knight in the world can draw it forth. Lancelot declares that the wonders of the Holy Grail are about to begin, but refuses even to try the sword. Gawain, Perceval and others try, but all fail. As the company sits down to eat, an old man enters leading a youth in red armour, whom he announces as the expected one, of the seed of David and Joseph of Arimathea, the one who will achieve the Grail. On the Seat Perilous is now written, 'This is Galahad's seat'. He is recognized as Lancelot's son and is successful in the test of the stone, from which he draws the sword intended for him. After Vespers a clap of thunder announces the Grail, floating through the hall, covered in white samite, borne by no visible hand. Everyone present receives the food they like best. Gawain leads the way in declaring that he will seek until he is able to see the Grail unveiled.

Next morning all set forth and a series of adventures now commences. Galahad earns the red cross shield, which once belonged to Mordrains, the story of which is retold as in *Le Grand Saint Graal*. He acquires a young follower Mellians, whom he knights and who suffers various adventures designed to point a moral. The story weaves a pattern of adventures concerning Gawain, Lancelot, Galahad and Perceval, whose paths cross and re-cross each other. Lancelot comes to an old chapel and sees an altar within, on which burn seven candles. He lies down to sleep outside and sees a sick knight who bitterly laments his fate. Lancelot pretends to be asleep and hears the knight ask to be healed by the Grail. It appears, and when he touches the table on which it stands, he is made whole. Lancelot finds himself unable to move, and a squire comes who arms the knight in Lancelot's armour and mounts him on his horse. Lancelot wonders whether all this was a dream, but hears a voice saying: 'Harder than stone, bitterer than wood, more despised than the fig-tree - depart and pollute the place of the Grail no more'. Weeping, Lancelot departs and, finding a hermitage, confesses his love for Guinevere.

Perceval, meanwhile, meets his aunt, who tells him that she was once Queen of the Waste Land and that he, Galahad, and Bors will win the Grail. He asks further about the knight in red armour (Galahad), and is told the story of the Three Tables: the first at which Christ sat with his disciples; the second the Table of the Holy Grail, made in likeness of the first by Joseph of Arimathea; and lastly the Round Table made by Merlin to show the roundness of the world and the firmament. And as at Whitsuntide the Holy Spirit came to the disciples as tongues of fire, so at the same time Galahad comes in red armour. Merlin had prophesied that the three of them would win the Grail. More of Joseph's adventures are related, much as in the *Grand Saint Graal*. To find Galahad, Perceval is instructed to seek out first Castle Gher, then Corbenic where lies the Maimed King. He sets out and arrives at a monastery where he sees the ancient King Evelach, blind and wounded, still waiting for the one who is to come.

Perceval has many other adventures, in one of which he dreams that he is visited by two women, one riding a lion, the other a serpent. This is later interpreted as being a reference to the New Law (Christianity) and the Old (Judaism), the woman on the Lion signifying the Church and she on the serpent Synagogia. An old man appears on a ship but a damsel warns Perceval against him and tries to make him sleep with her. But as Perceval catches sight of the cross-shaped hilt of his sword he makes the sign of the cross, whereat the damsel and her goods disappear in flames and smoke. The old man reappears, explains that she was a demon sent to try him and takes Perceval on board his craft, but not before Perceval has wounded himself in the thigh in contrition for almost allowing himself to be seduced from the way.

Returning to Lancelot we see him remorseful for seeing the Grail at work but not asking aught of it. He encounters a hermit who is later killed by a demon, and begins to wear a hair shirt beneath his armour. Dismounting at the foot of a cross where four roads meet he has a vision of a man surrounded by stars, crowned and accompanied by seven kings and two knights who pray to be taken to Heaven. Another man descends from Heaven and orders one of the knights away; to the other he gives the shape of a winged lion which flies up to Heaven and is admitted. Lancelot later has this vision interpreted thus: it represents his own lineage - the man surrounded by stars is Celidonel, nephew of Evelach and son of Nasciens, and the nine figures, the kings and knights, his descendants. Lancelot is the knight ordered away, and Galahad is the winged lion 'lion-like in power, deepest of all the streams'.

The story turns to Gawain and his companions, who endure various adventures, dreams and visions of an allegorical kind. Then to Bors, who is tested when he goes to the help of a damsel about to be raped and sees his brother bound naked to a horse being beaten by two men. In anguish Bors goes to the help of the damsel, saves her and meets with a seeming-monk who tells him his brother is dead. Bors then arrives at the Castle of Maidens, where after a vain attempt to get him to lie with any or all of them, they threaten to jump off the topmost tower of the castle. Bors still refuses, and they fall, vanishing along with the whole castle in flame and smoke. They were all devils, as was the monk, for next day Bors finds his brother safe and well at a monastery. He is angry with Bors for allowing the indignity of being beaten to go unpunished and attacks his brother. Bors will not defend himself, however, and two knights who come to his aid are slain. At last Bors draws his sword and prepares to defend himself, but a fiery blade descends from Heaven and comes between the two brothers. Bors is led away to the sea where Perceval waits him. A ship comes for them both, and soon collects Galahad also, led there by a damsel who turns out to be Perceval's sister. On board the ship is a rich bed with a crown at the head and at the foot a sword, two inches out of its scabbard, which has at its tip a stone of all the colours in the world. The hilt of the sword is made of the bones of two beasts, the serpent Papagast and the fish Orteniaus; it is covered with a cloth on which is written that only the last of his line may grasp the sword. Perceval and Bors both try, but fail. Galahad sees that it says only the one who may strike best should attempt it. The damsel explains that this is the sword with which Lambor was slain (as in the *Grand Saint Graal*). Examining the sword more closely Galahad finds the scabbard to be of serpent's skin but the belt of poor stuff.

On the scabbard it is written that only the daughter of a king, who is also a virgin, may renew the belt. Other details are explained by the earlier history of the sword as narrated in *Grand Saint Graal*.

They now examine the bed and find that it has three spindles: that in front, snow-white, that behind, blood-red; that above, emerald-green. These are explained as follows: the three spindles are from a tree grown from a cutting taken by Eve from the Tree of Good and Evil. Originally it was a white tree in token of Eve's innocence, but it turned green when Abel was born and red when Cain slew Abel. It survived the Flood and remained until the time of Solomon. In a dream Solomon learned that the last of his line was to be a virgin knight who would achieve a great wonder. He consulted his wife as to how he should let the knight know of his foreknowledge and she advised the building of a ship which should contain a rich bed with Solomon's own crown and the Sword of David with a new hilt and scabbard.

All these things are done and the great king has another dream in which he sees angels writing the various inscriptions on the sword and the ship. It is prophesied that a maiden will give a new girdle to the sword and this Perceval's sister now does, plaiting a belt from her own hair. She renames the blade 'The Sword with the Strange Hangings' and its scabbard 'Memory of Blood'. Galahad girds it upon himself. They leave the ship and journey onwards, meeting a white stag led by four lions which show the way to a hermitage. They hear Mass and the stag becomes a man who sits on the altar; the lions become an eagle, a lion, a man and an ox, all winged. Perceval now wears Galahad's old sword which he had drawn from the stone.

The travellers arrive at a castle where the custom is that any maiden who comes there must give a dish of blood from her right arm. Galahad, Perceval and Bors protect Perceval's sister against overwhelming odds but in the evening learn that the lady of the castle is suffering from leprosy. Perceval's sister then willingly offers her blood as a healing agency, but as a result dies. The lady is healed. Perceval's sister is put aboard the Ship of Solomon, which is to take her to the Spiritual Place in Sarras, there to be buried as was her wish. The three knights separate and the story now turns to Lancelot.

After many adventures Lancelot goes aboard a mysterious ship and finds there the body of the maiden with a letter explaining how she died. The ship turns again to land and Galahad joins his father. The two undergo more adventures together.

At Easter a white knight bids Galahad continue alone, and we follow Lancelot again. He comes to a castle guarded by lions and on entering finds a room where Mass is being celebrated with the Grail. He is warned not to enter, but when he sees the priest struggling to lift a wounded man onto the altar cannot resist going forward to help. He is struck by a fiery wind and remains fourteen days dumb and unmoving. He finds he is at Corbenic and a damsel tells him that his part in the Grail Quest is ended. Next day he returns to Camelot.

The story now returns to Galahad who comes to the abbey where Mordrains awaits. He heals the old pagan, and Mordrains dies in his arms. Galahad causes a fountain of boiling water to cool by putting his hand into it. He continues for a further five years with Perceval at his side, in which time they achieve the greatest adventures of the Kingdom of Logres. They meet Bors, and the three come at last to Corbenic and are welcomed by the Fisher King. The Maimed King is carried in on a litter; a hot wind strikes the castle and a voice orders all who have not taken part in the quest to depart. From Heaven comes a man clad like a Bishop, borne in a chair carried by four angels who place him before the altar of the Grail. He kneels and opens the ark and more angels issue forth bearing lights, a cloth of red samite, and a Lance bleeding so hard that the drops run down into a box in the angel's other hand. The lights are placed on the table and the cloth over the Grail. The bishop is Josephus, son of Joseph of Arimathea, not seen on earth for more than 300 years. He celebrates Mass, and on raising the Host a Child appears and smites himself into the wafer. Josephus kisses Galahad and bids him to be fed from the Saviour's own hand. He vanishes, but out of the vessel comes a man bleeding from his hands, feet and side who says he will reveal his secrets and give the rich food so long desired. He gives the Sacrament to Galahad, explains that the Grail is the Vessel of the Last Supper, and promises that Galahad shall know it more fully in Sarras to where it now goes - Britain being unworthy of it - and to where the three knights must now also travel.

But first Galahad heals the Maimed King with some of the blood from the Lance. They send messages to Arthur's court and depart in the Ship of Solomon wherein they find the Grail already housed. At Sarras they are at first imprisoned but fed by the Grail for a year, after which time Galahad is crowned king. He builds a tree of gold and precious stones over the Grail and prays before it daily.

A year from the day of his crowning the three go to the Holy Vessel and see a man clad in the robes of a bishop standing before it. He begins the Mass and calls Galahad to come and see what he has longed to see. Galahad looks within the Grail and trembles greatly to see what tongue may not tell nor heart think, and begs to be allowed to die. He takes leave of Perceval and Bors and sends greeting to Lancelot. He dies, and a hand from Heaven takes away the Grail and the Lance, since when no man may say that he has seen the Grail.

Galahad is buried. Perceval retires to a monastery and Bors returns to Camelot where he tells the adventures of the Holy Grail.

**Le Morte d'Arthur.** Many will be familiar with the preceding account because it is the source on which Sir Thomas Malory drew for his own 'Book of the Sangreal' contained in *Le Morte d'Arthur.* For this reason a full discussion of Malory's text is omitted here; though it must be said that his version is no mere re-telling. Everywhere he shapes and styles the original, making deft cuts which reduce the degree of theological and allegorical matter in favour of action. Some critics have attacked him for this, claiming that the result is a meaningless procession of symbols, but that this is far from the case will be recognized by any who reads the *Morte d'Arthur* with attention to the underlying detail. Malory fitted the Grail story into the framework of the Arthurian world with great sensitivity and understanding; and for the sake of the language alone - virtually unparalleled in English prose - he is worth reading. There are, besides, as Charles Williams noted, many clues and hints to be followed up in this text, just as the *Queste* itself also contains much to make the Grail seeker pause for thought. In the Vulgate cycle to which the *Queste* belongs is the first appearance of Galahad: a figure many have found difficulty in accepting due to his often seemingly bloodless actions. However, one has only to read the account of his last days spent alone with his father Lancelot to see that behind the facade of the pure knight is a profound figure who embodies many virtues, far from the priggish dolt that many have seen him to be. Indeed the 'invention' of Galahad may well be one of the more profound aspects of the Grail legend as a whole: he is born of the greatest secular knight and the daughter of the Grail King - and this is brought about through trickery, when Lancelot is made to think he is sleeping with Guinevere rather than Elaine. The outcome is Galahad, the man driven by inner knowledge and predestined from the start to achieve the greatest task ever undertaken by the Round Table knights. He is seen as expiating his father's sin in the manner of his begetting: his life is a triumph which knits together the two halves of the cycle - the spiritual and the secular.

All of this may well owe much to the influence of the teachings of St Bernard of Clairvaux, who founded the Cistercian order and whose thought has been shown to have had a marked effect on the compilers of the Vulgate cycle. Certainly the symbolism is very strongly Christianized, which makes it all the more surprising that the Church steadfastly refused to acknowledge the existence of the Grail at all - never actually attacking it, but simply ignoring the vast popular literature which grew up around it. In this dichotomy lies a great mystery, for the Grail is primarily a Christian symbol for all its provable pagan origins. Perhaps the silence of the Church may be seen as a desire to avoid giving support to a theme which might have become a focus of heretical belief. Or perhaps we are seeing something of the Grail's particular power - its ability to transcend both its origins and its elaboration and development in the mediaeval texts - the same power which keeps it fresh and alive for us today! Whatever the truth, both the *Queste* and Malory's reshaped version will bear careful study by the modern Grail seeker: in particular the episodes concerning Solomon's Ship with its elaborate symbolism could form the basis of long-term meditation; while to pursue the path of the three Grail Knights on the final stages of their journey is to undergo a profound experience. The blood sacrifice of Perceval's sister (better known as Dindraine) holds great significance for both male and female seekers - the latter might wish to consider their monthly offering of blood, while the former may see in this the esoteric value of sacrifice borne out at its deepest level. Whatever line is followed it is virtually impossible to enter the world of the *Queste* without experiencing something of its incantatory power. It is built upon a foundation of inner reality which everywhere looks out from amid the heavier theological interpretations of the various hermits who throng its pages. Even their words hold meanings more subtle than is at first obvious.

**Sone de Nansai.** This text is somewhat later than the majority of those we have been examining, and is often omitted from consideration as a Grail story because it has an historical setting and features real characters known to have existed. Nonetheless it adds important details to our understanding of the Grail, and is remarkable for the way in which it places the holy relic firmly in this world - albeit at a place that can no longer be identified. The story, as summarized by R. S. Loomis in *The Grail: From Celtic Myth to Christian Symbol*, is as follows.

Hearing news of the invasion of Norway by the Irish and Scots, Sone de Nansai takes service in the Norwegian army, defeating both the King of Ireland and a giant Scottish knight. He then takes ship with the King of Norway significantly called Alain, to an island off the coast where there is a monastic community. The object of this visit is to pray for victory, and the travellers are welcomed by the monks, who live not in a monastery but a castle - which furthermore has four towers at each corner and a central tower containing a great hall. Further details show a marked resemblance to the Grail Castle as described by Chrétien. Sone and the king are royally entertained and next day the abbot tells them the history of the monastery and of the Relics kept there. These include the Holy Grail and the Spear, as well as the body of Joseph of Arimathea and the Sword with which he protected Britain. The abbot then narrates the story of the Grail, more or less as found in the Vulgate cycle, but with a substantially different version of the life of Joseph.

Here we see the Grail Keeper discovering an empty boat near Askalon in Syria and being carried away in it to Italy and thence to Norway, where he later becomes king, fosters the Church and establishes the monastic settlement where Sone and the present king find themselves. To test his faith God causes Joseph to be wounded in the thighs and he is thenceforward known as the Fisher

King from his habit of fishing from a small boat by way of diversion. He is later healed by an unnamed knight, but so long as he remained wounded the Kingdom of Logres suffered also and was laid waste. Later the kingdom was renamed Norway.

The abbot then opens a casket and takes out the Grail, which sheds a light bright enough to illumine the world. He next produces a Spear-head which drips blood and shows Sone and the king two coffins, containing the bodies of Joseph and his son Adan. After a great feast Sone and the king depart for the mainland again and the abbot sends after them the Sword with which Joseph had guarded the land. Sone later uses it to slay the gigantic champion of the King of Scotland, and when the daughter of King Alain falls in love with him she gives him a drink from the cup once used by the Fisher King (presumably not the Grail). The name of the island was Galoche, which Loomis glosses as a corrupt form of galesche, i.e. 'Welsh' in Old French.

Here the Grail Kingdom has become identified with Norway, and the life of Sone de Nansai is set in a historical context of thirteenth-century Europe. The Relics of the Grail - Cup, Spear-head and the bodies of the first Keeper and his son - are found in an identifiable place operated on the lines of any monastic establishment and with the marvels reduced to a minimum. There are echoes here of the Lindisfarne community off the coast of Northumbria, which was for long a centre of Celtic Christianity, and of the Island of Gwales (Grassholm) off the Welsh coast where the Company of Bran the Blessed went after his death, and which became known for the Entertainment of the Noble Head because of the manner in which the head of Bran remained animate and provided for its followers. The most astonishing aspect of this text is the identification of Joseph of Arimathea with the Fisher King, which appears in no other surviving version, but which is here explicit. The events described take place long after the time of Arthur and the quest, but we see that the idea of the Grail and a belief that it still perhaps existed, like any other relic, in a geographical place, was still understood by the writers of romances like *Sone de Nansai*.

**Perlesvaus.** The final version we shall look at is also a profoundly rewarding one. It has been suggested that beneath its layers of meaning lies the fragmentary traces of an even older mystery - even of a ritual, and it may well be that prolonged study will reveal enough of this to enable a reconstruction of the original. At all events *Perlesvaus*, or, as it is sometimes called, *The High History of the Holy Grail*, makes fascinating reading. It contains a story which differs strongly from most of the other texts considered here, much of which will test the ability of the seeker to the utmost.

The story begins at Arthur's court on Ascension Day, when the king finds Guinevere sorrowing over the decline in the splendour and might of the Round Table. Arthur acknowledges that he is largely to blame, having lost heart and become enfeebled in spirit. Accordingly he determines to go to the Chapel of St Austin (Augustine?) in the forest and pray for guidance. He therefore bids a page, Chaus, to prepare his horse and accompany him the next day. But in the night the squire dreams that the king has gone ahead and hastens to follow him. In the forest he finds a chapel, and on entering sees the body of a knight covered in a rich cloth and surrounded by brightly burning candles. Determining to bring back something to prove that he has really been there the squire takes one of the golden candlesticks, but in the wood meets with a hideous black giant who demands its return. Chaus refuses and the giant strikes him down.

All this has been a dream, but the squire wakens and calls out that he has been slain. A real knife is sticking in him. The king is summoned and Chaus relates his dream before dying. Thus forewarned the king sets out for the chapel of St Austin. He arrives, and though not permitted to step across the threshold witnesses a Mass in which the Virgin first assists the priest and then offers her Son in the sacramental rite. Arthur learns from the resident hermit of the trouble brought upon the land of the Fisher King by Perceval's failure to ask concerning the Grail. On his way back to the court he has many other adventures, including a meeting with Perceval's sister who tells him of her brother's life up to that moment and of the straits of their mother at the hands of the red knight slain by Perceval. Just before he reaches home Arthur hears a voice proclaim that the state of the world, which has fallen sick through his recent neglect, is about to be improved and that he should summon his court as soon as possible.

The barons and knights duly assemble (at Penzance in Cornwall), and a new era of splendour for the Arthurian kingdom is ushered in by the greatest test of all - the Quest for the Grail. When the court is fully assembled a damsel rides in on a white mule. She is bald, her hair having fallen off as a result of Perceval's failure to ask the all-important Question. She is accompanied by a second damsel carrying a hound and a richly jewelled shield bearing a red cross. A third damsel, the most beautiful of the three, comes on foot, urging on her companions' mounts with a whip and with one hand attached to a star which hangs around her neck. The shield had once belonged to Joseph of Arimathea and it is now hung upon the wall of Arthur's court to await the coming of the Grail winner. The hound also must remain there, as it will only show signs of joy when the Grail Knight comes.

The bald damsel tells Arthur some of the horrors that have come about through Perceval's failure, including the sickness of the Fisher King and a wagon-load of heads, some sealed in gold, some in silver and some in lead, which stands outside the castle, harnessed to three white stags. The three damsels then depart, meeting Gawain in the forest and acquiring his protection past the castle of the black hermit. Many adventures now ensue, in which Gawain earns the gratitude of a pagan king and receives for reward the sword with which St John the Baptist was beheaded. It bleeds every day at noon, that being the time when the prophet was beheaded. Without it no one can enter the Grail Castle.

When Gawain does eventually arrive there he finds everything much as in Chrétien's version, and resolves to ask the Question at dinner. However, when the procession of the Grail takes place - including, in this version, a Child in the Cup who is transformed into the likeness of a Bleeding Man - Gawain is so overwhelmed that he forgets all about his intention, and when the procession has passed becomes involved in a game with the magic chessboard at the end of the hall. After losing twice it is taken from him and he falls asleep. Next morning he hears a mass celebrating the return of the Sword of St John but is not permitted to attend directly. He is reproached for not asking the question and learns that the castle must now defend itself against the advance of the evil King of Castle Mortal (who here occupies the roles of Klingsor and Garlon).

After Gawain's failure we hear of Lancelot's attempt to win the Grail, which is foredoomed by his love for Guinevere. He does succeed in reaching the castle but is not permitted to see the Grail.

After this narrative of failure the story turns at last to Perceval, now clearly identified through his adventures as the 'Good Knight' long expected to achieve the Grail. During his wanderings he learns that the King of Castle Mortal has murdered his uncle the Fisher King and seized the Grail Castle. Perceval lays siege to it and is so successful, killing so many of the evil king's knights, that he finally commits suicide. The Grail Knights then return, together with the priests and damsels who have fled from the evil king, and Perceval becomes the new Grail King.

Meanwhile one evening Arthur goes down to the sea-shore and there beholds a mysterious ship steered by an old man. Within it lies Perceval asleep, with a branched candelabra at his feet. He awakes and is led into the court by the old man, bearing the candlestick before him. Perceval claims the shield and hound as foretold, and departs again for an Elysian island of which he is rightly king and to where the ship will return with him in a future time. Meanwhile he must return to serve the Grail.

Arthur later visits him and sees the Grail, after which Perceval takes the Holy Relics and goes to live in the forest until in the course of time the ship returns and carries him away to the Blessed Isles - since when no man has seen the Grail. However, in a coda which admirably describes the experience of all Grail seekers, two young knights visit the castle years later when it has become an empty shell rumoured to be haunted, and after remaining there some time, emerge much changed. When asked about their experience they say nothing except 'Go there and you will see what we have seen'.

In this text we enter some of the deepest mysteries of the Grail. The Mass of the Virgin witnessed by Arthur and the repetition of the transformation of the Host into the actual body of a Wounded Man or Child, touch upon the most profound levels of mystical Christianity, while the passage of Perceval to and from the mysterious island identifies him with the otherworld mysteries - indeed, the whole passage in which Arthur witnesses him come ashore from the mysterious ship carrying the candelabra reads like an otherworld visitation. Perceval brings the light of the Grail into the halls of Camelot and establishes himself as the rightful claimant of the place filled by Galahad in texts such as the *Queste del Saint Graal*. The war between the Fisher King and the King of Castle Mortal fleshes out the fragmentary stories of Klingsor and Garlon in *Parzival* and the *Queste,* while the mysterious Sword of John the Baptist is also made clear as Gawain's personal quest - though here there is no mention of it being broken. The mysterious coda implies that there is still something remaining behind in the castle, even though Perceval has long since returned to the otherworld realm over which he is presumed to rule. It is this fact which is most clearly reflected in the modern quest: though seemingly withdrawn the Grail continues to exert a deep and powerful influence over all who seek it.

This completes our all-too-brief summary of the major Grail texts. Other references abound - not least in the Welsh *Preiddeu Annwn*, which though listed as one of the primary texts will, because of its peculiar nature, be discussed fully in Chapter 4. In this Arthur himself takes a leading role, sailing to the land of the Otherworld in search of the Cauldron of Rebirth, the earliest archetype of the Grail. Despite its fragmentary form it is still possible to reconstruct from this something of the original quest story and the heroes who took part in it.

The above summaries are intended to give some idea of the richness of the materials available, and some of the symbolism which, as we shall see, can become the basis of a lifelong Grail Quest for any who so wish it. It should be understood, however, that the summaries in no way replace an actual reading of the texts. Most are readily available and have been translated or are in the process of being so. The experience of the authors suggests that to attempt to read all those described here over a short period is equivalent to eating too much rich food - magical indigestion can be just as uncomfortable as physical overeating! Taken one at a time, read through once and then returned to for meditation on specific episodes or symbols, the texts will be found to be some of the most rewarding ways of beginning your own inner search. Certain characters, symbols and events will begin to have special appeal, and these are best used as springboards into the deeper waters of the quest.

# Chapter Two

## Of Forests and Wastes

### The Landscapes of the Grail

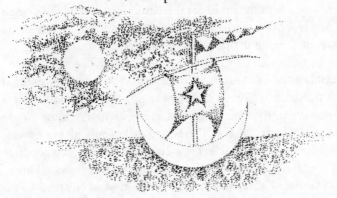

The world of the Grail seems to be our world — but superimposed upon it, penetrating it at certain points, the Other World is present.

P.L. Wilson: Angels

Once we have become accustomed to the world of the Grail texts we can begin establishing it as a living part of our own inner realm, that place where we move freely and at will, crossing vast distances of time and space, building castles and towers and demolishing them again, finding ever new and varied paths into stranger, richer, more wondrous places. For this is a realm that is larger within than without, it has no boundaries except those we ourselves impose, and its laws are always true to itself: nothing happens that has not been allowed for and everything that is allowed for has already happened. In this it resembles the outer world as seen through a mirror: everything is true, according to our understanding of reality, yet it is just a shade more real - our own world a copy of this far truer place.

We are all aware, at some level or another, of this inner place. It borders upon the Otherworld and we enter it nightly in our dreams. From it come all the myriad symbols, archetypes and mysteries with which our own world is peopled. It has its own reality, its own laws and its own purposes - some of which we can know while others remain totally unsuspected. It is not to be confused with the psychological world of the unconscious - though they do share certain points of similarity. The space between our own inner world and the Otherworld is minimal. The two are not the same, however, though it is comparatively easy to step from one to the other. In the quest for the Grail this can and does often occur, and it is plain from the clues scattered throughout the texts that what may begin in this world seldom remains so for long.

Places, names and situations convey much. The place of the Celtic Hallows is an Otherworld far different from that entered through the gates of Corbenic - though again there are many points of common identify. The four aspects or partitions of the Celtic realm: Finias, Gorias, Murias, Falias, and of the four cities or towers: Caer Golur, Caer Ochren, Caer Vandwy, Caer Siddi, each contains an aspect of the total mystery. Four guardians: Morfessa in Falias, Esras in Gorias, Uscias in Finias, Semias in Murias, stand guard over the identities of Stone, Spear, Sword and Cup. They may be contacted and questioned, and may or may not choose to answer, according to whether the intention of the asker is right and proper.

Theirs is a landscape of flat grasslands and standing corn; of massive green mounds and circular or four-square towers; of deep forests and tumbled stones; of swift-flowing streams and ancient moss-covered rocks. Here, in the shadows, when mists arise, or in the broad light of the sacred sun, the mysteries of the Grail in its earthly aspect are shaped and enacted for our wondering gaze. We walk the paths of Faery and see the shape of the inner Albion, the Logres of the Heart, forming around us.

These are enchanted realms, and to enter them is to become enchanted also. We may choose to set sail upon a mysterious, unmanned vessel for one of the island earths: Avalon, the Blessed Realms, Hy Brazil - or for one of those strange, unnamed places visited by the Irish St Brendan or the hero Bran son of Febal (not to be confused with Bran the Blessed in the *Mabinogion*). Or there is Spiral Castle, earlier echo of Corbenic, a mysterious, totally unpredictable place where anything may happen and few things are what they seem to be. Here at every level of the maze-like interior, at every turning of the winding stairs, a new adventure or test awaits, a new personage turns its gaze upon us, new questions await the asking and (sometimes) the answering. And below it, deep within the earth, a mirror-image of the over-earth castle lies, leading to cities beneath the sea where the Cauldrons are set bubbling and the god Mananaan mac Lir holds court in the kingdom of the watery Grail.

These are chancy places, where there is no guarantee that what is sought after will be found, or that what is not sought will not come seeking in its turn. But for some it is still the only way, with at its end a sip from the Cauldron, with all that that may bring. For this is a world of great riches, few of them physical; a world where the strong magic of myth works itself into the bloodstream of the seeker. And it is the home of the Grail, where everything is unexpected and wholly normal. Unless we enter it we shall be swiftly turned back upon our quest - for we can seldom see the outer world clearly without the perception of the inner realms to act as our focus.

Techniques and suggestions for working with all the archetypes of the Grail will be found in part 3 of the present work, so that the following gazetteer of places and sites may be considered as guide-posts to the country we seek. Once it is firmly established it will begin to work its own subtle magics and to transform our inner awareness of the mysteries which underlie all we have learned and will learn as we advance further and deeper into the realm of the Grail.

What follows here are no more than impressions, gleaned partly from the texts themselves, partly from extant historical evidence, partly from knowledge derived from inner quests, of the landmarks to be found within the Grail realm, where, as the poem has it, 'you and I will fare'.

The Waste Land The setting within which the quest most often begins is that of the wasted lands, once ruled over by the Fisher King. As we have seen from the texts this is usually brought into existence by the unthinking acts of one of the protagonists of the

story - be it the Maimed King, whose sterility is given outward
expression by the state of his kingdom, or some unfortunate knight
like Balin le Sauvage, who strikes the Dolorous Blow and lays
waste the whole country as well as its ruler.

In a deeper sense the Waste Land is within us all; it is that
barren place where imagination, love, charity have ceased to
function. It is the scar on the soul caused by some wrong, self-
inflicted or brought about through someone we love, where nothing
will grow thereafter. It is also an image of the world in which we
live, of the concrete jungle and of fundamentalist politics; the world
where everything is leveled or made to seem a weak copy of an
original, vibrant reality. It is the grey world where possessions are
all and love has died amid squalor and promiscuity. It is an ancient
world that has always existed, sometimes hidden within an outward
seeming fairness, sometimes with its sores and wounds exposed
for all to see. It is a place we all know and have all visited. Yet the
Grail exists at its heart, and therein lies the paradox with which
each and every one who sets forth on the quest, filled with high
ideals, has at some time to come to terms. For it is both necessary
and essential that we pass through the Waste Lands and see them
clearly for what they are, for the potential which lies within them,
for the opposite they represent, the perfect world hidden like a
crystal inside a rough-hewn rock.

The lesson they have to teach us is that it is no use setting forth
on the Quest filled with sweetness and light, believing that the
Grail exists in some never-never-land like a crock of gold at the
rainbow's end. The Grail is here, it is now, and it is often hidden
behind a surface of surpassing ugliness. Part of its mystery is
being able to see through the outer form to the crystal within. Like
the Loathly Lady who appears in the texts to mock and revile the
seeker, but who in the story of Gawain and Ragnall is revealed as
having another face of beauty and gentleness.

Thus a great part of the task for the Grail Seeker is to look
within at the reality behind the world of surface appearances and
to bring that reality out into the open, where it may be seen and
shared by all. Thus as when the question is asked by the seeker
and the wounds of king and land are healed, we must be able to
stand in the Waste Land and question what we appear to see - the
words 'quest' and 'question' are here synonymous.

**The Savage Forest** Another aspect of the Waste Land is the Forest Sauvage, or as it is sometimes called, the Wood Adventurous, a vast, uncharted tract of land bordering and adjoining the Waste. Likened to a maze by some who have walked its ways, it contains many strange and terrible things. Each road leads to a different part of this seemingly endless realm, and in each part are clearings, glades where castles sit, tenanted with strange monsters, beautiful women, tests and trials; perilous beds that move of their own volition and submit the onward traveler to showers of spears or attack by wild beasts; magic chessboards where the pieces move against you, and where to lose may be to summon strange visitants. Giants there are also, with one eye or one tooth; serpents hidden in towers or under the earth; maidens kept boiling in magic baths for a hundred years.

This is Broceliande, the magic wood where Merlin dreams in his Hawthorn Tower or appears to Arthur in the guise of a wondrous youth; where the Questing Beast, with the head of a serpent, the body of a lion, the feet of a hart, the tail of a boar, and the noise of thirty pairs of hounds issuing from its belly, leads the unwary down endless paths between the trees.

The forest is symptomatic of the quest which leads nowhere, pursued for its own sake like a dog chasing its own tail; the quest misused for reasons of personal desire, or as a place in which to hide from reality. It is an area which must be traversed before the true lands of the Grail are reached, and where it is perilous to linger. Many kinds of delusion await those who come without purpose or direction. And yet, at its heart, in some almost forgotten glade where the wanderer comes at last after many leagues in the dim greenness of the wood, lies the first rumour of the Grail. For here too is its home.

**The Grail Castle.** Here, bounded by water where the Fisher King glides in his strange craft, across a bridge that can become as narrow and sharp as a naked sword, lies the mysterious chamber where the Maimed King waits with ever-renewed hope for the coming of the one who will heal him - and who may well be one of us! But first we must cross the narrow bridge above water that bubbles and boils; must find entry by way of the revolving walls of the castle, which as it spins offers brief glimpses of gardens within; must face the gate-keeper, the Dweller-on-the-Threshold, who reads our true intent with terrible accuracy. And, when we are within, we must decide how to behave, what questions to ask and when to remain silent - must endure, indeed, all that the quest-knights endured, fail where they failed, and try to succeed where they did not.

Or we may find that we have entered another form of the castle - that which is called the Orgellus Castle, the place of pride, where we must overcome the most insidious trial of all - that spark of inner satisfaction which tells we are on a great quest and are therefore set apart from the rest of mankind.

**The Chessboard Castle** Is so called not only because those who enter are called upon to play out a game against usually invisible opponents, but also because its floor is marked out in chequered squares of black and white - echoing the design of most magical temples, where the two worlds, light and dark, are shown to overlap in our own world, where we must seek to balance both within ourselves, So, too, is the theme of balance wound into the shifting patterns of the Grail Castle, which tests us in so many ways, emphasizing both the positive and negative aspects of character, giving prominence to the foolish and the wise.

**The Castle of Maidens** Is the place of the feminine mysteries of the Grail. Here the Lady of the Lake and her entourage hold court, and it is thus sometimes found beneath the waters which surround the Castle of the Grail. Within it the positive, active and receptive aspects of the spirit find a home, and it is here that the Princess of the Grail holds sway, offering her blood for the healing of those who require it, making a belt for the Sword of Aspirations from her hair. Entrance may be had by way of the Fountain of Adventure, guarded by maidens who are bound to offer hospitality to all who come in search of the hidden realm of the Grail.

This castle should not be seen as the domain of women only, however: men with sufficient understanding of the feminine principle are welcome here also and can learn much from such a visit. Here are the mysteries of giving and taking, of service offered and accepted, of love and gentleness and strength, of woman as

Vessel, of virginity and marriage and sex. Here also is the flowering of the troubadour ethic as it might have been, seeing woman as Grail, as a way within to the realm of the perfect mirror of creation, the womb of life and of the world, the marriage of heaven and earth.

**The Grail Chapel** Those who traverse the Waste Land, who find their way through the diversity of the Savage Forest and the Castles of Wonder, come at last to the Chapel of the Grail, a simple room containing an altar, a candle which burns with a steady flame, and upon the altar a Cup and Spear. These are seen as the Hallows of the Spirit, which, in the words of Charles Williams, have been 'nearest the divine and living heart of all things'.

At the door to this chamber must be left all falsehood and vain intention, here the soul is as naked as a newborn child - indeed, it is as a child that one enters here: innocent, foolish and wise at once, open to the eye of God. No preparation is ever sufficient for what occurs in this place, for here one enters the most secret heart of the universe and beholds the unseeable, untenable truths.

**The Chapel in the Green** Others may see the Grail Chapel thus: as a simple mound with an entrance leading to a green-lit interior. Here the most ancient archetype of the Grail, the Cauldron of Rebirth, tended by nine maidens whose breath warms its rim, is found. Here is all knowledge and all wisdom - sometimes too terrible to bear. Here the seeker is stripped of all shadows, all doubts are taken from him, all questions asked and answered. The two are seen to be one, the mystery of the Grail as neither pagan nor Christian, simply itself. Like Lancelot, if we are not ready we should not look upon these things for fear of being struck down, blinded by truths too great to understand. For though the Grail may dwell here, in simple room or simple cave, it is also far greater, filling the whole world with its presence, appearing at once in the populous hall at Camelot, the hermit's forest cell, and the mysterious places of the Spirit.

**Sarras** The Holy City of the Grail, is such a place. It lies 'across the sea' divided from the land by a gulf which only the chosen may cross. Yet we are each given passage by our desire to see the higher mysteries of the Grail, and we may, in time, come to that fair city and walk its golden streets until we reach the great basilica on the hill. And, entering in, we may stand with the chosen three: Galahad, Perceval and Bors, before the altar on which the supreme mystery is enacted before our astonished gaze. And we may hear, as they heard, a voice saying:

'My knights and my sergeants, and my true children, who have come out of earthly life and into the spiritual life, I will no longer hide myself from you, but you shall see now a part of my secrets and of my hidden things . . . For this is the dish wherein I ate the lamb on Sher-Thursday, and now hast thou seen that thou most desired to see . . .' (*Malory: Morte d'Arthur*)

Here then we can make our choice: whether to dedicate ourselves to the service of the Grail, or to pass inward, 'further up and further in',[Footnote: C. S. Lewis: *The Last Battle* (Bodley Head, 1965).] to even greater mysteries. Or we may wish to return, bringing with us the light of the Grail, back into the world where we may become aware of the hidden Logres, the inner kingdom which lies always just beneath the surface of the everyday world in which we life.

The true home of the Grail is finally no more in the spirit than in a museum or between the pages of a book. It is multi-dimensional, its presence touching our lives through many levels at once, its country bordering on our own at every possible part. We enter there, knowing little; we go there to learn; and above all, we shall return with the knowledge thus gained impressed deeply upon our minds and hearts, so that we may tell it to others. All walk the paths alone, but it is still possible to share understanding in ways that may help others through stretches of difficult terrain. The Grail lands are often harsh at first, and the going may get easier or harder as we pass further or deeper into them. But at every point we will meet those who can help and advise us, who, though they seem to challenge, yet seek to send us onward, ever deeper into the magical country of the soul where we may find our own Grail. Some of these we will meet in the next chapter, but before that we must look further at the outer landscapes of the Grail, at the places the modern seeker might wish to visit in his quest.

There are indeed, many places scattered throughout the world which according to long-standing traditional ascription have connections with the Grail. Some, like Glastonbury in Somerset, or Valencia in Italy, even claim to possess the Sacred Vessel itself. For those concerned with the inner value of the quest, however, such places can enhance and focus the awareness in a unique way. Actual visits to Grail sites can thus be of considerable value, and meditations conducted there may well be more powerful than similar sessions at home (not, of course, that either should be held to be more effective than the other over a long period: the strengths and abilities of the individual seeker are what really counts, not the place where the realization may be sought). This being so, what places are there which possess actual Grail connections?

Glastonbury Must always figure largely in any such listing, not only for its obvious associations with Joseph of Arimathea and its possible claim to be the site of the oldest Christian foundation in Britain, but equally for the powerful inner resonances possessed by the hills which surround it on all sides. Glastonbury works very much like a burning glass, focusing and enlarging aspects of the personality - negative as well as positive. Thousands of pilgrims who make their way there every year, many in the hope of discovering the Grail for themselves - that some have claimed to do so is a testimony to the remarkable properties of the place.

Two great mystics who lived and worked there have given further testimony to the Glastonbury Grail phenomenon. The first of these, Wellesley Tudor-Pole, founded the Lamplighter Trust which opened a centre in Glastonbury at Chalice Well Gardens, reputedly the site of one of the three Holy Wells which rise in and around the area of the Tor. Chalice Well itself is certainly a remarkable spot by any criteria. When it was drained in the early part of this century it was found to be constructed from huge stone slabs, not unlike those used in the formation of Megalithic tombs or monuments, which formed a chamber inside the hillside. There is a small, unexplained niche just below the lip of the well where, according to tradition, a small blue glass bowl was discovered in the 1930s as the result of a dream experienced by a member of the Tudor-Pole household, who was told to go forth and search under the well-head. Subjected to vigorous archaeological tests the bowl was found to have originated in the Holy Land at a period near enough to the estimated date of the Crucifixion to cause further speculation that this might indeed be the Grail.

Nor was this belief contradicted by the later disclosure that the glass bowl had been placed in Chalice Well by Tudor-Pole himself, who had obtained it while traveling in the Middle East. For whatever its origins, the blue bowl was found to possess properties of healing and focusing energy. It is today kept in a bank vault, where it was placed to protect it against vandalism or theft - but until recently it was still to be seen, in private hands, and its genuine qualities attested to by those who made pilgrimage to see it.

Dion Fortune, the second great mystic to be active in Glastonbury is best known for her influential books on magic and Qabalah and as the founder of the Society of Inner Light, but in her book *Avalon of the Heart* she gives a penetrating and enlightening view of the area in all its aspects, revealing levels of understanding available only to those who live and work there. She gives her own version of the hiding of the Grail beneath Chalice Hill, in which the Fisher King, doubting the wisdom of allowing the sacred relic to remain in the hands of wicked men,

> took it to keep in his treasury, an underground chamber in the heart of Chalice Hill . . . There the Cup was guarded by three pure maidens, who watched it day and night, and only brought forth for high festival, when it passed from hand to hand in memory of Our Lord, and His death upon the Tree. Whosoever drank of it never thirsted again, for it was to him a well-spring of Waters of Life within his soul.

Drawing on deep esoteric sources, the book gives understanding not only of Glastonbury the physical place, but also its deep inner resonance as Avalon, place of wonders and final home of Arthur.

Apart from the Christian associations, there are older echoes, in which the Tor is seen as the gateway to Annwn and therefore the home of the earliest image of the Grail in Britain. Several writers have recently discussed the idea that the hill constitutes a natural maze around its sides, and that to follow this way brings a form of enlightenment. In the inner understanding of the Grail, the mystery of the Labyrinth is an initiatory one, in which the pattern itself conducts the soul of the seeker through levels of experience into other realms.

In the area surrounding Glastonbury, many seekers claim to be aware of great terrestrial figures representing the house of the zodiac, cut into the landscape. Katherine Maltwood, who rediscovered these figures in the 1930s, successfully established a connected narrative from these which she derived from the text of *Perlesvaus*. Much of that text appears to be set in and around the Somerset levels, and it is possible with the help of the maps provided in her book *Glastonbury, Temple of the Stars*, to follow the course of the quest adventures through the shaded lanes and green hillsides of the Summer Country

**Nanteos** According to local tradition the eighteenth-century mansion of Nanteos, just outside Aberystwyth in Wales, became the resting place of the Grail when monks from Glastonbury Abbey fled at the time of the Dissolution first to the Abbey of Strata Florida and finally to Nanteos itself. The 'Grail' which the monks carried with them was a plain bowl made of ancient wood. It was certainly very old in the sixteenth century, when members of the Powell family still maintained guardianship of it, and it was widely believed to possess healing properties. Water poured into it was sent around the world to those suffering from various diseases or ailments, and as recently as our own era letters and cards were to be seen at the house attesting to its miraculous cures.

As nearly always in such cases, it is in all probability belief in the sacredness of the object which affected the cures, rather than any supernatural properties - however, the Grail takes many forms and works through more than one agency so it would be rash to dismiss the claims of the cup out of hand. The Nanteos Cup is no longer to be seen, being kept, like its fellow in Glastonbury, in the safety of a bank vault, but at least one early visitor known to have seen it was Richard Wagner, whose inspiration to write his mystical Grail opera *Parsifal* dates from this time.

**Langport** Not far from Glastonbury, the church at Langport contains a window depicting Joseph of Arimathea carrying two 'cruets' containing the blood and sweat of Christ. This dates from the late fifteenth century and probably derives from local tradition concerning the arrival of Joseph in Britain. There is a strong peaceful aura about the place, and to sit in meditation before the window can bring valuable realizations.

Castell Dinas Bran. Further North in the fastness of Wales, near Llangollen, stands the steep-sided hill linked with the Grail since at least the Middle Ages. The noted Arthurian scholar R. S. Loomis pointed out that it fitted several descriptions of the Grail Castle, while its name, which associates it with the Celtic deity Bran the Blessed who possessed a Cauldron of Abundance, strengthens its association with the earlier aspects of the Grail. As late as 1794 Dinas Bran was known as Crow Castle, and since the name Bran also means Raven, and the Grail Castle is sometimes referred to as Corbyn (also meaning Crow), there is cearly a well-founded connection here.

Dinas Bran is certainly a powerful spot, as those who make the long climb to the top will testify. The present ruins which occupy part of the hill are mediaeval, but there are echoes of much earlier occupation just beneath the surface. Like the harsher outcrop of Dinas Emrys, it is a place where the presence of Merlin can still be felt, and this may indeed, for some, lead to a deeper understanding of the origins of the Grail tradition.

Further afield, in the haunted landscapes of Brittany, are several sites worthy of visiting. The tiny church of **Cleden-Poher** in Finistère has an extraordinary Calvary in its graveyard which depicts, in miniature, the Crucifixion scene with two angels holding vessels to catch blood pouring from Christ's wounds, while a figure of Joseph of Arimathea kneels at the foot of the Cross with another larger Cup in which he is also collecting blood. The whole carving has a feeling of extraordinary power emanating from it, and though it probably dates from no earlier than the sixteenth century is imbued with far earlier and more primitive energies.

This is the case at **Trehorentenc** in Morbihan, where the entire church contains a rich collection of Arthurian and Grail images. The church is dedicated to the seventh-century St Onenne, but it is the Arthurian figures whose pictures throng the walls who catch the attention. They are like living icons and every bit as powerful as any depictions of the lives of the saint.

At the western end of the church is a huge mosaic depicting the Fountain of Barenton, where Merlin was long believed to dwell, and a great red rock known as Merlin's Threshold, which is strongly reminiscent of the block of red marble which floated down to Camelot and from which Galahad drew his sword at the start of his quest. That too had been placed there by Merlin earlier in the story, so the connection seems valid.

An east window also carries the weight of Grail symbolism, with Joseph of Arimathea kneeling before Christ while the Holy Vessel floats overhead. Above the sacristry door is a painting depicting the Round Table with twenty-one knights seated around it and the Grail, shown as a chalice, appearing before them. The whole church is thus redolent with the imagery of the Grail and provides hours of study and revelation for those engaged on the quest.

Bruges In Belgium, has been named by one writer 'the City of the Grail'. This title is in part generated by the presence of a relic of the Holy Blood kept in the church of that name in the heart of the city. It is, indeed, still possible to venerate this sacred object which is displayed daily at certain times. It looks like dry red dust inside its glass container - but it radiates energy. At least one of the authors can testify to the extraordinary power of the realisations made in meditation in the beautiful mediaeval church which is its home.

Apart from this central connection with the imagery of the Grail, the author Paul de Saint-Hilaire, in his book *Bruges, Citie du Graal*, has found numerous other visual references throughout the city - to, amongst others, the Swan Knights, the Templars (who are reputed to have brought the Holy Blood to Bruges), and the same St Elizabeth of Hungary whose crystal cup, kept in a museum in Coburg, is reputed to have performed miracles akin to those of the Grail. Even if you don't accept M. Saint-Hilaire's theories, Bruges is still worth a visit by all engaged on the quest. Note in the church of the Holy Blood a small carving, high up on the wall of the crypt, which shows the motif of the two cruets found in Somerset on the shield of Joseph of Arimathea.

**Montségur** A full discussion of this site is held over to Chapter 4 where we deal with the Cathar connections with the Grail, but mention must be made here of its long-standing association with the Grail and of its undoubted power. One sensitive investigator reports that on visiting the site shortly after the Second World War he was appalled by the aura of pain and suffering still emanating from the area where hundreds of Cathars were burned to death by the Inquisition (the infamous remark of the Bishop who condemned women and children to the flames without trial is often quoted: 'Burn them all, God will know His own') - and others have since borne witness to this, although it does seem to have abated in more recent years.

Whatever the truth of the Cathar theory, the fact remains that the sacred mountain where the Castle of the Grail stood, according to Wolfram von Eschenbach, was called Muntsalvach and this has caused other, similarly named sites, including Monserrat in Spain, to be connected with the mysterious castle.

Three other sites worthy of mention, also draw upon the imagery of the Grail Castle for their support as claimants for our attention. These are the Castel del Monte in the Apulia region of Italy, Karlstein Castle in Poland, and the ruined Taq-di-Taqdis in what is now Iran.

The first of these, **Castel del Monte**, was built for the Emperor Frederic II, Emperor of Germany, King of the Romans, King of Sicily and Jerusalem. Known by the title *Stupor Mundi*, King of the World, Frederic had a reputation as a confirmed heretic, hater of Christianity and practitioner of the black arts. In reality he was a highly educated polymath whose keen mind led him to investigate many curious and arcane areas of knowledge, including the prophesies of Merlin and the beliefs of the Sufi orders of Islam. He surrounded himself with experts in the Qabalah, astrologers and alchemists. His court probably became the most sophisticated in the Western world at that time (the beginning of the thirteenth century), and a knowledge of the Arthurian legends and of the Grail in particular figured largely.

The castle, constructed to Frederic's personal specifications by the architect Philippe Chinard, is octagonal, composed of two concentric octagons divided by lines running outward from the centre to the points of each angle - thus providing eight wedge-shaped rooms. The only entrance gate, facing south-east towards Jerusalem, leads to a central chamber known simply as 'the Master's chamber'. At each point of the octagon is a massive tower rising from the surrounding wall.

Apart from its curious architecture, Castel del Monte is clearly not built to be lived in - it has no kitchens, pantries, or bedrooms: yet it was built to house something. Tradition says this to be the Grail, and while there is no evidence to prove this, enough strange stories are related to suggest that something odd was once housed there. Rumours of hoards of alchemical gold, of strange statues, and of its association with the Templars may have given rise to its Grail memories. It is still worth a visit.

Karlstein Castle Near Prague was built for another king, Charles IV of Bohemia, in 1348. Like Castel del Monte it contains some curious architecture, in particular a massive tower connected to the rest of the castle by a slender bridge, which contains at its top the Chapel of the Holy Cross, better known, according to local tradition, as the Chapel of the Holy Grail. Within its huge walls a spiral stairway winds upwards past wonderful frescoes depicting episodes from the lives of Bohemian saints. The chapel itself is a masterpiece of ornate symbolism, with patterns inscribed in semi-precious stones from the floor almost to roof level. The windows are of translucent crystal and the entire ceiling is gilded, representing the dome of the heavens with sun, moon and stars. Here Charles IV, who has been described by Rudolf Steiner as the last initiate to sit upon the throne of kings, used to withdraw for private meditation every year from Good Friday to Easter Saturday. It is reported that he used to contemplate a marvellous crystal cup which was kept there, and that he believed it to be the Grail.

Whether any of this is true, those who have visited Karlstein Castle speak of its overpowering splendour and deep meditative echoes, making it an important point on the outer itinerary of the Grail seeker.

Taq-di-Taqdis The last of the three castles of the Grail, is the most ancient, dating from the seventh century AD, when it was built for the Persian King Chosroes II. All that remains of this once imposing palace (its name means Throne of Arches) is a ring of broken and crumbling walls and the foundations of once fabulous buildings. Its claim to be included in the list of Grail sites has to do with the remarkable similarity between this ancient Eastern palace and the Temple of the Grail as described by a twelfth-century German poet named Alberecht von Scharfenburg. In his work *Der Jungëre Titters*, Alberecht describes the Grail Chapel and its setting in considerable detail. It included a high, circular building, surmounted by a dome of gold and with constellations and planets painted upon it and outlined in jewels. He is also specific in describing the mountain upon which the chapel stands as being made of onyx, which shone like the sun when it reflected the light.

In the 1930s the Persian scholar Arthur Upham Pope visited the site of Taq-di-Taqdis and found that it had been built around a lake which left a mineral deposit around the edge which looked like onyx. He investigated further and found contemporary sources which described the palace as it had once been. It included a high, round temple surmounted by a golden dome, on which were painted depictions of stars and planets. Other points of similarity convinced Pope that he was looking at the original Grail Chapel - though how word of it come to the ears of a twelfth-century poet was another matter. It is no longer easy to visit the site of the palace, but the story may serve as a pointer to the way in which the Grail surfaces in the most unlikely places and under the oddest of forms.

Other sites do exist, though we have no space to investigate them here. The Prentice Pillar in Melrose Abbey, Scotland, is rumoured to contain clues to the whereabouts of the Grail, or even to contain the Vessel itself; there is a plain wooden bowl encased in a rich gold container and kept in the Cathedral at Valencia in Spain which it is claimed is the actual Cup used by Christ for the celebration of the first Eucharist and therefore the actual Holy Grail. All others are false ... but in reality, of course, all and none are the 'real' Grail, whose true country is the landscape of the Soul.

One final site needs to be considered: the so-called **Extern Stones** in the Tutoburg Forest in Germany. These vast stone monuments, carved out of the rock by prehistoric hands, contain two chambers aligned respectively with the rising of the sun at midsummer and its setting at midwinter. Beneath these is a third, empty, chamber, with ancient runic inscriptions long since partially defaced. Nearby on the face of a massive granite boulder is a carving which depicts the descent from the Cross. Joseph of Arimathea, depicted as of almost giant stature, lifts the body of the dead Saviour; aided by Nicodemus. Sun and moon watch upon either hand, and a smaller picture of the Risen Christ dominates the whole scene. The shapes and design of the carvings are significant, forming several spherical figures when seen from a distance. This, together with the possible meaning of the name Extemsteine (as it appears in full) which may be read as 'Star-Stones of the River', suggests ancient astrological intent. Noted followers of Rudolf Steiner, Dr Alfred Heindenreich and Emil Bock both identify this site as the centre of Grail energy in Germany. Once again personal testimony indicates that the stones and their fantastic carvings are a meeting place of the old and the new, the very nexus-point of which the Grail itself is a symbol.

The truth is that wherever one looks there are images which remind one of the sought-after object. So rich is the lore of the Grail that it is bound to find echoes in many forms and places. Inner journeys in search of the sacred things may be balanced by actual pilgrimages to the sites thus associated; and there are always others awaiting personal discovery. Those discussed here are only a few of the major sites where echoes of the Grail may be felt most strongly. Others as yet unknown may appear in the lives of the seekers who go in search of these mysterious things.

# Chapter Three

## Of Damsels, Knights and Lords:

### The People of the Grail

*"The Knights and their Ladies, who form the fellowship, are archetypes of different sorts of force as expressed through human experience, and at the same time each one of them, as a particular type of force, is present within us all."*
Gareth Knight: Secret Tradition in Arthurian Legend

having looked first at the texts as a way into the country of the Grail, and secondly at the strange and yet wholly consistent landscape itself, we come now to a consideration of the characters who people it: the seekers and finders, the successful and those who fail, the knights and damsels, dwarfs and hermits, squires and evil magicians who populate the wondrous world of the Grail.

As Gareth Knight so ably expresses it in the quotation which heads this chapter, the people of the Arthurian world are more than types; they are present within each of us. In time, it is hoped, those who go in search of the Grail will encounter some at least of these folk for themselves, will come to know them as friendly guides or doughty adversaries. Meditation, either in a direct fashion as participants in the ongoing quest, or from a more remote position as watchers of the events described, can bring one quickly into the realm of the mysteries, and can deepen the awareness of their true nature.

Perceval, Galahad, Gawain, Lancelot, Merlin and Bors - these are archetypes. Like the god-forms of higher mysteries they can be worked with directly, their personalities put on and taken off like cloaks, their adventures experienced directly through the use of the active imagination in meditation or path-working. They are, we repeat, archetypes, not aspects of the seeker's own personality - though they may well draw on that personality to add flesh to the impalpable stuff of inner reality.

Working with one character over a length of time can establish a close rapport, but should never be permitted to take over or become too deeply embedded in the consciousness of the quester. Those who walk the paths of the Grail-search will find themselves - as we have seen - in a strange land where the laws are not those of our own everyday world. The best guides to this inner place are those who already know it best - its native inhabitants. We may find ourselves in the company of Gawain or Galahad, Elaine the Grail Maiden, or even Joseph of Arimathea himself. Always attend to what they have to say - they know the ways of the Grail lands far better than we ever will and may save us many fruitless hours following roads that lead nowhere. Or, if we wish to explore a particular aspect of the stories in detail - the court of the Fisher King or one of the four cities of Annwn - a character associated with that place will often act as a guide through the complex, shifting realm within.

You may wish to write path-workings in which you meet with and are led by one character, and to aid in this we have given brief descriptions of the foremost people to be found in association with the Grail lands - their ways and manners, their general appearance and insignia (where appropriate), and their function within the world of the quest. In the instance of the knights we have given their heraldic devices (where these are known) as another means of establishing them fully in the consciousness of the seeker, and at the end of the book there will be found family trees indicating the sometimes complex relationships within the various groups.

The list is by no means exhaustive, and it may be found useful to add to it both in the instance of those you may intend to work with but who are not included here, or by adding to the necessarily brief portraits found here. You may also wish to draw a picture of your chosen companion: perhaps the shield of the knight who accompanies you; or again you may wish to devise insignia of your own, symbols which rise readily enough to the mind once the Quest is begun. Our list is divided roughly into three sections: the Grail Family; the Grail heroes - seekers and guides; and others who fall into neither of the above categories but who are nonetheless actively concerned with the Grail.

## 1: The Grail Family

These are the traditional guardians of the Grail, stemming from the line of Joseph of Arimathea who was given the custody of the Vessel of the Last Supper by Christ. He and his descendants wander through the world, arriving at last in Britain, where they establish a permanent home, traditionally at Glastonbury and later in the mysterious Grail Castle. Perceval, Galahad and Lancelot are all of this line, and they are ruled over by a mysterious king: the **Fisher King**. The first to bear this title was Brons, brother-in-law to Joseph of Arimathea, who at the behest of a mysterious voice caught a single fish and from it fed all the followers of the Grail Company. Brons himself may well be named after Bran the Blessed, who in Celtic mythology was the possessor of a magic Cauldron which provided food for as many as needed it. After Brons, the next to hold the title was Josephus, followed by Alain le Gros and descending through seven sons to Pelles, who bore the title in Arthur's day. The Fisher King is primarily the Guardian of the Grail, and is usually first seen fishing from a small boat in the lake which surrounds the Castle of the Grail. He directs the quester to his home but is always there before him, waiting to greet him and lead him to the Table of the Grail, where he will witness the procession of the Hallows: Spear, Cup, Sword and Dish. It is his task to initiate the mysteries, but he may never guide the seeker in the actions which must be completed before the Grail gives up its secrets. He may be seen as a tall, stern but welcoming figure, of

almost any age, clad in the red mantle of the Grail Kings, fishing
from his small craft or standing at the doorway of the castle.

The Fisher King is sometimes confused with the Maimed King,
to whom he is related by blood in varying degrees. Unlike the
Fisher King, however, whose title is hereditary, the latter is seen
as living on, awaiting the appearance of the Grail winner who will
heal him of a dreadful wound, usually in the thighs or the genitalia.
Until then he remains in constant torment, unable to die or find
rest. The Waste Land, through which all must pass to gain entry
to the Grail, is seen as a direct result of this wound, for according
to ancient tradition the king and the land were one, and when the
king bled the land suffered accordingly. Behind this lies the belief
that the monarch married the sovereignty of the land, personified
as a goddess, and that he must always be perfect in body as must
all such offerings.

The cause of the Maimed King's wound is variously attributed
to pride, evil custom or accident. In some versions of the story it
is brought about through his attempt to approach too near the
Hallows; in others he undertakes service to a lady, thus weakening
his responsibility to God and the Grail, and is struck down by an
angelic messenger. Perhaps the most significant version is that in
which he is wounded by the knight Balin le Sauvage, who in
ignorance of its true identity takes up the Grail Lance in order to
defend himself, and thus strikes the Dolorous Blow which lays
waste both king and country.

The Maimed or Wounded King is, then, usually depicted as an
ancient, white-haired patriarch, carried to and fro in a litter, or laid
upon a bier in the antechamber of the Grail Chapel. He is kept
alive only through the receipt of a Host, brought to him daily by a
dove from Heaven. Healing takes place either through the touching
of his wound with the Spear which drips blood, or through his
being anointed with blood from the Grail itself. In this are echoes
of blood rituals which are very ancient. Blood was regarded as
sacred, as the seat of the spirit in the human animal. Its spilling
meant more than physical death, and  where the blood was holy -
it could effect miraculous cures (cf. Dindraine, who gave up her
blood to cure a woman suffering from leprosy). For obvious reasons

the Maimed King is not recommended for direct working, but meditation on his plight and its causes can be rewarding.

Garlon, sometimes referred to as 'the Invisible Knight' is the Fisher King's brother or, as some have it, his dark aspect. He represents the forces opposed to the Grail and is indirectly responsible for the Dolorous Blow which wounds the Grail King in the thighs and brings about the Waste Land. In the text known as The Elucidation (see Chapter 1) he is named Amangons and brings about the wasting of Logres when he rapes one of the Maidens of the Wells, Otherworld women who are part of the court of the Rich Fisher. As in many of the characters associated with the Grail, there is a good deal of overlap between one figure and another, so that it is no longer easy to define the personality of this anti-Grail king - indeed, like Garlon himself, he is so shadowy as to have almost earned the title invisible (this invisibility may well refer back to an earlier character who after some evil action was given a geasa or prohibition which meant that he became invisible to everyone - that is, no longer acknowledged even though he might be present).

In another text he is known as the **King of Castel Mortal** and is described as an evil magician. In Wolfram von Eschenbach's Parzival (see Chapter 1) he becomes **Klingsor**, a haunting figure who emasculates himself in order to gain greater power, and who is pledged to the destruction of the Grail or the misuse of its powers. Behind this lies a dark tale of ancient dualism, the battle between light and dark, good and evil, truth and falsehood. Needless to say, the authors do not recommend working directly with any of these figures, but some knowledge of them may well be advisable if the Grail seeker is to avoid the pitfalls along the path to the Castle.

The three important female members of the Grail Family are **Elaine**, daughter of the Fisher King, also known as Repanse de Schoy; **Kundrie, the** Loathly Damsel, and **Dindraine**, the sister of Perceval. In almost all of the texts the Grail is carried by a woman, a fact which must of itself set the Vessel beyond the pale in the eyes of the established Church. At first she is not named, but with the gradual elaboration of the stories a desire to know more of her produced a name and character to accompany the role. In the Queste (see Chapter 1) Lancelot is brought to her bed through the connivance of her father King Pelles, who orders that he be given drugged wine which will convince him that he is being entertained by Guinevere. As remarked already, thus by subterfuge and substitution is brought about the birth of Galahad, the destined Grail winner.

We are not told of Elaine's feelings in this, and presumably as with most young women in the Middle Ages her assent was not required. But she seems willing enough to give up her virginity to Lancelot, and when he discovers the truth and is about to kill her in anger she makes it clear that she has been acting in the name of the Grail so that the 'Good Knight' may be conceived. Her role is therefore of considerable importance and interest, and though not always an easy archetype to work with, she has much to teach regarding the deeper meaning of esoteric service.

In a similar, though essentially different, way her sister **Kundrie** also serves the Grail. She is in many ways one of the most mysterious figures in the whole cycle of stories - she is portrayed in most of these as an ugly, misshapen, black-skinned hag who appears always after the failure of Perceval or Gawain to ask the ritual Question during their first visit to the Grail Castle. She mocks and unbraids them unmercifully, and yet always gives sound advice as to the best course of action open to them next. In Wolfram's Parzival her role is more highly developed, and at the end she accompanies the young hero to the Grail Castle and is able to see the sacred objects herself. Behind her lie a whole gallery of Loathly Damsels, Black Hags, and Proud (Orgellous) Ladies, who in turn reflect an even older icon - that of the Black Goddess of Wisdom and Sovereignty, one of the most powerful archetypes to be met with anywhere in the mysteries. As such she is an extremely difficult character to work with, though capable of imparting great wisdom and knowledge to aid the seeker on the path. As with all such dark-aspected figures, behind the terrible outer form lie beauty and divine love, aspects to be met with when the 'loathly' qualities have been faced and transmuted. A thoughtful reading of the non-Grail story of Gawain and Ragnell will reveal much to the serious student.*

---

*See *Sophia: the Bride of God*, by Caitlin Matthews.

Dindraine, Perceval's sister, plays an important part in the higher Grail mysteries. As sister to Elaine she is also a Grail Maiden, permitted to carry the sacred Vessel, and she is knowledgeable in its ways when she journeys with Galahad, Perceval and Bors in Solomon's Ship (see Chapter 1). On that fateful voyage she makes a new belt for the Sword of St John the Baptist from her own hair and renames it 'The Sword with the Strange Hangings'. But her most significant act is to volunteer her blood for the healing of a leprous lady - this when her knight companions would have fought to defend her - which subsequently causes her death. In this she not only reflects the degree of selfless service required by those who follow the way of the Grail, but also connects with the overall mystery of blood which plays such an important part in the Grail mysteries. W.G. Gray has written extensively on this theme, seeing it as a symbolic representation of the Royal Blood of the King which must be shed for the good of all men and of the land. Much has also been made of the play on words which transposes San Greal (Holy Grail) into Sang Reale (Royal Blood), though this is undoubtedly less important than it is made to seem.

Nor should one overlook the monthly giving of blood by all women, which surely makes Dindraine the most ideal symbol for the female Grail seeker - though by no means confined to women only for study and meditation. Her importance in the mysteries is confirmed by the fact that her uncorrupt body is carried by the Ship of Solomon to the sacred city of Sarras, where it awaits the coming of the Grail winners. It is interred there with great ceremony.

Dindraine appears in most of the major texts, though she is often nameless, being called either 'Perceval's sister' or 'the Grail Maiden' throughout. She is often to be met with on the tideless and timeless sea of the Grail country, standing at the prow of the Great Ship which takes the seeker over the water to Sarras and to the highest mysteries of all.

The Family of the Grail does not end with the achieving of these mysteries however; any more than the quest itself ends here. In Parzival the hero's half-brother Feirefitz, who is half Arab, marries the Grail Maiden, Repanse de Schoy, and their son is Prester John, the mysterious Christian king whose rumoured kingdom somewhere in the east became almost as keenly sought-after as the Grail itself. In the inner world he is known as the Keeper of the Grail for our own age, and as such may be encountered most often by those engaged in the quest today. He is an archetype of great potency whose influence extends over vast areas of inner-plane teaching. Visualized as seated on a great ivory throne carved with the likeness of phoenixes and eagles, wearing the triple crown of the East, he is a powerful influence for good and a keen instructor of current Grail seekers.

Also in Wolfram's poem Parzival has a son, **Lohengrin**, the Swan Knight; and though his story, perhaps best known today through Wagner's opera, has least to do with the Grail in the true sense, he is nonetheless an important aspect of the figure of the Grail Knight. The story of his appearance, in a boat drawn by a swan, to aid the Countess of Brabant on condition that his origins are never questioned, is reminiscent in some ways of the Cupid and Psyche story - as there, when his lineage is revealed he departs as he came, mysteriously and without explanation. His actions indicate the way in which those dedicated to the Grail may find themselves sent out into the world to perform some task and to depart once it is accomplished, and he shows that the work of the Grail Knights continued after the apparent ending of the quest. In all cases he is recognized by the great silver swan emblazoned on shield and surcoat.

These, then, are the members of the Grail Family most often met with on the quest. Their founder **Joseph of Arimathea** has been referred to throughout and his story narrated in some detail in Chapter 1. It is necessary only to add here that he is the overall guardian of all mysteries relating to the Grail and keeps a keen eye upon all who seek it, in the world and out of the world. His presence is still to be felt very strongly at Glastonbury, particularly at Wearyall Hill, where the Holy Thorn, supposed scion of his staff which flowered on Christmas Day when he arrived with his company, still stands guard over the quiet town. Joseph is unique in having an outward site attached to his name, and for this reason may make a good point from which to begin the quest. However, it must be said that Glastonbury has been perhaps over-used in recent years, and that its energies are unpredictable. It still has much to offer as a place of pilgrimage, it offers no final advantage over the quest begun within the self and followed onto the inner planes.

## 2: The Grail Heroes - Seekers and Guides

Many set out on the quest but few arrive - such, at least, is the story told in the primary texts. Of all the knights who depart from Arthur's court of Camelot only three succeed in achieving the final mysteries - though it should be said that this does not mean that the rest were totally negligible or that there is not a good deal to be learned from their efforts. Among the latter two are of particular interest: Lancelot and Gawain, the former for his tragic and somehow glorious failure, the latter because, although he is never wholly successful he at times comes closer than any of the successful three to the heart of the Grail.

Gawain is, in many ways, one of the most attractive figures in the entire Arthurian cycle. Hot-headed, impulsive, charming, he possesses a fatal attraction to women which over and over again lands him in trouble. In later texts his character undergoes a decline until he is little better than a noble savage, but he was once the most popular figure among the Round Table Knights, renowned for his chivalry and strength of arms, his courage and fairness to all. In the Middle English poem *Sir Gawain and the Green Knight* he is a splendid, if flawed, hero - splendidly human, that is, and it is partly these qualities which make him such a sympathetic figure to accompany one on the quest. It is indeed more than probable that he was originally a Grail winner himself, and although no text exists which makes him precisely this, he does come again and again within a hairsbreadth of achieving his goal. He is the first to pledge himself to the quest, and the last to give up.

There are fragmentary references, also, to a lost story concentrating on Gawain's search for the Sword of the Grail. In many of the oldest versions he is offered a broken blade which he must succeed in mending before he can continue to the second stage of the quest. In at least one version, Diu Crone of Heinrich von dem Tülin (see Chapter 1) Gawain does succeed in undoing the enchantments which lie upon the Grail Castle and its inhabitants, succeeding where Perceval had failed before him; and while this reflects a later tradition there are echoes of earlier Celtic material throughout. Gawain has indeed long been recognized, by his flaming red hair and his strength that waxes and wanes around the middle of the day, as a Solar Hero, and he is also the Knight of the Goddess, bringing with him the whole matter of the Celtic mysteries into the Grail stream. His colours are green and gold, and his insignia the five-pointed star or pentagram which makes his connection with the Goddess, the five joys and five sorrows of the Virgin (he is called Mary's Knight in some texts), and with the five aspects of the Grail.

Lancelot, who ousted Gawain in all the later texts as the Best Knight in the World, is actually of the lineage of Joseph of Arimathea. It was originally intended that he should achieve the Grail himself, and for this reason he was christened Galahad. This was changed to Lancelot when he was given into the care of the Lady of the Lake, an Otherworld guardian who provided Arthur with his magical sword Excalibur. Lancelot is trained to become not only the greatest of the Round Table Knights but also to heal the breach between the Christian Grail and the pagan Cauldron which preceded it. It is thus doubly tragic that, through his fatal and unlawful love of Arthur's queen, he is prevented from achieving the higher mysteries - thus necessitating the begetting of Galahad upon the Grail Princess, Elaine. Lancelot becomes thereafter a type of all who aspire to the greatest heights of mystical awareness but who fail because of a single fault in their make-up.

In a terrible scene Lancelot comes to the very door of the chapel where the Grail Mass is being celebrated. Despite the warning which had told him to remain outside, he enters in order to help the priest whom he sees struggling to raise the body of a wounded man onto the altar. For his greatness of heart and desire to help Lancelot receives a blow from the Grail which renders him temporarily blind and paralysed. Like many before him and many since, who seek to enter the place of the mysteries before they are summoned, he is shut out and it is terrible for him - 'He wept as he had been a little child', says Malory, and we feel how deep is Lancelot's suffering. Yet it is for this reason that he makes a great companion upon the quest, one who has suffered and grown wise because of it, a truly human figure with whom it is all too easy to identify. His colours are red and silver and his insignia three bends (stripes) of gules (red) on an argent (silver) shield, signifying that he had three times the strength of normal men in battle.

And so we come to the three Grail heroes who succeed in attaining the highest point in the quest. In reality they are aspects of a single character, the archetypal Grail winner. Separately they represent individual merits and abilities, which is why in versions where all three appear (the Queste del Saint Graal in particular) they often seem to lack humanity.

Bors de Ganis, the third of the successful heroes, is Lancelot's cousin, and is generally represented as the most human of the three, the 'ordinary man', married where both his fellows remain single, always seeming slightly puzzled by the events of the quest.

In one episode he is forced to choose between either rescuing his brother Lionel, whom he sees tied naked to the back of a horse, being beaten with a stick, or going to the help of a maiden in distress. He chooses the latter and earns much trouble for himself as a result, but the act is typical of a man who consistently tries to do good at the expense of his own fortunes, while always seeming worried, preoccupied with the many choices and tests to which he is subjected. In another incident he allows several women to jump from the tower of their castle rather than be seduced by them - he is proved right when they turn into demons and vanish in flame and smoke.

As a guide and companion for the Grail seeker Bors is the most accessible and easy to identify with - while he never aspired to the heights of attainment yet achieved much and is possessed of deep wisdom and gentleness. His greatest attributes are loyalty, a balanced outlook on life, a sense of discipline which makes him given to action rather than words, and his ability to reason even in the most challenging of situations. His colour is deep red and his shield silver with three bends (stripes) and chevrons in red.

Perceval has been ousted from the place he once held by the rise of Galahad. In all the earliest versions it is he who overcomes all tests and trials to become the outright Grail winner, while in the later more detailed texts he becomes largely secondary to his younger luminary. Yet his role was always subtly different to Galahad's: it was never his part to expire in spiritual glory: rather, he takes up the burden of Grail Guardian after the healing and freeing of the Maimed King and the Waste Land. In most versions it is implicitly understood that he will return to the Grail Castle and take up his duties - incidentally making it clear that the Grail does return there also, despite the claims that it was taken up to Heaven and never seen again by mortal man.

Perceval's title is 'the Perfect Fool' and this links him with the Fool in the Tarot as well as with the idea of God's Holy Fools, the saints. His innocence of worldly matters cause him to do many things which seem comical (his burning the body of the red knight to get his armour being a macabre instance) but which often carry a deeper meaning. He is, above all, the archetypal seeker, the innocent abroad in a strange land where anything may happen that only intuition will help him to understand. His name has been variously interpreted - a favourite being Pierce-the-veil, but like all neophytes he has many titles until he finds his True Name through the mystery of the Grail.

In some versions of the story he is referred to as the Son of the Widow, an esoteric term also applied to Christ and found in many mystery lodges. Indeed, it could be said that all who seek the Grail are sons and daughters of the Widow, seeking to atone for their ill-treatment of Mother Earth, the Widow of the Stars. Perceval, then, is the most ideal guise to adopt along the way, each episode of his story having within it the seeds of knowledge. Study his response to the advice he is given along the way, to ask no questions, to help all women, to take from them only a jewel or a kiss. Observe his wanderings and his slow growth towards experience which yet leaves his innocence untouched. His colour is red and he carries a plain shield. See him mounted upon an ancient steed with a clutch of hunting spears rather than the traditional sword and lance of the knight.

Galahad. In all the later, specifically Christian, texts Galahad is the supreme Grail winner. Born to the Grail Princess, fathered by Lancelot, he combines physical knighthood with spiritual chivalry. Destined from birth to achieve the mysteries of the Grail, he fulfils every test or sign laid down to indicate the commencement of the quest. Like Arthur at the beginning of his kingship, Galahad draws a sword from the stone, here found floating in the river outside Camelot. No one but he can do this, and he approaches it with the supreme confidence of one who already knows his destiny. Indeed, this certitude is a feature of his entire career and gives him the somewhat bloodless reputation of a character without heart or feeling - belied somewhat by his relationship with Lancelot, his father, which is a loving one despite all that separates them. In the Christianized texts in which he appears, especially the *Queste del Saint Graal*, he is often identified as a type of Christ - who also possessed the same certitude of action, of destiny to be fulfilled. Yet there is something unsatisfactory about Galahad's success.

To be sure, he achieves the mysteries, heals the Maimed King and restores the Waste Land; but in the end, when he comes to Sarras and is allowed to look into the Grail, he dies, no longer able to cling on to this world. The Grail is then withdrawn. But is this the real object of the quest? The Enchantments of Britain may well be at an end, but the vessel is no longer at hand to heal and to provide the inner fire at the heart of the kingdom. Arthur's realm begins to fade from this point on - the old sin of Lancelot and Guinevere breaks out again, despite their vows not to be alone together again, bringing madness and ruin to the Round Table Fellowship, which is broken for all time.

The truth is that the Grail is for no one person - not even for the three who win through - to achieve and then pass away within an odour of sanctity - it is for all men to find and recognize within themselves, for we are all Grails when all is said and done. The Grail brings the gifts of life and death (see Chapter 7) but Galahad cannot resolve them. His is a difficult archetype to work with, requiring a special kind of dedication to the quest; yet beneath the cold exterior burns a deep and lasting flame which can be released under the right conditions, and it is worth remembering that a derivation of his name, from the Irish Gal, means power.

As with all the Grail heroes, Galahad can learn from us, just as we can learn from him. He is high and noble and serious in his silver armour with the Grail device on his breast. His shield is white with a red cross upon it.

## 3: Other Characters

The figures who fall into this group are all ones who are indirectly part of the Grail quest, but who seldom play a leading role, either as guardians or guides (though most can perform this function at need). All are, however, important in their own right, and should not be ignored in favour of the Grail Family and its heroes.

ARTHUR. Implicit, though never clearly stated in any of the texts, is the fact that it is really Arthur who is the Maimed King, and that the figure encountered by the Grail seekers is really his surrogate. The Waste Land is, therefore, not a small enclave within Logres, but the Kingdom itself, the Inner Britain grown sick, suffering with him until the mysteries of the Grail are achieved. Herein lies a seeming paradox, for it is the Grail Quest which, in a certain sense, brings about the downfall of Arthur's realm, which is portrayed as lacking the inner strength to contain the power of the Grail, which therefore, in passing to and fro in the land, causes the break-up of all that Arthur had striven for. Yet in fact this is less paradoxical than it seems. The outer realm, the Round Table chivalry, Lancelot and Guinevere, Gawain, and of course Arthur's son Mordred, all perish. But Arthur himself, we must remember, does not. He passes, wounded, into the Vale of Avalon, the Otherworld realm where he awaits the time when he is called again to salvage his land from the darkness of ignorance and savagery. He is, indeed, following all the precepts of the Maimed King, who also waited for release and healing for the good of the Land: the Once and Future King.

And, while the kingdom of Logres stands, the Grail is there, sometimes seeming to cause the strange enchantments which occur so bewilderingly throughout the realm, sometimes representing the means by which they will end. Arthur stands at the centre, playing an outwardly static role, yet in reality holding within himself the secret heart of Logres.

Few, today, would attempt to work directly with this archetype: he is Britain, and to identify too closely with this source of national energy can easily lead to unbalanced thinking and actions. He is, therefore, best adopted as a subject for prolonged meditation and study: the elements of kingship, his relationship to the Wounded King, are all important parts of the quest, knowledge of which can only further the attempts of the seeker. He can, too, connect with the later echoes of the Grail and its part in the history of this land - his later manifestations as Alfred, Hereward, Drake and others, are all present within the one archetype, knowledge of them opened in the same study. Arthur's colours are blue and gold, and his shield bears either a red dragon or thirteen crowns.

Merlin. Always behind Arthur stands the figure of the arch-mage of Britain, Merlin the enchanter, the prophet and the bard, by some believed to hail from Atlantis whence he fled before its inundation, carrying with him many of its secrets and, it is believed, a priestess who became Arthur's mother Igraine.

Thereafter, he becomes many things: magician, wise-man, soothsayer, his long life a bright thread in the tapestry of Britain. His activity within the story of the Grail is crucial. He sets up the Round Table which will give birth to an earthly chivalry reflecting that of the Grail Knights, and he further arranges the coming of many miracles. Galahad and Perceval are very much his 'children', as much as is Arthur, for the part he plays in the nascency of all three. Yet he fails to prevent the birth of Mordred.

He is perhaps the greatest inner-plane teacher we have ever seen in this land, his Prophecies every bit as valid as those of Nostradamus and his ilk - yet he remains a figure in shadow, seldom seen except when least looked for. In Arthur's time he is the builder of far more than the Round Table (which he is said to have constructed magically as he is also credited with the building of Stonehenge). Not only does he arrange the birth of the future king, he is also, as several of the texts bear witness, a prime mover in the matter of the Grail. As with the sword in the stone which Arthur drew to prove his kingship, it is Merlin who arranges for the second such weapon which Galahad is destined to pull forth.

He endows the seats of the Table with the ability to show the names of those destined to sit there - including the Siege Perilous which will one day bear Galahad's name. Though he has withdrawn - some say to the Isle of Bardsey, where he lives in a house of glass; others to enchanted sleep beneath a hawthorn tree or an earth-delved cave - his presence is yet felt throughout the quest as though he remained, ever aware of the events which take shape in the outer world.

In reality of course this is the case - Merlin's tower of glass, his hawthorn bower, his cave, are all metaphors of the inner world where he moves at will through time and space. The story of his enchantment at the hands of the fairy Nimuë, so powerfully evoked by Tennyson that it has almost become a reality, is little more than an episode in a life filled with far stranger events.

A Welsh legend relates that Merlin keeps watch over the Thirteen Treasures of Britain within his glass home - and if this is so then the counterpart of the Grail, one of the Cauldrons of Rebirth, is certainly among them.

The mage can, indeed, offer a new and powerful way into the mysteries of the Grail, and while few would seek directly to approach him, Merlin often comes unbidden to seek out those who take up the quest. He is unpredictable and acts largely according to his own will; but for those fortunate enough to encounter him, the way may never be the same for them thereafter.

Blaise. Behind the figure of Merlin, shadowy and insubstantial as a ghost, stands that of his 'master' Blaise, portrayed at times as a monk or hermit, but always as older and deeper, sunk in the veils of time. His origins are obscure and few have succeeded in making contact with him. Those who do are at once possessed of a potential access to the entire Grail corpus - since Merlin is believed to have told him all that occurred during the quest, and Blaise to have written it down. In the *Didot Perceval*, where he makes a memorable appearance, he is brought into the presence of the Grail and becomes one of the company who guard it. For when the mysteries are completed Merlin comes to Blaise where he dwells in Northumbria and tells him all that has befallen.

> And he said 'Merlin, you told me that when these works were completed you would put me in the company of the Grail'. And Merlin answered him: 'Blaise, know that you will be there by tomorrow'. (trans. D. Skeeles)

The pupil has surpassed the master, but Blaise still has much to offer the Grail seeker. See him as a monkish figure in a brown habit, seated in a whitewashed cell poring over a beautifully illuminated tome. What does that book have to tell..?

Balin le Sauvage, and to a lesser extent his brother **Balan**, are both important characters within the Grail cycle, Balin because he is the cause of the Dolorous Blow which wounds the Fisher King, Balan because he causes the working-out of the brothers' destiny.

Their story rings with all the old tragic-heroic values of an ancient Greek drama. Balin (named le Sauvage because of his wild and uncouth behaviour) is one of the first Knights of the Round Table

- he serves Arthur faithfully and well. But after many adventures he comes one day, by chance it seems, to the Grail Castle. He is not witness to its mysteries, but he does see a knight struck down by Garlon, the sinister brother of the Grail King, who is called the 'Invisible Knight'. Believing this to be an evil deed perpetrated by an enemy of his host, Balin slays Garlon and finds himself pursued by an outraged king through hall and chamber, stairway and tower, until he arrives at the place where the Relics of the Grail are kept and, knowing nothing of their history, seizes what he takes to be an ordinary spear to protect himself. He thus strikes the Grail King through the thighs, and with this blow both the castle and all its people are destroyed.

Balin wakes to find himself alone amid desolation, and sets out to discover its reason. Not long after, he meets with an adventure which requires that he fight a defending champion with a plain shield - and thus, unknowingly, he fights with his own brother Balan, and the two wound each other to the death before they realize the truth. Merlin builds a tomb over them and writes on the gravestone part of the Grail mysteries.

Thus the Blow is seen as a destined act, its outcome beyond the control of the participants. The mutual death of the brothers becomes an inevitable working-out of their lives (when Balin hears a horn blow for the death of a stag he feels it foretells his own death).

As an inner-plane archetype Balin has remained restless and unredeemed, and some work has been required to help him find rest. At this stage he remains a difficult and sometimes painful aspect to work with, his knowledge of the Grail obscured by the memory of his deed. Yet for those who wish to know more of the nature of the Dolorous Blow, he is still the most immediate source into that complex knot of symbolism and sorrow. Care should be taken when working with what is still, in some senses, an unbalanced force.

Only two figures now remain to complete this brief gathering. Though in some texts they do bear names (Nasciens or Repanse de Schoy) they are more usually known simply as **The Grail Hermit** and **The Grail Maiden**. Their roles are really those of guide and way-shower. At almost every turn of the way one or other will appear to advise, interpret and point the path towards the next adventure. Often they may seem like many different people, and this is part of their mystery: they are, like all guides one meets across the threshold of the shadowy realm, both one and many, existing to show us how we may best proceed upon our own adventure. Here, where the goal we seek is the Grail, they will be ever-present along the way. The Hermit is closely related to both the Fisher King and the Maimed Lord - and may indeed be an aspect of both - and is also, as will not be lost to those already familiar with its symbolism, connected with the Hermit of the Tarot. His lantern-light of wisdom is ours to call upon, once we have earned it, though he can be a stern judge and taskmaster until we have done so.

The Grail Maiden may seem to play a more passive role, but in reality she holds the reins of many mysteries. She it is who commands us to follow the white stag or the red-eared otherworldly hounds; and she will both guide us and interpret our confusions upon the path. For those just starting out these two roles are of great importance, holding the keys to so many of the other archetypal figures we have looked at.

As we said before, these are archetypes, located neither precisely within ourselves nor in some realm of fantasy. They possess their own reality, which may overlap with our own at certain times and in certain conditions. When you have read the brief biographies above, turn to the bibliography and find the books listed there which will tell you more of them. Learn all you can in this way before you begin to meditate upon them or build pathworkings in which they figure. Once a full understanding of the part each one plays in the mystery of the Grail has been attained, fresh understanding and realizations will unfold. The people of the stories will become friends, guides and guardians upon the way of our own quest.

# Chapter Four

## Of Cranks and Angels

### Theories of the Grail

. . . above all (the Grail) is a symbol of symbolism itself. It
represents the very potency by which a symbol symbolizes.

P.L. Wilson: *Angels*

I t is a well-known and well-attested fact that the Grail is all
things to all people. Almost as many as there are seekers will
be found the varied theories put forward down the ages which

have attempted to explain or confine the sacred vessel within a single shape or system of belief. That such attempts have frequently proved unsuccessful or unsatisfactory need not surprise us. As well try to catch smoke or moonlight as to tie the Grail to a single form or a single doctrine. Yet people continue to try, and it is part of the nature of the Grail that it blends all of these theories in such a way as to allow something of value to emerge again and again.

In a famous and much quoted passage from the *Perlesvaus*, it is said that at the performance of the Mass 'the Grail underwent Five Miraculous Changes which ought not to be spoken of, the last of which was into a Cup'. Later we shall look deeper at the meaning of this key statement, but for now let it stand as a heading to a brief look at some of the theories - serious and silly - which have been applied to the Grail throughout its long history.

The mere existence of so many variations upon one theme can lead to confusion in the would-be seeker. Which one is right, which will bring us closest to the truth? The answer is that any or all may do so, and that only we, having looked at them, can make our own judgement upon which we feel most drawn to - not which is right or true, wise or foolish, but that which has most to say to us personally. Only thus does the Grail work.

The truth, when all discussion and argument is done, is that the Grail is more than either an idea or an object. Far more. This enables it to be so many things, to undergo so many changes, while yet remaining essentially the same.

Che Celtic Cheory The way in which we view the Grail is inextricably bound up with its origins. Even the mediaeval authors who gave us most of what we know of the Sacred Vessel in written form, though they gave it a Christian interpretation that has shaped our understanding ever since, betrayed knowledge of earlier archetypes. Thus many of the stranger elements within the stories - such as the Chessboard Castle, or the ability of the Grail to provide food for everyone - are traceable to earlier, probably Celtic origins. A number of scholars and commentators have drawn attention to this, notably Alfred Nutt, Roger Sherman Loomis, Jean Markale and A. C. L. Brown. Each has provided us with a minutely detailed comparison of the major elements within the cycles with the ancient saga and myth of Celtic descent.

The most common element in this is the identification of the Grail with one or other (possibly all) of the various Cauldrons which appear within the ancient literature of Ireland and Wales. Chief among these is the Cauldron of Annwn, the Celtic Otherworld, which has the property of restoring the dead to life again - though bereft of speech so that they may not speak of what they have seen. An important early Welsh text, known as the *Preiddeu Annwn* or *Spoils of Annwn*, tells how Arthur, accompanied by three shiploads of warriors, set off to take this Cauldron and return with it to our world. The present text dates from the ninth or tenth century, and as such must be the earliest recorded quest for a sacred vessel (at least in our culture) that we possess. That it undoubtedly contains much of an earlier nature is beyond question: the riddling exchanges between Arthur's men and the mysterious unseen characters who guard the four caers or castles of the otherworld, are alone enough to send shivers of recognition and part-comprehension up the spine.

'Except seven none returned . . .' is the refrain repeated at the end of most verses of the poem, and we are not told if the attempt was successful or not. But here is much that we can recognize from the later texts - the quest led by Arthur (here taking an active role), the strange castle or castles encountered on the way, the sense of otherworldliness which hangs over the text's every word.

There are even references to the freeing of a prisoner, which may be taken as a distant echo of the freeing of the Maimed King. *Preiddeu Annwn* is a mystery text of the most powerful kind, and if meditated upon could form the background of a whole system of magical operation - as well as a rich and fascinating journey. Since the text is so important and not always easy to come by we have included both an early translation and a reconstructed version at the end of the book.

The second Cauldron is that of Inspiration or Awen, and it is an essential part of the mysteries of Taliesin, the sixth-century bard who is the outward projection of a far older force, active still within the framework of Celtic magic. The story is told that the goddess Ceridwen desired to give the gift of wisdom to her son Avagddu, who was famed for his ugliness. To this end she collected herbs and elements with which to brew a draught of inspiration in her great Cauldron, and set the child Gwion Bach to watch over it until the time when it should be distilled. As he stirred the brew three drops fell upon his thumb, which he automatically thrust into his mouth to stem the pain. Gwion thus became possessed of knowledge, divine wisdom and inspiration - he became a poet. Ceridwen, in her anger, pursued him, and the two went through a series of shape-changes until Gwion finally became a grain of wheat and Ceridwen a hen. Swallowing him, she then bore him in her womb nine months until he was reborn, then threw him into the sea in a leather bag. But the child survived, being pulled from a salmon-weir (the salmon is itself a symbol of wisdom) by Prince Elphin ap Gwyddno, who renamed him Taliesin (Radiant Brow) for the light of knowledge which he saw in the child.

Behind all of this lies an ancient ritual where the initiate drinks a draught such as that prepared by the priests of Eleusis, which causes him to see true and to experience the feeling of changing shape. Out of this he finds understanding, perception and wisdom, and is reborn with a new mystery name. The Cauldron which gives this gift is much like the Grail in this: it changes those who drink from it, who indeed become as new men.

At a still deeper level Taliesin reflects the ancient wisdom of the Druids, from whom he learned much in the long years of training required of one who was destined to become a chief bard. In a poem ascribed to him he says that 'My true home is the Region of the Summer Stars', and from the starry depths he speaks still, speaks profoundly of the Grail-as-Cauldron, which has its home in the far-off depths of the timeless realm. For those who seek this particular aspect, his is the first voice to listen for in the silence of the Green Chapel.

Other possessors of life-giving or wisdom-dispensing Cauldrons are Gwernach the Giant, who figures in the Culhwch and Olwen story of the *Mabinogion*; Bran the Blessed, whose story appears in the same source; and the Dagda, chief of the Irish pantheon of gods. The various properties of these magical vessels included the serving of food to a whole company, except those without courage; the ability to bring the dead back to life; and the ability to produce endless riches. In Peredur, alongside the proto-Grail procession containing the head in the Dish and the bleeding Spear, is also a tub in which is placed the corpse of a man who when he has been washed and anointed springs forth again alive.

Yet as we shall see in Chapter 7 the Grail and the Cauldron can also offer the gift of death, so closely akin to that of initiation. Thus in the Irish tale *The Adventure of Nera*, when a prisoner drinks from the Cauldron the last remaining drops spray over the people in the castle and kill them all - in the same way that the brew from Ceridwen's Cauldron (other than the three drops imbibed by Taliesin) is deadly poison.

In all of the stories relating to the magical and mystical Cauldrons there is a common theme: those who seek them seek life itself, sometimes reflected in its other face - death. All who find them are those who have faced many trials and tests, who are no cowards, not to be served by the generous vessels. These are powerful lessons to be learned by all who seek the Grail, under whatever form it may reveal itself.

Another writer, Marko Michell, has interpreted, in a series of articles, certain scenes from the life of Christ from the point of Celtic Christianity and fairy lore. Concentrating on Christ's conception and on the period shortly before the Crucifixion, Michell sees these two key moments as deeply representative of the Celtic mysteries.

Gabriel, one of whose symbols is the horn, and who is remembered in the name attached to the white, red-eared hounds of the Otherworld sometimes called Gabriel Hounds, conducts the Virgin Mary through the rite of the Immaculate Conception, in which she herself becomes a Grail and the bearer of the Sacred Blood. Later another Mary, the Magdalen, who was an initiate of the ancient Druid order of Abaris (as was Joseph of Arimathea, here called 'of the Abari'), ushers Christ into the realm of the Otherworld when she anoints his feet before the Last Supper. Here they both drink from the Cauldron/Grail of Eternal Knowledge, which may also be seen as the 'bitter cup' of Gethsemene - like Ceridwen's Cauldron its contents poison save for the first three drops which distilled all knowledge.

Again, during his three days of entombment Christ visits the Otherworld and like Arthur raiding Annwn 'harrows hell', visiting the deep places under the earth to free the waters of life.

These important articles draw deeply on the well-spring of traditional lore, opening up many layers of deeper understanding of the relationship between the ancient Cauldrons and their later Christian counterpart. They could well form the basis of further investigation and study.

The Grail is not alone of the four Hallows to appear in earlier forms. The Four Treasures said to have been brought to earth by the Tuatha de Dannan, gods of ancient Ireland, included a Sword, a Stone, a Cauldron and a Spear - precisely the forms which the later Grail texts feature again and again. Here, the Sword, which belongs to the god Nuada, gives off a brilliant light; the Spear, property of Lug, bursts into flames when used; the Cauldron, of the Dagda, we have already examined; and the Stone of Fal, the last of the four treasures, was said to roar aloud if anyone but the rightful King of Ireland sat upon it. It is thus both a distant echo of the stone from which Arthur drew the sword to proclaim himself sovereign of Britain, and of the stone which split asunder with a loud noise in the *Didot Perceval*. The Grail itself is, of course, a stone in Wolfram's *Parzival*.

Much ink has been spilled in trying to prove that these objects are the original Hallows, upon which all subsequent versions are based. But this is an over-simplification of the true state of affairs - which is that the Grail is none of these things, and is yet all of them; that as an active symbol it draws upon them all, shares in their properties, and reflects the power and might of each one. Thus the fiery Spear is also the bleeding Lance; the Sword of lightning also the Sword of the Spirit, broken and re-forged; the Stone of Fal also the Grail-Stone; and the Cauldron of the Dagda, along with all the Cauldrons of Celtic myth, also the Grail - and yet not the Grail.

Once this single truth has been grasped, much that seems strange or confusing falls away. The Vessel is far too subtle to retain any single form for long. As the quotation at the head of this chapter so clearly puts it: the Grail 'is a symbol of symbolism itself'.

The mediaeval writers of the Grail texts clearly understood this. The mysterious changes which it undergoes in *Perlesvaus*, the endlessly changing views of its properties, abilities, and purpose throughout all the stories, make this abundantly clear.

Nor has this ceased to be so. From the Middle Ages until the present, seekers have continued to reinterpret the Grail according to their own understanding and needs - sometimes casting fresh light upon the path, sometimes obscuring it and making it harder to follow. In a sense this is a necessary part of the quest - every seeker has to see the object of the search in a fresh light and with unclouded vision - the theories discussed here are neither meant to be accepted or denied, simply looked at objectively before the seeker moves on to the actual business of the Quest - which may very well lead along quite other lines than any of those mentioned below.

The Vegetation Theory. This was originally put forward by Jessie L. Weston as long ago as 1906, and it found sufficient initial favour to become an influence on several creative writers - including T. S. Eliot, whose poem *The Waste Land* shows the effect of Weston's writing throughout. The thesis, briefly stated by the author herself in a paper to the Folk-Lore Society, is that 'the god Adonis, or Tammuz, or whatever he was called in the land where the rites were celebrated, typified the revivifying principle of vegetation; his death was mourned as the death of vegetation in winter, his restoration to life was hailed as its restoration in spring. An effigy representing the dead god was honoured with all the rites of mourning, and subsequently committed to the waves. Women especially played so large a part in these rites that an Arabic writer of the 10th century refers to the festival as El-Brigat, the Festival of the Weeping Women'. (*Grail rites of Adonis. Folklore, vol.* 19, 1908).

Miss Weston saw reflected in these events a source for the Grail stories, which also commemorate the demise and restoration of the vegetative aspect of life (the Waste Land), featured the body on a bier (the Maimed King) mourned by women, and had several other details in common. The theory has, of late, fallen somewhat into disrepute, but it still offers a good deal to the Grail seeker who wishes to tread the winding path between pagan and Christian versions of the Divine Vessel. Without doubt the Grail is an object of ritual significance, the stories which surround it are rites expressing the triumph of life and Light over death and Darkness. The dying and resurrected god, mourned alike in the rites of Adonis, Tammuz, Osiris or Christ, are all mirrors of this mystery.

The Tarot and the Qabalah. Miss Weston was also one of the first scholars to notice the similarity between the Grail Hallows and the Suits of the Tarot. In her celebrated book *From Ritual to Romance*, in which she declared her indebtedness to Golden Dawn luminaries G. R. S. Mead, A. E. Waite and W. B. Yeats, she notes that the Cup, Lance, Sword and Pentangle (Coins) of the Tarot suits exactly correspond to the objects in the Grail procession. We would go further to say that many of the archetypes to be discovered in the Tarot trumps derive from Grail sources (or are themselves such sources), and that a further examination of these, with meditational skills, will reveal further important correspondences. This is not the place to go into a lengthy discussion of the esoteric import of the Tarot, but using it as a system of related images it is more than possible to construct an archetypal Grail story which may then be explored in depth. As a suggested beginning to this line of exploration, we have appended a list of correspondences between Tarot trumps and Grail characters and symbols in part 3 of this volume.

While on the subject of the Tarot it seems relevant to mention that the placing of primary Grail images on the Qabalistic Tree of Life brings the relatedness of certain characters and images into relief. Several authors have investigated this in some depth, notably Alan Richardson in his *Introduction to the Mystical Qabalah* and *The Gate of Moon*. In the former he projects a speculative Arthurian Tree in which the Grail appears at Yesod, the Foundation. This is interesting in that it places the Grail Sphere close to Malkuth, the Sphere of Earth; though of course this 'closeness' is illusory and the traversing of the whole Tree is still called for - a way of showing what must already be clear to those involved in the quest: that the shortest way to the Grail is also the longest.

Gareth Knight, in his seminal book on the Qabalah, associates the Grail with Binah - Understanding, Daath - Knowledge, Geburah - Severity, and also with Yesod, as a sphere of receptivity and a point of fusion between the planes.

It will be clear from the above that there is a great deal to be learned from placing the elements of the Grail quest on the various

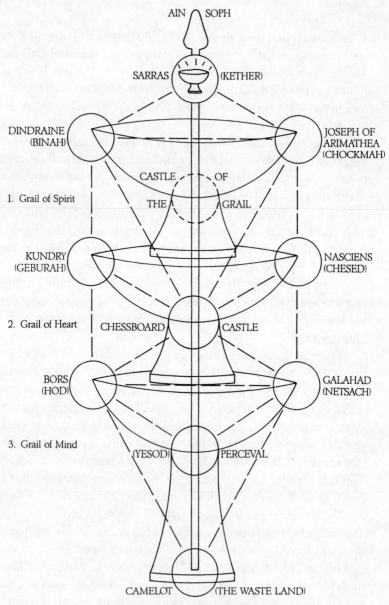

Fig. 3 The Grail on the Qabalistic Tree of Life

spheres of the Tree. One might (for example) place some of the castles or cities of the Grail at various points: Camelot being Malkuth (or indeed the Waste Land), the Chessboard Castle at Tiphareth (Beauty), the Grail Castle at Daath, and the Holy City of Sarras at Kether (the Crown). Or again, the characters may be found to fit well at various spheres: Kundry, the fearsome Grail Messenger, at Geburah (Severity) ; Nasciens, the Grail Hermit who balances her, at Chesed (Mercy); Galahad at Netzach (Victory); Perceval at Yesod (the Foundation) ; Bors at Hod (Glory) - these last three forming a triangle which is expressed again by their higher selves at Tipareth, Geburah, Chesed, and again at Binah, Chokmah and Kether.

Thus we have in effect three levels of the Grail which may be (very generally) called the levels of Mind, Heart, and Spirit, each of which is needed if our approach to the Grail is not to be unbalanced. It is as well to note here, by way of warning, that from this the path to the Black Grail, which is nothingness, extinction, rather than fullness and fulfilment, matches our proposed Grail Tree in reverse: Klingsor's dark castle being situated at Daath and the negative aspects of the protagonists at the same spheres, but in shadow, falling away into the qlippothic realm where the Grail serves only to empty out wisdom, love, mercy and so forth that have been gained through the journey. The way to the Grail is not without its perils, and the symbolism of the Tree demonstrates these perhaps more clearly than anywhere.

These ascriptions are, of course, only suggestions, it being a well-known fact that one may put anything at all on the Tree with virtually endless permutations. Much work remains to be done in the placing of the Grail symbols within this framework; only patient study and meditation on each of the spheres and their qualities, together with those related aspects of Grail-lore can make this clear in time.

The Zodiacal Grail. While discussing the relatedness of the Grail to other symbol systems, it is worth noting that the cycles and houses of the zodiac may also be adopted in this way. Much work has already been done by writers such as Katherine Maltwood and Mary Caine, whose investigations have tended to centre more or less exclusively on terrestrial zodiacs - particularly in the area of the Somerset levels around Glastonbury. It has been suggested in *The Western Way, vol.1*, by Caitlin and John Matthews that these may reflect an ancient folk-memory of the archetypal characters themselves, many of whom have hidden associations with the landscape itself, rather than a clearly defined pattern on zodiacal symbols on the land itself. This is very much a matter for personal preference, relating more to the search for a physical Grail or sites associated with it (see Chapter 2) ; however, one could do worse than attempt a relating of the key figures from the cycle to the zodiacal symbols and to follow this with either an imaginary or physical visit to one of the sites, where the character in question, bearing the appropriate symbol on his or her brow, awaits your enquiry.

Another way of working with the Arthurian zodiac might be suggested by Edward Matchett in the book he wrote with Sir George Trevelyan, *Twelve Seats at the Table Round*. Here he provides various correspondences - Knight of Taurus = Intelligent Openness; Knight of Libra = Inner Vision; Knight of Capricorn = Conscious Control - which may be worked with either indirectly or in a small group. Still another possibility would be the making of a Round Table, either physically or in meditation, at which you might take your place and where each seat would be related to either a zodiacal sign or a symbolic reference connected with the Grail. A suggested scenario for such a Table of the Grail will be found in exercise 7 of part 3.

All the themes discussed so far can be said to pertain to the inner quest and the meaning inherent within the symbols. We should perhaps now look at some speculations which have endeavoured to set the Grail within a larger, historical context, or which have associated it with a physical object or place.

There has been, indeed, a steady movement away from the inner realms in which the Grail first finds its home, towards a point within the outer world. That this is at times an uneasy position will be seen from the sometimes bizarre lengths to which various writers or investigators have gone to establish a precise lineage for the Grail and at least a possible resting place where it might (if one were clever or lucky) be found to still lie.

This tendency can be seen as manifesting as long ago as the Middle Ages, where various chalices were depicted as 'the' Grail, and marvellous properties were attributed to them in accordance. At Valencia in Italy was a cup believed to have been given by King Solomon to Sheba, and which was later believed to have been used at the Last Supper; while in Coburg is another cup, said to have belonged to Elizabeth of Hungary, which has also been attributed with Grail-like properties. Since Elizabeth, who was later canonised, has for her father the patron of Walfram von Eschenbach, it may well be that we have here an example of the transference of an idea from a literary source to the character of a spiritually developed personage.

The Onomastic Theory. Many attempts have been made to identify the origin of the word Grail, but without success. It seems to have appeared literally out of the blue at the end of the eleventh century with the writing of the first of the surviving texts. Whether it derives from a scribal misreading of a now lost original, or whether it was coined by Chrétien himself we cannot know. Perhaps it simply entered the consciousness of the mediaeval world at the time it was required to describe the indescribable. Nevertheless, lack of firm evidence has not prevented numerous attempts on the part of Grail experts, ancient and modern, from speculating - sometimes with amusing results, as the following quotation from R. S. Loomis' *Celtic myth and Arthurian romance* (1927) shows.

Perhaps the best-known piece of onomastic ingenuity is Helinandus' endeavour to find the origin of the word Gradale, a Latin form of our word Grail. Unaware of its true derivation from Latin cratalis or cratale, a shallow dish, he suggests first that the word gradale is connected with gradatim, because food was placed in the dish 'in succession, one morsel after another'. Then he says that the word is popularly pronounced greal because it is 'agreeable and acceptable to him who eats from it'. A later attempt to read a meaning into the *Saint Graal* is found in Jacopo da Voragine, who towards the close of the thirteenth century says that 'the English in their books call that vessel Sanguialia'! And an even more ingenious corruption found in England is the Sank Real or 'Royal Blood'.

None of these seem especially enlightening, but this should not deter determined Grail seekers from attempting their own interpretations!

The Narta Monga. In more recent times a whole plethora of theories have been put forward in an attempt to pin down the Grail to a specific place or time. One of the most interesting of these concerns an ancient vessel originating in what is now part of Russia. Several scholars, including in particular Helmut Nickel, C. Scott Littleton and Ann C. Thomas, have drawn attention to certain similarities which exist between the stories of Arthur and the Grail and those of a little-known group of people from the region of the Caucasus Mountains. Known as the Ossetes, they are believed to have seceded from the ancient Persian Samatians and to have inherited from them several cycles of stories which deal with a band of heroes known as the Narts. Among the significant points in common between the Arthurian heroes and the Narts are the death of their leader, Batardez, who cannot rest until his magical sword has been cast into the waters of a lake, and the possession of a wonder-working cauldron known as the Amonga. This vessel shares with the earliest versions of the Grail, already dealt with, its ability to serve food only to heroes, to select those good enough to serve it, and to impart prophetic wisdom.

All this being so, what further connection can there be between the obscure Ossetes and the Arthurian Grail tradition? According to Littleton and Thomas, some 5,000 Ossetes were stationed as part of the Roman army of occupation, at Ribchester, near York, where substantial archaeological evidence has been unearthed to prove that they were there during the period AD 238-244.

The suggestion which follows from all this is that the Ossetes brought with them their native tales of the Narts and that these, cross-fertilizing with Celtic and other sources, produced stories of both Arthur and the Grail. Whether or not this theory holds water is not our concern here - what is interesting, however, are the almost incredible connections with Persian traditions (the Ossetes are Iranian-speakers) and with the ancient Shamanic practices of the Caucasus. These things may seem a far cry from the Grail stories as we have them today - but, as has already been pointed out at some length, the site of the great Samatian temple in what is now Iran may in all probability have provided a model for the Grail Temple; while the Shamanic practices current in the Caucasian Mountains not only bear a close resemblance to those practiced in Celtic lands but also possess much that is familiar from the stories of the Preiddeu Annwn and the Story of Taliesin. Living when we do, any theory which, however obliquely, connects the Grail with Russia, must be of interest. Whatever the truth of the Ossetes and their heroic Narts, the parallels do exist and are worthy of exploration. Any Grail seeker concerned with world peace might do worse than approach the problem of the healing Grail from this direction, gaining a greater and deeper understanding of the traditions which are still active within the vast body of Mother Russia.

The Adams Family Theory. Another curious and thought-provoking speculation, advanced by researcher Andrew Rothovius in 1977, connects the Grail with a family which has produced two presidents of America - John Adams (1735-1826) and John Quincy Adams (1767-1848) - as well as one of the seminal books on the mediaeval mystical tradition (of which the Grail was a central part: *Mont St Michel and Chartres* by Henry Adams (1838-1918).

Rothovius' theory is based around some words carved on the tombstone of Henry Adams, grandfather of the first member of the family to be president and the first to emigrate to the then recently founded American colonies. His tomb, erected by John Adams, refers to the reason for this as 'flight from the Dragon persecution in Devonshire'. From this phrase Rothovius traces a curious story. It seems that there existed a secret society known by some as 'the Dragons' and by others as 'the School of Night', which numbered among its ranks Sir Walter Raleigh, John Dee and Christopher Marlowe. During the reigns of Queen Elizabeth I and James I this group were dedicated to, among other things, restoring a way of life more common to Megalithic times, and which was reflected by their interest in star-lore. Dee had already discovered the terrestrial figures around Glastonbury while visiting Somerset, and nearby lived the Adams family - at the centre of the projected circle of the zodiac. From this heart of Grail tradition, Rothovius believes the Adams family took their guiding principles, which aimed at establishing a New World where the ancient laws of the Megalithic period would hold good. Political adversaries, backed by those with money to lose, prevented John Quincy Adams' grand design to build a series of observatories which he called 'lighthouses of the skies' from ever taking place. His dreams of a harmonious world based upon meditative cycles of planetary influence was stillborn, though his grandson Henry preserved some of its light in his famous book.

Whether or not we set any store by Rothovius' findings, his theory gives a covert glimpse of the way in which the Grail is perceived, and how its spirit continues to hold sway despite political change or bias away from the interior realm in favour of materialism. The notion of the zodiacal connections with the myth, as we have seen, illumines much that might otherwise remain dark, and the star-patterns sought by the Adams clan hold many secrets for those willing to study them at length.

The Holy Blood. Another theory which has found a good deal of support in the last few years, and which also involves a political slant, is that advanced by three authors: Henry Lincoln, Michael Baigent and Richard Leigh. Their book *The Holy Blood and the Holy Grail* (1982), started a veritable avalanche of follow-up volumes, each one aimed at expanding the original idea. Thus the old pattern of Grail Quest material germinating from a single seed and giving birth to numerous more complex offshoots is again seen to be in operation - though in a very different way.

Lincoln, Baigent and Leigh became overnight celebrities when their book appeared, and for several months afterward the name of the Grail was upon everyone's lips, though in a manner never before envisaged. Their carefully researched book set out to investigate an ancient mystery - that of the sacred bloodlines of European royalty - and to connect it with the Grail by way of the scribal error which changed 'San Greal', Holy Grail, to 'Sang Real', Royal Blood. From this, by dint of a complex web of evidence, which connected the Cathars, Templars and an ancient French dynasty, the authors set out to prove that the Grail really referred to the blood-line of Christ, who has escaped death on the Cross, married Mary Magdalen and gone on to produce the ill-fated dynasty of Dagobert I, known as the Merovingian line.

Much of this had already been worked on by a German Grail

expert named Walter Johannes Stein, and latterly by William G. Gray. But Lincoln, Baigent and Leigh took it all a step further and brought the story up to date with the inclusion of a mysterious sect known as the Priory of Sion. This group, for which no documentary evidence seems to exist any earlier than the 1930s, claims descent from both the Merovingians and the Knights Templar. They are also, according to Lincoln, Baigent and Leigh, the inheritors of the Holy Blood - that of Christ, whom they portray as a king and a charismatic leader rather than as Messiah or Son of God.

Thus the Grail becomes diminished to a bloodline rather than an actual object, and the archetypal character of the participants on the quest is replaced by actual figures who played sometimes leading roles in the history of the world. It is, so far as one may see, nowhere suggested that these historical personages were overshadowed, in the esoteric sense, by the inner archetypes of the Grail - which would certainly be an interesting notion. Instead we have something like a political jigsaw crossed with a treasure hunt. The story of the priest Berenger Saunière, who seems to have discovered either documents or actual treasure while renovating his church at Rennes-le-Chateau in 1891, has become the subject of numerous books, essays and studies seeking to relate his finds to this secret history of the European bloodlines. But these seem rather to detract from any serious understanding of the Grail tradition, and to trivialize it into physical treasure-trove rather than helping to penetrate its true mystery.

The Spear of Destiny. Walter Stein, whose book *World History in the Light of the Grail* (1928), traced the major characters of the Grail cycle to the Merovingian and Carolingian dynasties, is not quoted by Lincoln, Baigent and Leigh - though one would suppose that his researches must parallel those of the more recent authors. Unfortunately, Stein's one-time association with the Nazis has caused his work to lie under shadow - even though he left Germany soon after the start of the Second World War and came to work for Winston Churchill as his sometime occult advisor.

Stein's theories, which relate also to the whereabouts of the so-called Lance of Longinus, are elaborated by Travor Ravenscroft in his book *The Spear of Destiny*. Here we are shown how the powers of Light can be, and sometimes are, used by those who serve the Dark. Hitler, who believed implicitly in the value of occult attack as a reinforcement of physical war, sent teams of researchers and picked SS men in search of the Hallows - Grail and Spear. The ruins of the Cathar outpost at Montségur were excavated in expectation of discovering one or other. The Spear, fragments of which had been traced to Rome and the Austro-Hungarian Empire, did find its way into Nazi hands for a time, and the infamous Heinrich Himmler formed an élite core of SS troops around it in a castle which had been aptly named 'Black Camelot*.

Part of the Spear now resides in the Vatican, though it is not known whether it is the true original, or, like many of the 'Grails' to be found scattered throughout the world, simply a relic which has become invested with power through the belief of those who formed it into a receptacle of power.

Cathars and Knights Templar. Connection of the Grail ethos with the Cathars or the Knights Templar may prove rewarding, since there is clear evidence, introduced by various writers, of a reflection of what may be termed Grail energy in both these organizations.

The Cathars, who were mercilessly obliterated in a crusade launched against them in 1179 at the instigation of Pope Alexander III, reflected in their gentle way of life a deep understanding of the links between Christianity and religions of the past. The ultimate origin of the Cathars, or Albigensians as they were known by outsiders, remains obscure. They seem to have inherited certain of the doctrines and beliefs of the ancient Manichean sect which originated in Persia in AD 61 and was in turn based on an even earlier religion known as Mazdanism. This has given us the heritage of dualism, where the powers of Light and Dark exist in a state of perpetual war, and was later fleshed out in the beliefs of the Gnostic sects who flourished in Greece and elsewhere from the fifth century onwards. The Cathars' belief in a dualistic creation, formed by Lucifer, the Demiurge, rather than by Gods, caused them to reject the orthodox idea of the Incarnation and earned them the title of heretics. Yet their way of life, simple and austere, could well have served as a model for the Grail Knights.

* in the novel of that name by Duncan Kyle (1978)

The Cathars' connection with the Sacred Vessel was so well established in the minds of their oppressors, that when, during the siege of Montségur, their last stronghold, one of their leaders put on silver armour and stood forth on the battlements, the crusading armies withdrew in the belief that 'the Grail Knight' had come to aid the beleaguered citadel.

Rumours continue to exist of a treasure, far richer than mere gold or jewels, which was smuggled out of Montségur the night before the castle fell, and which was then taken across the mountains into Italy where it vanished from sight. Whether this was the Grail or documents relating to Cathar beliefs will probably never be known - though there is still an active order based in what was once Cathar country, which practices the same beliefs and bases much of its teaching around the mysteries of the Grail.

As for the Templars, the connection here, apart from the claims of the Holy Blood theory, is derived chiefly from the fact that Wolfram von Eschenbach in his *Parzival* referred to the guardians of the Grail as 'Templiessen'. This can be taken to mean, simply, servants of the temple - in this instance the Grail Temple which Wolfram describes elsewhere in some detail. Or it may indeed be a reference to a once widely-accepted understanding that the Knights Templar, ostensibly founded by a group of knights to escort pilgrims to the Holy Land, were also the guardians of a hidden body of knowledge, centered upon the Grail.

It has been suggested several times that St Bernard of Clairvaux, who was related to one of the founding knights and who helped write the Rule of the order, may have communicated some knowledge to them which is also to be found in coded form in the pages of the *Queste del Saint Graal* (See Chapter 1) which, as we have already indicated, was written by Cistercian monks of whose order St Bernard was both founder and head. But, once again, no real evidence exists to support this theory.

The Holy Shroud. Another, very recent, theory which again connects the Templars with the Grail, has been put forward by Noel Currer-Briggs in a book called *The Holy Grail and the Shroud of Christ*. This is once again a skilful piece of detective work which, convincingly enough, traces the ownership of the Holy Shroud, with which Christ's body was wrapped and which is said to bear his image impressed upon it, from the Holy Land to the city of Turin where it now resides.

The keys to the whereabouts of this most holy relic, particularly between 1204 and 1350, have been plausibly charted by Currer-Briggs to the Templars, and he had identified the Shroud, folded so that only the image of the face was visible, both with another wonder-working image of Christ, the Mandilion, and with the infamous 'Head' which heresy-hunters ascribed to the Templars as an idol which they were believed to worship.

Taking this as a jumping-off point Currer-Briggs turns his attention to the Grail texts which describe light emanating from it and the form of a child within it. He then suggests that the word Grail, subject to so many different interpretations and meanings, actually refers to the grill with which the Mandilion (in reality the folded Shroud) was covered or framed. Thus one could indeed be said to 'look into' the Grail and see the form of Christ, or even a holy radiance, as Galahad was said to do.

This very ingenious theory is yet another attempt to identify the Grail as a physical object, and if nothing else it does suggest a very plausible explanation of the Templar connection. Whether the Shroud and the Grail are really one and the same, there can be little doubt that their effect on those open to receive such things was much the same.

The Grail Pyramid. We have looked at more than one theory relating the Grail to mysterious geometric patterns in the landscape. Michael Beckett, in his short book *The Pyramid and the Grail* adds yet another dimension to these by advancing a new contender, 'the Pyramid of Albion', which he discovers in the landscape in and around Glastonbury Abbey, and which precisely reflects the dimensions of the original Great Pyramid of Giza. This is further extended to include significant Megalithic sites, notably Avebury and Callanish; a famous mediaeval painting *L'agneau mystique*, itself redolent with Grail symbolism; and with the fall of Atlantis.

The answer to the riddle of the Grail, says Becket, 'is likely to be mathematics in its purest form ... where the Grail will be shown to be the ultimate resolution of the conflict between that which exists and that which does not; between matter and spirit'.

Beckett is opening up the truth of the Grail into areas of cosmic proportion. The existence of the Pyramid of Albion, points to there being something unique hidden within these islands - the reasons, Beckett believes, for their being so often identified with the Otherworld and, of course, with the home of the Grail. He hints, interestingly, at there being a recurring pattern of salvific restoration, at intervals of 5,000 years, in which the exhausted energies of the earth are renewed by the sacrifice of a god or messiah. In this Osiris, Christ and the Wounded King become high points in a continuing process. A great deal is based upon this theory, much of which will bear further investigation. There is something more than a little exciting about the idea of a 'fourth dimensional shadow' on the land which may possibly form a link between the inner and outer worlds - a function which the Grail itself performs - and this does indeed give one pause for thought regarding other landscape figures, such as the Glastonbury zodiac, or indeed the several other such that have been discovered in recent years. If they are viewed as inner rather than outer shapes they become instantly more understandable as well as more worthy of careful study.

The Grail Stones. Most writers and investigators have adopted the Grail as Vessel, or at least receptacle, in their researches. Few have followed up the suggestion of the Grail as Stone, though the obvious connection here with the alchemical Philosopher's Stone, with which the Grail as depicted by Wolfram showed considerable similarity, must surely bear investigation. Some arguments for identifying the Lapis Philosophorum with Wolfram's Lapsit Exillis (stone of exile) will be found in *The Grail: Quest for Eternal Life* by John Matthews, and in Emma Jung and Marie-Louise von Franz' *The Grail Legends*; while another important aspect is dealt with by Lady Flavia Anderson in her classic study of the Grail entitled *The Ancient Secret*.

In this book Lady Flavia sets out to follow a particular aspect of the Grail as a light-bringer. To this end she has gathered numerous references to light-reflecting, light-focusing, light-preserving objects found in myth and ancient history, and classes the Grail, which she sees as a kind of burning-glass or crystal, amongst them. Mirror magic, moon vessels, the Glass Islands of the Arthurian world; the 'nine pearls about the Cauldron's rim' of the Celtic Otherworld vessel; and the seemingly endless proliferation of fiery swords which appear, as we have seen, throughout the Grail romances are shown to relate to the mysterious inner world of the Grail. Finally the most ancient wonder of fire itself - the ancient secret of the title - is invoked as the original spark from which all subsequent visions of the Grail derive.

This book is a veritable treasure-trove of esoteric lore - the chapter on Candlemas alone should make one look with new eyes at that ancient festival. Nor does Lady Flavia fight shy of the spiritual side of her theory: the fire which the Grail lights is, after all, more often than not a spiritual one.

This brings us almost to the end of our brief survey of some of the theories relating to the Grail - but no such consideration would be complete without mention of the ideas expressed in the work and teaching of Rudolf Steiner and certain of his followers. Indeed, we have already encountered one of these in the person of Walter Jonannes Stein, who with Maria Schindler developed the cosmic insights of Steiner in their own work.

Another follower, Dr Alfred Heidenrich, describes Steiner's method of working as rooted firmly in 'thought' - that is to say that he began from an opposite position to that of most mystics or occultists, who begin by contacting the level of the spiritual, and by seeking to transfer their thinking and feeling selves into pure vehicles of the spirit. Steiner aimed at the raising of pure reason to a point where it becomes liberated from the cerebral and enters into a new level of reality, supersensible rather than realistic. Thus he chose to describe his work as spiritual science, to signify that his approach was philosophical rather than purely esoteric.

Steiner was born on 27 February 1861 at Kraljevic in what is now Yugoslavia, the son of a gamekeeper turned railway official and a housemaid from the estate of a Hungarian nobleman with estates in Austria. He went to school and later to university in Vienna where he became the editor of the scientific works of Goethe. During his time at the university he met a mysterious figure, usually referred to as 'Father Felix', a man of humble background who yet knew of the lore of plants and herbs, of the natural sciences and the mysteries of the mineral world. He in turn introduced the young Steiner to another character, not named, who was to exert a profound effect over the future founder of Anthroposophy.

This happened in approximately 1901, and became the beginning of a world-wide movement. This is not the place to enter into a history of Anthroposophy; apart from Steiner's own books there is a wealth of material available by other writers. Steiner was undoubtedly a gifted psychic, and his huge output of material, mostly in the form of lectures, lays before us the vast structure of world history seen from a completely different viewpoint to that of the historian who deals only with documented facts. Steiner's approach freed him from such a necessity and enabled him to rewrite much of what is accepted as historical truth.

His works are laced throughout with references to the Grail, which was undoubtedly an important symbol in his thought. We have already looked at the theory of Walter Stein, which is further borne out in that of Maria Schindler. According to these writers the point of the Grail's direct entry into the theatre of world history was during the eighth century AD at the beginning of the formation of the main European states and kingdoms. Almost all the royal houses of Europe can claim descent from Charlemagne, who according to Stein and Schindler was directly influenced by the Grail - embodying as it did the fullness of knowledge guarded by the mystery schools of earlier times.

Eleusis itself knew of the Grail, Steiner believed, and its mysteries were reborn in the School of Chartres, which continued the secrets of those earlier times and bodied them forth in the first written Grail texts and in the foundation of certain hidden orders of the Grail.

However, according to Steiner and his followers, there were certain antiGrail forces which sought to frustrate the object of the Grail-orders in their desire to propagate the esoteric teachings of Christianity. Despite the strength of the Carolingian dynasty, various of its members married into the opposing forces, and the dynasty ended in ruin. Yet as Maria Schindler says, in her book *Europe: a Cosmic Picture*,

> So great had been the spiritual impulse of their beginning that in spite of their tragic end ... for centuries all the kingdoms of Europe felt that they owed much of their dignity to it.

So, exactly as was later to be mirrored in the Arthurian legends, the great plan was frustrated. Arthur's dream of a united Christian kingdom extending from Denmark to Rome perished from within through the tragic error of his incestuous union with his sister which resulted in the birth of Mordred, the human embodiment of the anti-Grail forces.

Steiner draws attention to several centres of Grail activity in Europe, including Chartres Cathedral, which was constructed according to clearly defined esoteric plans including the circle, the square and the triangle - a motif reflecting the history of the three Tables of the Grail (see Chapter 1). The Divine Plan upon which Chartres was built is contained within these three shapes, as will be found further outlined in *The Mysteries of Chartres Cathedral* by Louis Charpentier.

Steiner also had much to say about both Castle Karlstein and the Extern Stones, already discussed in Chapter 2. Long before these centres existed, however, the spiritual power which was to guide and help in the formation of mankind's consciousness was latent in the racial inheritance of the different peoples of the world. Such centres as Chartres, Glastonbury or Karlstein are merely the manifestation of that power; the Grail its most profound symbol. As Maria Schindler puts it:

> The Grail Temple was the temple of the divine Sophia, the world-embracing cosmic star wisdom. In the 9th century, Scotus Eregina, himself probably a Knight of the Holy Grail, wrote of the Temple: 'If to celestial heights thou dost thyself uplift, with shining eyes thou wilt behold the Temple of Sophia.

It was to these 'celestial heights' that Rudolf Steiner looked for the message of the Grail. Of all symbols for the operation of divine gnosis, the action of which helped form the very existence of the world, the Grail was to him the most profound. Throughout his work, in the many hundreds of lectures he delivered at the centre he designed at Dornach in Switzerland, references to the Grail appear again and again. Always the symbol is interpreted as a luminous archetype of man's spiritual ascent, his sacrifice and rebirth. In a lecture entitled What is the Holy Grail? given on 23 October 1905 in Berlin, Steiner had this to say:

> Up to the present man has mastered the lifeless in nature. The transformation of the living forces in the world of plants, the mastery of the animal forces as they are active in the reproductive instincts, is still outside his power today. As true as it is today that man has acquired mastery over lifeless nature, it is also true

that in the future he will master through himself what works in the other three kingdoms of nature ... in as much as that cultural age has not been reached yet ... this is already being prepared through the movement which one calls the Lodge of the Holy Grail.

Steiner is not only referring to the work of the Anthroposophical movement, but to those other schools which are working to bring the message of the Grail to fruition, and which seems to be approaching completion in our own age.

In whatever way one chooses to perceive this - and we can see clearly enough from the foregoing views of many theorists that it can manifest on any number of levels - it must be admitted that without Steiner's profound contribution to our understanding of what we may call the inner history of the world, we should be less equipped to deal with the advent of the Grail - were it to appear before us at the next moment.

If that were indeed to happen, how should we prepare ourselves? Some, perhaps all, of the theories discussed here have some valid point to make which, taken up, amplified, studied and meditated upon, can bring us closer to the state where we would know how to react in the presence of the Grail. These 'glances' at the Grail demonstrate its ability to change at will, to bemuse and bewilder, to bestow degrees of knowledge and understanding beyond those attainable by everyday means. This is one of the sublime mysteries of the Grail, with which we must each learn to work as we travel our particular paths towards it. After all, the quest may one day come to an end; we may achieve our desires, receive our just dues.

The foregoing should, then, be seen as providing a set of tools with which to work upon the inner side of our natures. What follows, in the second part of the book, are some possible ways to put what has been learned to practical use in our own time. From there onward the quest leads into other areas which we must chart for ourselves.

# PART TWO: MYSTERIES

# Chapter Five

## Ways to the Grail Today

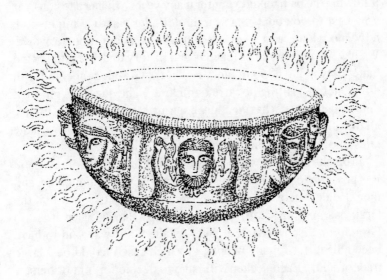

...Celtic poetry, German mysticism, Christian chivalry, and ideas of magic which still cling to the rude stone monuments of Western Europe – all these combined to make the story of the grail, and to endow it with the strange attraction which has led to its recreation by artist after artist for seven hundred yuears. And who, even now, can say that its course is run at last, and the towers of Montsalvat dissolved into the mist from which they sprang?

T.W.Rolleston: Myths and Legends
of the Celtic Race. 1911

The power of the Grail still has its thrall over us - though many ages have passed and the tales have been altered and diminished, the magic has not faded and its force can still be felt by us. Magic plays a key role in the matter of the Grail in a number of ways. The Grail is a magical vessel, appearing and disappearing with a will of its own. Many of the mysteries surrounding it have been preserved among the magical lodges, which even now, use the symbolism and power in their rituals. Magic will be needed by those who seek the Grail, for by using these ancient technologies of heart and mind and spirit shall the Grail be recovered, and its healing energies shared.

We, who are taking up the quest now, or who may have been following the path unknowing for many years, will need to consider how best to go about this search, defining what we might find, how and where, and what use it might be to our modern world. We have a rich source of legends and history to delve into to find material which will point the way, but the Grail is concerned with doing, not just sitting down and thinking. The quest has physical dimensions, just as it has emotional, spiritual and rational dimensions, all of which will help us on our journey of exploration through the tales of old and the inner reaches of our beings.

From the ancient legends described in the first part of this book it is possible to see what physical forms the Grail might take, and then decide where such might be hidden. It is also clear that the Grail has non-physical forms, or perhaps shapes when it is too large to be discovered in a cave, for the Grail was said to have been able to feed many people, in which case it could be a large tract of land. Each seeker will have to decide for him or herself what form the Grail they are seeking might take - for hard as it may be to accomplish the quest, to have no defined goal will make it far harder.

Another factor to consider at the outset of the journey is whether or not to travel alone. In the stories, many Grail seekers set out alone and then sought or discovered companions on their travels. It is possible to make a solo assay into the unseen worlds, or to follow the faint paths from their mythical sources on your own, but often a companion can help with the journey, unravel clues which are a mystery to you, or help guide you on those inner journeys which lead to the Grail of the Heart or Spirit.

In some ways this brings us back to the matter of magic. The orders whose rituals and philosophy has been shaped by the Quest for the Grail and whose practices involve the concepts of chivalry, honour and brotherhood may still be encountered in the modern world. The path they point will involve hard work, dedication and persistence, but they offer in return companionship; a well-trodden path which they have pioneered, and guidance to the inner roads of the mind in a safe and effective way. Many of the arts of inner voyaging have spread from the secret cloister and the lodge library to the text-book on psychology, the work of the personal-growth movement, and many other sources of self-awareness and creativity. Arts and skills which used to be termed 'magic' have become quite commonplace for they are seen as techniques which can free the individual from his self-imposed prison, develop insight and intuition and bring calm and relaxation in a stressful world.

If you set upon this quest you will need to understand something about magic and the most basic techniques for its use. We are not saying that you will abandon family and friends and join some remote fraternity in the hills of Tibet, nor will you have to wear red and chant strange mantras night and morning. The arts are basically very simple, and most of them require little more than a quiet place. Perhaps you can find a cassette recorder to tape the narrative of some of the inner journeys or any ideas which you may uncover as you go along, a large notebook to jot thoughts in, and, most important, a spacious diary in which you can enter your dreams, meditation themes, and all the stages through which your personal quest may pass. This record-keeping is important, for only by looking back can you chart your progress, and discover when you have been inspired with information which becomes real in the future.

The most important art to master is that of 'creative visualization', 'grownup story-telling' or 'path-working'. This is a very simple technique whereby a journey narrative is followed in the imagination to some secret place; a scene from one of the Arthurian legends or some other location which is pertinent to the Grail Quest. As in meditation, where a concept, symbol, phrase or word is allowed to become the centre of a growing blossom of ideas and insights, it is necessary to find a quiet place, where you won't be disturbed for about half an hour, and set aside mundane concerns. You will learn to enter an 'altered state of awareness' in which, whilst physically relaxed and still, you find your mind is full of clear information and buzzing with inspiration. There is a knack to mastering this very basic magical skill, and it can only be gained by practical work. You will find that you will have to try a variety of methods until you discover one that works well for you, but do be patient. The inner mind is not very pleased to discover you, whose mind it is, delving about in the depths of memory, past experience or future happenings. You will find all manner of things will try to distract you when you start. This can be small itches, internal gurgles or persistent thoughts about trivial things which will not allow you to become totally focused inwardly. You may become more sensitive to external sounds, the physical sensation of pressure on the chair you are sitting in, your pulse rate or breathing. All these feelings are excellent signs and indicate that you are relaxing a little.

It will help you, if you have never tried either meditation or 'path-working' before, to choose a firm, upright chair which is both supportive and comfortable - for following some of these inner journeys may take some time. Ensure that your feet are firmly on the floor, or on a box etc., and that when you relax your head doesn't slump forward and restrict your breathing. Make certain you have no tight belts or collars and that your hands and ankles are not crossed as this can give you pins and needles rather than meditative inspiration. Dim the lights, or if you prefer, light a single night-light or candle in a secure holder. You may like the atmosphere you get from incense or joss sticks, and perhaps, if you are living in a noisy environment, some quiet background music will banish the interference from outside. Take a few slow, deep breaths and as you breathe out each time, allow tension and unwanted thoughts to be expelled from within you. Relax and mentally slow down, become physically still, and try very hard to remain quite impassive, no matter what tingles, itches or coughs want to disturb you. This is particularly important if you are sharing your explorations with others, for once someone gives in to disturbance and moves, the rustle he makes may interfere with the relaxation of others, who in turn move or cough, and that is the end of the peace and quiet so vital to these inner journeys.

Become still and allow the image of the part of the Grail Quest which you want to investigate to rise up before your point of consciousness. This is a safe and well-tried experiment, but if you are troubled by the new experience, and fear you may lose control or sink into some unpleasant state, use the following technique. Look at whatever familiar scene is before you and see clearly the door to the room, a piece of furniture or an ornament which you know well, then close your eyes and relax. If you 'see' or sense anything which upsets you, see clearly that same door etc and gently open your eyes, and you will discover you are still quite safe and at home. Certainly some of the journeys you may take are long ones, leading both through time (if, for example, you wish to trace the Grail images back into the past to the Age of Arthur, or seek the Cauldron of Rebirth from earlier times), and through distance when you seek out the Grail Castle, the Cave of Merlin or any of the other myriad landscapes of this mysterious legendary world.

From the earlier chapters of this book you will have glimpsed this 'otherwhere-and-when', and a little reading of any of the texts which appeal to you will fill in the details. The method of recreating these within your own experience is quite simple, but it requires patience and perseverance to acquire the knack. Ideally you should share some of these early adventures with a friend as you then have a narrator who can relate the tale, describe the environment, create the atmosphere for you, and, judging by your reactions, pace the dialogue to suit your inward journey. If you are alone at this stage in your quest, then it is worth the effort of recording on tape the aspects of the journey so that you are gently led forward, into the land of legend. Speak quietly and firmly, pausing now and again to permit the images to form before your mind's eye, or to allow your inner senses to detect the ambience of the 'other where' if pictures do not immediately spring to mind. Some people see instantly with clear and fully 'real' images, and are able to feel the climate, the atmosphere, and enter totally into the experience, whilst others see still pictures, without colour, or hear snatches of the dialogue without images at all, although they can detect the path with senses other than sight. Some people feel they are witnessing a film which they are unable to enter into or interact with whilst others get the sensation of totally being elsewhere only during dreams, which they cannot recall at will.

It may well be a new art form for you to discover, the making of an effective narrative for your journey on the Grail Quest, and you may choose to embellish the tape with sound effects, music, singing and all manner of material which will help you enter the safe, 'relaxed-yet-aware' state which is the magical key to true exploration of the matter of myths. If you have a companion you will quickly learn how to proceed with building the images and sharing the experience, for you have instant feedback. You will also discover how you can also enter the relaxed altered state of awareness and see the pictures and scenes build up behind your closed eyelids as you describe them to your companion. Take it in turn, watching and speaking, and if there are a group of you see how different people react to the same image journey.

Become still and enter the Otherworld by leaving your own place and following a well-known road which passes back through time, becoming more rural and ancient in aspect, or by going through a door you recognize yet which, in your own experience is closed to you. Travel slowly envisaging the path beneath your feet, as well as the scene around you. Perhaps you will choose to start in a familiar road near your home, and pass into the 'otherwhere' through a gate, doorway or entrance which you have never explored in real life, or maybe, by allowing a few moments of peaceful contemplation, you can open your inner eyes to a different time-scale, when the local landscape was unaltered by the works of modern mankind. Do be patient with these first steps, giving your mind's eye a good chance to focus on the new landscape around you.

From the starting off place you can follow one of the traditional magical journeys through a forest, across a desert, or even by boat over the sea to a distant island. Keep the initial voyage simple, exploring the texture of the rock or soil beneath your feet, the nature of the land and its plants and trees, or the types of birds and animals which may be discovered there. It is far safer to become used to the gentle yet definite switch of attention from the 'real' world you live in to the world of inner vision, which can become just as real as you get to know it. Look closely at the details of flowers or trees as these can clearly indicate the season, or perhaps the place, if your travels have led you to some other land. If you don't 'see' at first, sense the feeling of the place, the climate, the texture of any object you can touch, the sounds which may whisper to your inner hearing, perhaps even voices or the songs of birds.

There need not be any time limit to such explorations, but if you are new to this or any other meditation technique, try for only about ten minutes at first. By lengthening the narrative, or by focusing more attention on a particular place or object you will find that in time, given patience and a bit of perseverance, you will be able to go on comfortably for thirty to forty-five minutes. Later on you will also learn to reach a certain stage in the planned narrative and then be silent so that new ideas, views or information can filter through into your mind from the place you are visiting. After a pause of a few minutes, or longer if it feels right to you, you will need to retrace your journey home. With practice it is not necessary to return exactly as you went, for the detached part of your awareness doesn't need to follow the entire trip in reverse to bring you back to your own place, but it is worth allowing the extra time to begin with. A slow return, examining the stages of the path as you come back, will help you to fix the ideas and scenes fully in your memory, whereas a swift return can have the effect of a sudden awakening which sweeps from you the memory of the dream in which you were immersed. Add a sentence to this effect into your narrative, that you will clearly recall all that you have experienced. When you are back again do remember to jot down any information, even fragments or hints, for these will help build up a clear picture as you become more capable of exploring deeply.

You may find that you can use this technique to get to sleep, or you may deliberately choose to follow a journey into the land of dreams, but, again, make notes of the things you dreamt as soon as you wake, for otherwise they melt like summer mists. There are no sure ways of learning to recall dreams, but one useful tip is to try to wake up naturally rather than being shocked awake by the alarm clock. Most people can discipline their subconscious minds to awaken them at any given moment, but it does take a degree of self-confidence. As most people sleep in cycles of about ninety minutes, when sleep passes through a number of stages of dreaming and peaceful sleep (when dreams may occur in a different form), you can often improve your dreaming ability by going to sleep either four and a half, six, seven and a half or nine hours before you need to wake. If you work backwards from your waking time you can soon discover at what hour you should be asleep for the best results, taking into account the number of hours of sleep you need and how long it takes you to get to sleep in the first place.

All this may seem a far cry from the idea of mounting your horse and galloping into the Forêt Sauvage to find the Grail Castle, but it is far easier to make the physical exploration once you have tuned up your inner sight and senses, which may be your only guide in that unmapped land. From your initial reading and interest in whichever aspect of the legends has led you this far you will already have begun to stock the images, the characters, the symbols and the ancient landscapes in the files of memory so that you can use them to lead on to new and personal advances in the quest. You will also need to decide which of the many possible paths in the world your quest will take - that of the individual, the modern hermit, who, though living in the world, can put aside its affairs and concentrate solely on the journey. You may choose to be one of many, and seek out an order, society or companionship whose works and philosophies centre around the Western Mystery of the Grail. Another option is to become one of a few, to discover a small number of companions who will share the quest, be it an outer journey, seeking in the world, or an inner, spiritual adventure, searching for the Grail within. From your own knowledge of your life, your aims, commitments and situation you alone can decide.

Dion Fortune is best known to many for her books *The Mystical Qabalah* and *Cosmic Doctrine*, the philosophy of spiritual evolution, but she also wrote a number of esoteric novels, revealing to the astute reader much about the rituals, powers and ancient traditions of Britain. She also founded, in the early 1920s, the Fraternity of the Inner Light. Always interested in the mysteries and their magical application, especially those based on the legends of Britain, Dion Fortune was one of the most important influences on the contemporary occult scene. Her Fraternity (now Society) was the training lodge for many important writers and thinkers, some of whom have gone on to initiate their own groups which teach students to this day. One of her own branches of teaching was closely linked with the Arthurian Mysteries, using the form of the Grail Temple in their rituals. Some of the people her order trained or influenced include W. E. Butler (who in turn taught Dolores Ashcroft-Nowicki - the Director of Studies of the Servants of the Light Association), W. G. Gray, author of the *San Graal*

*Sacrament*, Gareth Knight, author of *The Secret Tradition in Arthurian Legend*, and many other writers and teachers whose lodges are more secret, or whose works are better known in other fields of literature, poetry or history.

If you want to immerse yourself in the magical aspects of the Grail legends from a modern point of view, any of the books by the above-mentioned writers will provide valuable and comprehensible reading. If you want to enter one of the training schools attached to these orders or share with other students a postal or part-time course there are frequent details readily available, either in the books or in current magazines on Western magical traditions. You will need to be prepared to set aside time each day for regular study and meditation and to attend lectures or send in written reports of your progress for at least one year, and in some cases far longer.

Like any other subject, the practical mastery of magic, through the techniques of which you will be able to unlock the secrets of the Holy Grail, takes both time and effort. To become competent and self-assured will require persistence and dedication, for, as with sporting prowess or musical skill, there are many theoretical and practical matters to learn, and consistent practice alone will ensure success. You cannot dabble with magic because that just opens doors to your psyche, your inner vision, over which you have no control. Magic teaches control and self-discipline so that you remain the master of your own destiny.

If you are serious about your interest and wish to train your inner sight, intuition and magical will, these will all benefit you in everyday matters as well. You will discover abilities for growth, for self-healing and perhaps healing for those around you or the world at large. Creativity will flower, and the gifts of the Grail, which include sufficiency, peace, silence and health, even if you don't feel you have gone very far on your quest, will be revealed to you. All those who seek this mystery will be rewarded in ways which suit their needs.

From your reading of the legends and the history of the Grail seekers you will realise that it isn't the most intellectual, the strongest nor necessarily the apparently most likely seeker who got furthest in the quest. The same applies today. Even if you feel you have very little chance of achieving the Grail, whatever that may mean to you in personal terms, there is no denying the fact that if that is your aim you will get some distance towards your goal. There was never an archetype for the Grail finder in the past - those who got closest to fulfilling the quest were those who appeared to have the least chance. The quest is still to be completed, but now another phase in the Changes of the Grail may have occurred, so that the nature and value of the achievement may well have changed from that which pertained in the time of King Arthur.

To venture into the worlds within your own being is just as dangerous and difficult an adventure as to set out without maps or guides into the great unknown of the world at large. Inner spaces can include whole universes, not merely all the things which are upon the face of the earth. You alone can dictate your direction, how far and fast you dare to travel and the companions with whom you may share the exploration, but if you follow a few basic common-sense instructions there is no limit as to what you may, in time, achieve.

The two most important and simple steps can be taken at any moment. You will not need elaborate equipment, just a little time and space. As explained before, the narrative of a journey can both lead you into the mental state of altered awareness and provide the landscape for you to explore in a way that remains totally within your control. Become lost or tired and you only need call to mind the object in your physical environment, which is the key to return, and you are back home safely. You cannot stray on to any path which is not guarded by the Keepers of the Grail, the angels or elementals which protect both the Grail and those who seek it, and though you may face dangers and fears these are all within your own ability to cope. They may stretch your imagination, patience and determination, but you will be safe on every step of the way, and soon you will learn that those things which threaten come from within and that they have a power to guard as well as to alarm. You will take nothing into the Grail landscape save what is already within you, and will experience only the inner parts of your own character that you or your life-style have forced into the dungeons of repression. The dragons which confront you within the forest are your own unforgiven faults, guilt or unaccepted attitudes. Face them honestly, in the secrecy of your own Castle of the Heart, look clear-eyed into the mirror of experience, and those which you most feared, which troubled your sleep or invaded your peace can be turned from the dread Dweller on the Threshold to the guardian of your gate; from ravening wolf to pet dog.

The other important art is that of meditation. This may be deliberate, directed contemplation of a scene, word, symbol, character or other part of the quest, or it may be a more relaxed examination of the meaning to you of one facet of this complex pattern. Whereas in the creative art of pathworking you direct and control most of the landscape, in meditation you allow it to tell its own story. Be willing to become still and listen. Permit thoughts to arise and follow gently the stream of ideas that flows past your point of awareness. Don't try to grab hold of images, concepts, symbols or actions which drift or swirl past you. Gradually you will find ways of slowing down the current, seeing or sensing more clearly, holding in memory those elusive messages from the infinite within. There is no way to do this by strength but only by gentleness, subtlety and patience. Meditation is an art which awakens butterflies and you will need to try for them with a delicate net of controlled awareness, not the heavy stick of grim determination.

# Chapter Six

## The Grail of Aquarius

To me (Marian Green) the Aquarian Grail is signified by the Tarot
Trump Temperance. Like all Tarot cards it has many interpretations,
but most of these do seem to agree that it is a symbol of uniting divided
forces to achieve harmony. The patterns from the past, reflected in
the mirror of today, to foreshadow tomorrow . . . Reconciliation,
combination, purification, distillation, renewal and the creation of the
Philosopher's Stone from the separate elements.

Bill Butler: The Definitive Tarot: Temperance

We know that the Grail Quest was not totally completed.
We can see that the Waste Land is still with us from the
ecologists' reports of 'acid rain', the destruction of
climate-controlling forests turning to arid desert, the greed and
thoughtlessness which has raped the surface of the Earth for mineral
riches with no thought of the cost to future generations. We cannot

even realize half the problems the upsurge of short-term planning and human rapacity has brought about, and little is done, as yet, to stop this wanton misuse of human power over Nature. The purpose of the Grail has always been seen as that which returns fertility, which restores the Waste Land, bringing health and plenty to all around.

Whatever form the Grail may take in this technological age its virtues are still beneficial to us, not only in the West where apparent plenty still reigns, but in other desolate lands where many have few of the most basic needs we take for granted - clean water, a roof over our heads, clothing, cooking facilities and food in more varieties than we can actually eat. If the Grail could be used in its form of the Cauldron of Plenty then all the starving could be fed, and gradually the stricken and barren lands could have their fertility restored. If the Grail takes the form of the Healing Cup then the sick may be healed, to take their full places in the affairs of the world, and the hospitals turned into gardens where all may find peace and fulfilment. If the modern Grail should be in the form of the Philosopher's Stone it could instil true wisdom into the minds of all who direct the lives of others, so that from the dross of their existence might emerge the shining spiritual gold of human creativity, love, hope and happiness. Perhaps there is a new Grail, a form born out of the previous ones which could combine all its priceless gifts for the true benefit of all creation, people, animals, the land and even outer space.

There is also the Spiritual Waste Land, which in many ways is far more desolate than the ruined lands and spreading deserts, for it has sapped the will of many people, who do not know what they have lost. This is shown in general apathy, violence within the community, separation of families, despair and in many a feeling of desperate hopelessness. We have all become divorced from the forces of Nature, and cannot find either the will to use her perpetual bounty for good or the wits we were given to solve the problems which plague both the advanced lands of the West and poorer lands of Africa. There are ways to improve the share that all Earth's children receive from her, but only if we are willing to face the causes, the greed, the thoughtlessness with which the technological lands use their power for immediate profit rather than long-term sufficiency.

We seem to be living in the times of the Grail as a Cauldron of Inspiration, like the one which the goddess/enchantress Ceridwen brewed for her son, Avagddu, the ugliest man in the world. She wished to give Avagddu the blessings of Inspiration and Science, and knowledge of the mysteries of the future state of the world. During the year and a day needed for the making of the potion, a boy called Gwion was set to stir the pot, and a blind man, Morda, kindled the fire beneath it. Just before the potion was completed it seems to have boiled over or Gwion stirred too hard, so that three drops of the precious brew flew out and scalded his finger. Like many a burned child he put his finger in his mouth to cool it and so drank the magical drops. The Cauldron then burst and the rest of its liquor poured out and ran into a stream, where it poisoned the horses of Gwyddno Garanhir.

How close is this tale to what has happened to our application of knowledge and science? Researchers in many fields sought new chemicals, metals, minerals and drugs which were aimed to have miraculous effects on energy, nuclear power, building and the treatment of disease. In how many cases can we now discover traces of the 'waters of poison to horses' syndrome? In many cases there has been a great leap forward in technology, science and medicine, yet, given a few years foresight how many harmful side-effects could have been predicted and solutions found, or different approaches tried?

Even in the most common matter of food there have been many mistakes. We have to maintain food mountains or wine lakes while in other countries children starve. Our land is losing its fertility because continual mono-culture (growing only corn, for example, instead of rotating different crops and livestock) has taken the heart out of the soil, while agri-chemicals by their expensive bagful do not replace the natural humus, the dung and gentle treading of cattle which enrich and break up the soil. Heavy machinery causes ruts down which streams of rain, laden with displaced fertile soil, run off to pollute streams, silt them up and kill the fish to whom nitrates are poison. More and more people are developing allergies to food, its preservatives, artificial colourings and flavourings. A whole new science of 'clinical ecology' has sprung up to investigate many diseases like arthritis, 'irritable bowel syndrome', colitis, skin rashes, and manic behaviour in children, and has traced the causes of these frightening complaints to such widely used things as wheat flour, milk, eggs, sugar and artificial colourings. How much suffering may have been caused by our modern diet of processed foods, deprived of their roughage, texture, flavour and naturally beneficial minerals and salts?

Energy, too, is an area which is likely to bequeath problems to our children and grandchildren, and for thousands of years to come. Nuclear power may be cheap but the resulting waste cannot safely be stored on land, nor destroyed, nor easily be turned into any useful end-product, and its radioactivity may last for hundreds if not thousands of years. Is that the sort of problem you want to pass on to the unborn generations? Shouldn't we, who are still living in the Waste Land, try to find some solutions now? Should we not encourage in any way we can research into other unpolluting and safe methods of providing energy? The Creator gave us the perpetual sun to shine its enormous energy upon us, and caused the tides to ebb and flow, the winds to fan our hills and the fast streams to run into the valleys. These are all eternal, free and available for use as the powerhouses of the future. We do not need to drain the last drops of fossil fuels either as oil or as coal from under the earth, and cause who knows what problems when the empty spaces left under the North Sea and in coal-bearing areas have to be filled in, by man or Nature, in times to come.

Medicine is another field in which the gifts of the Cauldron of Life have been matched by its deadly dregs. In many areas science has produced 'miracle drugs' and saved many lives, but equally fears about side-effects, long-term addiction and unexpected reactions found in human patients which were not apparent in laboratory animals have caused much concern in medical circles and the world at large. No one can deny that the sick child given many years of happy and worthwhile life as a result of a new drug, organ-swap surgery or some other technical advance has a right to be treated, but sadly not all these experiments have similar happy conclusions. Who can tell what medicines, food additives or other unnatural substances to which the mother of those children was exposed caused them to be unwell or physically damaged at birth? These are not light matters, but no one who has any thought for the possible Gifts of the Grail in the time to come can ignore the state of the world and the people around them now.

Today many people are seeking the freedom of choice to overcome some of the problems which they attribute to incomplete science. The field of alternative or complementary medicine is expanding because people with problems have found that the 'miracle' cure of allopathic medicine could not work in their case. Homeopathy, where minute amounts of substances seem to spark off the healing power of the individual's system on a 'like cures like' basis, has no side-effects, it is holistic, treating the entire patient not just the stiff knee, upset stomach or headache, and in many cases has dramatic results. Osteopathy and chiropractic allow the manipulation of the spine, joints and muscles, often bringing relief to long-standing painful conditions which orthodox medicine can only treat with painkillers and anti-inflammatory drugs - it cannot attempt to cure, only to alleviate the symptoms. Acupuncture, massage, floral, herbal, naturopathic and aromatic therapies all strive to heal the entire individual. The Grail is the ultimate holistic therapy, for it can cure the ills of the entire world and all its people.

Religion, with its underlying tradition of spiritual care, has also lost out in the technological age. From the elegant and inspirational language of the Holy Books God's words have been rendered into modern jargon, alienating the traditionalists in many religious communities, and contemporary theologians have expressed their own personal doubts about the validity of the religious founder's message by preaching these as doctrine. Others have turned away from the faith of their fathers and sought Eastern paths to Nirvana, Samahdi or Shanti. Some have sought solace in reviving cults of the most ancient gods and goddesses, becoming pagans, and fulfilling their individual religious fervour in ritual, song and dance. As well as the familiar Christian symbolism, in that the Grail is both the Cup of the Last Supper and the Sacred Vessel in which Joseph of Arimathea caught the blood and sweat of the dying Jesus, its older form of the Cauldron is decidedly pagan. There are several Cauldrons in Welsh legend, not only the Cauldron Awen of Ceridwen in which she brewed the magical potion, but there is also the Cauldron of Rebirth, brought by Arthur from Annwn, the Celtic Otherworld, whose draught restored life and yet inflicted dumbness upon the rebirth in the drama of death and reawakening which forms an important aspect of initiation. Many pagan or magical groups require of their initiates who have undergone the ritual an oath of silence, or these days, of discretion in speech - is that not close to being struck dumb?

The pagan aspect of the Grail story has given it a new lease of life and several interpretations allow it to have been in the keeping of pre-Christian gods or goddesses. The Cauldron of Awen was used by Ceridwen, and the Cauldron of Annwn was wrested by Arthur and his companions from Pwll, the Welsh God-King of the Under/Otherworld. The entry to the Otherworld is another part of the most ancient rituals of initiation, and it is quite likely that many of the structures we find called burial mounds or long barrows, like Wayland's Smithy or the West Kennet Long Barrow, were originally not tombs for the dead but tombs for the living, as were the pyramids of Egypt in antiquity. Today the magical or sacred influence of ancient sites, be they circles of standing stones, the lone monolith, the henge, the vast earthwork or the almost time-obliterated tump, the ancient ford or dewpond, is being rediscovered and the new pagans are trying to understand the power and uses of these charged areas. The land too may hold aspects of the Grail mysteries.

Forests in the tropics are being destroyed, just as we are beginning to appreciate the value of plants and trees, for building, for gums, drugs and foodstuffs. The cover they give protects the fertility of the soil, provides food and shelter for many species of animals, birds and insects which may yet prove to be of value to modern mankind. Woodlands, hedgerows, single trees and sheltering copses in Britain have been grubbed up for quick profit from their timber, to make larger fields so that heavy and deep cutting ploughs may be driven over the face of the Earth, with no thought for the homeless birds and insects and small animals which feed on pests and their larvae. Poisonous chemicals are used on crops, taking us all one step closer to that final 'silent spring'.

In inner cities there is wasteland influence at work too, in the decaying and derelict buildings, once comfortable homes, workshops or businesses. If every existing home was restored and made dry and habitable there would be little need to gobble up more green fields for housing. If small workshops could be provided then much of the creativity and hidden talent could be put to use, and the Grail's gift for inspiration in art, in jewellery-making, in pottery, basketwork, weaving, sculpture, poetry, writing and music could be practised and shared. Those who know these sometimes dying arts could teach, and new students expand their own skills of doing and making.

Human kind was not designed to live in concrete piles reaching up to the sky. If contact with Earth is lost so too is the power and stability it gives us as her children, born of her substances, fed of her bounty. Here again we see how misplaced are the greed and keenness to demonstrate the value of newly found substances now that we know the harm done by asbestos, that curious mineral attributed in some traditions as a gift, with bees, from the planet Venus. Modern reinforced concrete's steel skeletons suffer from the wet in our climate, and develop 'concrete cancer', while some mixes of cement have not been as strong as they should be.

Modern pagans are taking as part of their newly discovered faith the need to respect the Earth, to learn to use her gifts wisely, to replace woods and treat these as the sacred groves they once were in the pre-Roman time of the Druids. Some of them seek knowledge of the many uses of plants, as natural foods, for healing, wine-making, aromatics, dyes and incenses. They are trying to live up to the commandment to honour their Mother and Father, being well aware that the Earth Mother offers our only support and nourishment and that her benificence has been overtaxed and misused, thus probably many of her valuable products have become extinct and so lost to us forever. Now we are living at a great crossroads in time, be it the Dawning of the Age of Aquarius or the rising tide of Alvin Toffler's Third Wave. Change is all around us, but so is choice. We do not have to adhere to the convention of lifestyle, religion, medical treatment or diet. We can face our own destinies by accepting all the gifts of the technological world, ignoring pollution, destruction, starvation, sickness, apathy and the breakdown of culture and civilization, as if by turning our backs on them they will quietly creep away and never bother us again - or aspiring to the inherent courage of the Grail seeker we may choose to set upon a dangerous road that leads directly into the Waste Land.

That is what this book is about. In the time of Arthur the land was being overrun by invaders. The Celtic people, returning to their individual tribes after the Romans left, were hard to unite again, even against a common foe, yet somehow by the magic of Merlin and the unifying concept of the Round Table a loyal and brave band of companions was formed. By using their warlike training they pushed back the Saxons and bought a spell of peace and prosperity. In order that these redundant warriors should not seek civil disturbance as a peacetime pastime the Quest for the Holy Grail became the focus of their energy, ingenuity and courage. We, who are living in the interim between the last war and the Last War (if the nuclear debate is not settled peaceably once and for all), need to find a cause which will employ our time and skill, our outer ability and our inner needs in a personal and constructive way. Such is the Grail Quest now. From what I have said above, the life-giving and restorative powers of the Grail are just as relevant today, if not more so. We have so much to lose.

The first step of any journey may in time lead to its completion, yet before that step can be taken a wise man will consider the purpose of his journey, he will prepare his equipment, consider his route, and perhaps ask others what conditions he is likely to expect when he arrives. This is just as true for the person indulging in a package holiday to the Costa del Sol as it is to one setting out on the greatest quest of all. Unfortunately, although quite a few people living today are in some way already engaged upon this quest, they are scattered and do not generally announce to the media the object or direction of their travels. The quest can lead through some strange places, not only the Forest of Broceliande, but many a modern city or pleasant country path. Here there are plenty of distractions. Not only the outer journey leads past a variety of diversions, but the harder, lonelier inner path does too. Apathy and hesitation, a lack of commitment or a clear direction can often prevent anyone taking the first actions to cross the boundary from the everyday world to enter the land of legend and seek out the matter of myths.

If you are truly willing to devote a little of your time, or perhaps the whole of your life to the Grail Quest, then you will need to make some sort of personal dedication. This may take many forms, from the simplest, a silent inner promise to set about the search for the Grail, to an elaborate ceremony whereby you make a formal pledge before witnesses to go forth upon the quest. If you are part of a training school this could be a part of your initiation oath, or when you take a magical name or motto this could be important. One way in which anyone could go about this would be to write a letter of personal dedication, which in its own way is a magical talisman - a statement of intent to fulfil or bring about some future event, a simple act of will. If you have already begun the meditations or path-threading journeys discussed in the previous chapter you will be clearly informed when to make this formal undertaking.

In time past, the knight who was to receive the accolade was well prepared for his advanced status. He would have served time as a page, perhaps in a strange household, learning his letters and the gentle arts of courtesy. Later he would be taught the warlike skills of the battle, to master his horse, hunt with hawks, fight with sword and lance, which were probably balanced by playing a musical instrument, writing poetry or singing ballads for his chosen lady. At last the time would come for him to set aside his childhood and youth and take on the weapons and responsibilities of a man of his age. He would be bathed and dressed in new clothes by his sponsor and peers, and then spend the night in silent vigil over the sword and armour to which he was earning entitlement. Perhaps he would be plagued with doubts, or be arrogant about his new status. In time the symbolically light but technically killing blows of the accolade would be awarded him and he would become a true knight.

In these modern days of unisex and equal opportunities where growing up seems to be something to be got over as fast as possible, we may well be losing out on the 'rites of passage' which still continue in simpler communities. To become an adult, with all the responsibilities and expectations of a 'person of the world' is now unmarked except by leaving school, college or university - a very feeble way to indicate this important phase of life. It may be that in later life individuals can reflect on what they have missed and by setting out upon some journey of inner exploration, or even an outer assay to some unexplored continent, they are seeking to fulfil the rites of passage which they have hitherto been denied.

The Grail Quest may be taken up at any time, or age, in any place, by those who are rich in worldly possessions and by those who have little. But seekers must not ignore the world around them. The first stage must be to know and acknowledge the situation which they are putting behind them and to honestly strive to see the surrounding Waste Land, the ruined country and unhappy planet. Only by seeing its true horror can you gain the courage and determination to do something about it. There may be fertile fields, bright gardens, flowing streams, sun-drenched cornfields, rich orchards, but there are also spoil heaps, polluted rivers and seas, sulphuric vapours in the air, dark smoke, acid rain, scarred and ravaged workings, derelict inner cities, and, worst of all, soul-lost people. These are the twin streams which the Angel of Temperance strives to unite between the cups of past and future. The Grail may offer healing but it can also pour out the draught of death. Unless we, whose lifetime spans the bridge of time when the harm of the dark and deadly draught may be refined, dissolved and blended into a pure and wholesome stream, begin the quest now, then we are too late to find the Grail. We are the alchemists, the Fferyllt, the Fairyfolk, the heirs of Wayland Smith, who may be willing to relearn the ancient arts which came to us from the Black Lands of the Nile so that we may in time make Green the Earth anew.

There may be no simple solution that can be poured forth from the Aquarian Grail but it can offer us the gift of Time. If we dare to seek answers to the many problems to which our flesh is heir, and wander into the unknown and hidden lands of the world at large, or the unexplored territory of the inner landscape, we will be able to discover the Elixir, the new drops of Inspiration and Science from the restored Cauldron of Ceridwen, and bring this back to offer others. We are not denied the Philosopher's Stone, nor the magical Grail cup, nor shall we be prevented from sharing their bounty with all in need. That need grows more urgent with every passing day, and the changes that are sweeping over the whole world as the tide of the Age of Aquarius gathers strength will have to be directed in a controlled and healing way, lest the recreative essence which such changes bring is swept away unused.

Let us find ways to empty the cup of our present being of all its dregs: anxieties, failings, faults and despairs, that we may be pure and whole vessels, ready to receive the outpourings of the new

# Chapter Seven

## The Gifts of the Grail

...In some mysterious way, there is only one task that the seeker after the Grail must perform, and that is to ask a question. To ask the Question is to perform the quest. If the Question is not asked, the Fisher King and the Land die, and the Quester fails to find the Grail which is Life. But it may be if the Question IS asked, and the King and the Land live, and the Quester finds the Grail which is Death.

M Krisdottir: *John Cowper Powys and the Magical Quest*

It is already clear that the Grail is a Mystery within a Mystery. It has many forms in the many accounts, and is said to pass through Five Changes. It may well still be amongst us in one form or another, for example, as the Cup or Chalice, the Christian symbol. Is not the Cup of the Communion in every church, high and low, Catholic, Protestant or non-conformist, that same container of Christ's blood? May the spirit of the Grail not be found in every kitchen where wholesome and enjoyable food is cooked, in that even the Grail of Arthur's court provided those dishes that the knights loved most? Anyone who prepares food with care for those they love, are they not partaking of the gifts of the Grail? Could not the Grail be seen in every meteorite that flies burning to earth, like the emerald which fell from the crown of Lucifer, Star of the Morning? Does it now rest, honoured as the Ka'aba at Mecca?

Is the Grail lying lost in some treasure hoard, shrouded by time in a forgotten cave among the Roman silver dishes, or the Saxon gold, the plunder of a mediaeval pirate or the spoils of war? Is it the sacred blood that runs down from a high historic past, yet those who bear it now have little power or position and pay little heed to such a potent inheritance? Are you not proud of your ancestors, preserving their memory as faded photographs, copperplate letters and family trees? Although they are ordinary you cherish their memory, so if they were sacred would not your pride be greater?

If you add all the symbols together you can certainly describe something which occurs all through the legends, which came with Joseph from his home across the sea, and can bear all the gifts which the Grail is known to share. Take the Dish or Cup, place upright in it the Lance, hang from that Lance the Holy Shroud, and set the Stone inside - here is the Ark of the Covenant of the Grail, set to sail upon the oceans of the world bearing its gifts. Science is gradually allowing us to see that boats, those earliest 'holy vessels', could voyage the seas long before man bestrode a horse, or hacked chariot-ways through the forests of Europe. Noah was not the only one to build a great ship and set out to save the population of the world. From the hot lands of the Nile and the inner regions of the Mediterranean travellers have set off in safe, unsinkable reed ships, to follow the ceaseless waterways which flow river-like across the Atlantic and the Pacific, touching fertile islands as they go, and above which blow helpful winds. With the wisdom gained by watching birds and whales migrating the ancient people set sail to find and settle in distant lands.

The special Stone is the anchor before the time of metals, or the hearth to protect the flammable hull from cooking fires. The dish or Cup is the dense, unsinkable hull of buoyant reeds bundles or great logs, the foundation of ships or rafts on which peoples from many lands made epic voyages and took their crops, their cattle and their wisdom to the world's other hemisphere. The only fear of sailors then and now is a lee shore, the unknown rocks of a strange landfall - the safest place in a storm is in a sound ship in deep water! This, too, could be the vessel of the Grail, that bore Joseph from his home, with whatever treasures of spirit or body he had with him, to these misty islands, to find safe haven in the watery Vale of Avalon or on the mysterious island on the shore of Britain described in *Sone de Nansai* (cf.Chapter 1).

Boats are also part of the quest, for just as in magical symbolism the Earth is both mother and foundation, then Water is the element of feelings, travel and emotion. The Lady of the Lake gave Arthur his sword, and he used a boat to go to her. At the end of his work, after the battle with Mordred, it was into a dark barge steered by three queens that Arthur departed for the other land. Heroes in all continents have sailed into the setting sun, their first tasks completed but their return promised when the need should be great.

You may well wish to travel the world, explore caves and dig for buried treasure as part of your quest. You may be guided to sacred sites or forgotten hiding places, to museums or to wild moorlands, where the rocks have never been shaped by man. Such journeying is a valuable part of the experience of the search for the Grail, for it will allow you to meet with strangers who may become your friends, to taste of exotic cauldrons and share the cups of companionship in distant places, for the stories of the Grail are spread throughout the world, from Western Cup to Eastern Pearl, each a precious object in its own setting.

You may prefer to make your journeys in the mind, through treading magical paths in the secrecy and stillness of your own place, or learn the arts of dowsing, which, as many a God-given talent, few develop. Once you have determined what for you is the form of the Grail, you can hold such a concept or image in your mind and dowse with a pendulum over a map of your own area, Europe or the world, and use a progressively larger scale until you can focus on a certain spot.

Dowsing (its name comes from the Cornish word down - to seek) is another way in which you can use magical skills in your quest. Most of the earliest dowsers were looking for water, those in the Middle Ages for metal ores, and these days for 'ley lines' those invisible power cables which appear to link ancient sacred sites of all types. In its simplest form, dowsing involves learning to hold a Y-shaped twig, preferably of hazel or willow (because they grow near water, and don't split when under pressure at the join), and walking slowly across ground under which you believe there to be a spring or waterpipe. Hold the twig with one hand at the end of each branch of the Y by turning the palm up, with the thumb outwards. Curl your fingers gently around the twig and you will feel a slight tension against the join of the Y. By flexing your wrists to increase this and cause the third arm of the Y to point upwards, you may begin to walk over the water source. Once you get the knack, which like meditation you have to practise till you succeed, you will find that the point of the twig will turn violently downwards over the water - be careful, you can grip too tightly if you resist this feeling, and raise blisters on your hands when the twig wants to twist!

The other, indoor, form of dowsing, which will work more subtly, is with a pendulum made of a heavy bead or small symmetrical object to which some thin twine can be attached. Woven cord, like thin picture cord, is best as it will not unravel and you can seal the nylon ends with a match. Have about a foot of cord between the bob and the bit you hold, again palm up, with the cord running over your index finger. To use a pendulum for dowsing for water, minerals, lost items or the Grail you will need to establish a personal code for 'yes' and 'no' or positive and negative. The easiest way to do this is to hold the bob, swinging gently, over your other hand and say 'Is my name . . . . . (whatever it is)?' You will soon find that from the idle, undirected swing, it may change to a firm straight-line swing, either left to right, or back and forth, or to a circle. If its movements are unclear ask it to 'speak louder' or indicate more surely what it is doing. Once you have a clear movement, ask a negative question and you will find that, again, from an idling swing it will make another definite sort of line or circle which should be different from the 'yes' answer. Do be patient and practise until you get consistent answering swings which you call 'yes' and 'no'. The next test is to hide a coin or similar under one of several upturned cups, shuffle them around, or get someone else to do it so you aren't sure where the object is. Hold the pendulum over each cup in turn, asking yourself 'Is this the coin, etc.?'. See how well you do.

This might seem a rather useless game, but it does help you open up those inner channels of communication within your mind, by which means it is eventually possible to locate unseen objects or to dowse over a map and locate areas containing sources of water or other substances. Unless you can become proficient at simple tasks then map or even real land dowsing will prove fruitless. Learn to trust your power to discover things in this basic way. Practise asking questions to which the answers must be 'yes' or' no' and finding out if your inner sense can tell you truly. Don't expect this skill to be able to predict the future, though, for as you will come to realize the pattern of individual destiny is as changeable as the sands on the strand of time.

You may discover that you can help other people through this simple skill by locating lost objects for them or the source of some pain or sickness. You might find if you are dowsing answers for another person that the pattern of 'yes' and 'no' answers you get for yourself are reversed for someone of the opposite sex. Do check this out first, as it could be very confusing to get a row of positive answers when asking about locations of illness or reasons for food allergy or similar. By dowsing down lists, or even menus, you might find ways of improving your diet and thus your total health if you get really good with your pendulum.

If you believe in a physical Grail which exists in some hidden location then you might well be able to put your new-found skill to map dowsing over areas in which you feel the Grail might lie. Certainly experts have located water and oil deposits from maps rather than having the bother of exploring large areas on the ground. By fixing your mind on whatever image you may have of the Grail and dowsing slowly over the maps of Glastonbury, or Wales, Scotland, Brittany, or around Rennes-le-Chateau, wherever you feel to be relevant, you might uncover the mysterious hiding place - who knows? The Grail Quest is open to all, and by its magical nature should be pursued by all reasonable means.

You can also use the art of dowsing to pin down other aspects of the quest. You could list possible attributes of either the effective Grail finder, or yourself, and try to discover which are the most useful, or even properties of the Grail itself, locations in which it might be concealed or methods by which you might be guided to find it.

Because the quest and the seeker cannot be totally separated from each other, and because each is dependent on the other, any art which gives help to the seeker will also aid the quest. If you make some progress as an individual it might help others who are also on the path to go forward. Your findings may make easier the way for those who follow, for the path to the Grail is the path of Life.

Another factor which is important is that you cannot set aside the quest from other aspects of your life. Many people set out to discover one or other of the magical traditions, imagining that this will be a hobby to fill in the idle hours when there is nothing of interest to them on television. What they soon learn, if they persist beyond the most basic reading, is that magic will affect all parts of their lives. It is not something like embroidery or carpentry which can be done at a set time and place and then put aside and forgotten about, its effects will influence everyday affairs as well as those times which are specifically magical. If you begin to train your psychism then it will work in the office or workplace just as it will in the temple or sacred sanctuary. If you start to meditate then your visions and insights will continue into dreams and idle moments. Once you learn to control and direct those inner resources which are what real magic is all about, then you will develop a number of very practical and useful skills, both for the inner journeyings and the outer world. Control is the key factor. though, for uncontrolled psychic powers are a great danger.

Anyone wishing to study magic is always warned against dabbling, and those warnings should be heeded. Any inner probings, be it through simple meditation, path-working or any of the most basic techniques, will cause doors to open. Through those doors will flood both information and power, and unless you are very careful about holding fast to the key these can completely overwhelm any novice. Grail Questing is also bound to open some of these previously firmly fastened doors to the inner realms. Be very careful to set aside specific times to work on what ever aspect of the Grail Quest most interests you. If you are even just re-reading the literature do it in a responsible and careful way, for it contains many potent symbols which will not affect the unawakened mind, but once you have started seriously on the quest, those symbols will haunt you until you come to understand them in your own terms. You will find them turning up, time and again, in the most unexpected places, urging you to continue your search. Only by acknowledging the potency of such symbols, and when you stop reading firmly closing the book, or completing your meditation or path journey with a sincerely meant closing gesture or word, will you be able to keep their influence from flooding through at what can become inconvenient moments. Certainly your quest will require persistence and dedication, but it must be prevented from becoming an overwhelming obsession and invading your every waking, and even sleeping, moment.

As with any practical skill you might learn, start with simple things. If you begin by tackling the image of the Waste Land and its Maimed King you will be working with most potent images which can have a profound, and often exceedingly unsettling effect upon you. Choose a small and well-documented aspect to begin work with, and test each step of the way for your own reactions to it. Magical work can magnify your emotions and feelings because it will start to work on that level. The Grail is commonly seen as a Cup and that is the controller of the emotions. Within a magical training school the novice is gently led through a series of encounters with different aspects of his own personality as symbolized by the four elements - Earth, Water, Fire and Air. In the Grail Quest you will encounter these alone, without the help in tackling them which you might like and perhaps need. The quest will prove to be an initiation to any who set upon it at all seriously, and the outcome may be very different from what you might expect.

It is always safest to work with the element of Earth, and in human terms that is your physical self. Get to know your state of health and if you know you are not totally well then do something about it. Although the quest will do a great deal to tone up your mental and psychic muscles it isn't likely to do a lot for your physical ones, unless you set out on foot for Shamballah or Tir nan Og - in the latter case it would be your rowing muscles which would get exercised!

Look hard at your life in the past - where on the road of this incarnation do you stand? At the beginning, in the middle, or well along the way? Consult your Life-lines on both hands - are they long and strong, or weak and often broken? How runs the Line of Fate or Destiny down the middle of your palm? Does it indicate fame or fortune? It is never too late to set out upon the quest, and though many modern magical arts equip you well for life, they would in earlier times also equip you for death. The legends of the Grail will certainly make clear to you that many of those who sought were harvested by the Grim Reaper before their quest was completed, and even those who achieved the ultimate goal sometimes lost their life in the process.

We, in today's society, have overcome many of the old taboos of sex and status to the point that the once forbidden topic is now the commonplace, displayed in the media daily. We have yet to dispel the last great fear of the unknown, and that is death - an integral part of the Grail Quest. To many the Grail was the bringer of a seemingly untimely end, and it may still be, whatever form, material or spiritual, it may take now. There is no way we can deny that fact, just as we ultimately have to face the undeniable fact that we are mortal and some day we shall die.

Each night when we go to sleep we are entering an unknown yet generally unfeared zone. Our dreams may take us to weird landscapes, strange and perhaps even frightening situations, yet most of us lie down each night without too many qualms. In the old schools of magic the novices were taught that to sleep is a reasonable comparison to dying, and by learning to be unafraid of sleep, and the special sleeps of magical work, the novice did not fear death. Those who tread the secret ways now will have to face again the dark door of initiation and the cave of descent into the inner world, just as Arthur sought to bring forth the Cauldron of Rebirth from the caverns of Pwll, Lord of the Underworld, in Annwn. That which offers Life promises Death, too.

Dying, in this technological age, may often be without dignity and in unfamiliar circumstances. Many die as a result of the way they have lived, and go forth unknowing into limbo. Others train themselves to be able to withdraw and so pass gently and certainly into whatever part of Paradise they have prepared themselves for - that is the way of the magician and the Grail finder. The spiral of many lives may bring back past questers and set them on the path of achievement in this life, and so by recalling something of what we have been we might find yet more answers to the work.

Life could be looked upon as a preparation for death. To some this is a shocking and gloomy view, for death is surely the end, but to others death is but sleep and a new awakening. Those who seek the Grail must think about this for themselves. There is no certain answer to the matter of afterlife, Heaven or reincarnation. Most magicians accept that they have lived before, some recalling clearly other places, other faces and other times. Some of their meditational arts help them to recover such information in a gentle and effective way, rather as those who regularly record their dreams find them easier to remember each morning.

Those who take care of the dying also need to be taught some of the forgotten ways of sending forth the souls of the patients under their care. Any sensitive nurse will recognize when some spirit is set to depart and a few kind words, even to the deeply comatose, can bring comfort and guidance. In harsher times one of the gifts of the Grail would have been a peaceful and painless parting which was like going forth from one family into the arms of another. Many who in these days of scientific medicine have been recalled to life after physical death report a similar vision of passing through a dark tunnel to the place of great light, or a garden of delight, into the company of loved ones who have already passed through the thin veil that separates life and death. This too may be part of the Grail Quest, for in at least one of its forms, the Grail which heals also created the Waste Land which we seek to make green again through our search and achievement.

It may seem extremely callous to talk about death, to say that it is necessary to think hard about dying, preferably of extreme old age, at peace in our own beds, and that the Grail seeker, if he is successful, might bring about the death of a society we know and accept, yet this is a definite possibility. The work of the healer, in the old days, was also that of the practitioner of euthanasia, which is already becoming an accepted idea in some Western societies. To know how to send forth the spirit of the dying one gently and peacefully, by laying on of hands, or at a distance, is not a form of magic discussed in popular books, yet its secrets may be revealed to the Grail quester at some time.

Another factor which concerns death is the suffering of those left behind. People can be happy to see the end of an old, sick but beloved pet - though they may grieve there is something satisfying about knowing that the cat or dog has found a painless peace, and so they can accept the situation. When the dying one is a person, a very different reaction often comes into play. We all know that we have never really opened our hearts to our nearest and dearest and shared with them the words of love, or thanked them for the joy they have brought us - perhaps this, too, should be a lesson of the Grail, to speak honestly with the quiet voice of emotion whilst you have the chance. We find it hard to accept the loss, are affronted by the power of our own feelings, and blame ourselves in some way for the inevitable. It is usually not sorrow for the departed which most wrenches at our heart strings and dries our throat, but a selfish feeling, 'Why have they done this to me?' It takes great courage to face these feelings in the open, weep for the loss of a dear one, and then get on with living our lives as they would have wished. Those who tread the paths of magic should have this courage, or seek to find it within themselves, just as they should have compassion for others who are suffering the pangs of bereavement.

If you can follow further the inner way to an acceptance of reincarnation, the pain following a death may be eased by the certainty that the beloved will live again, and perhaps your lives will be united in the years to come. The quest is certainly something which transcends death, and many who seek now may have lived the lives of other seekers long ago. Through meditation and other magical arts it may be possible to recall steps on the quest that you took before, remember clues and symbols from the distant past which are still relevant on today's journey.

There are many aspects to the ways the Grail Quest may affect contemporary seekers, for esoteric philosophy teaches that all things are inter-linked and interconnected so that one life or one action can have farreaching consequences. To solve the Grail mystery, to heal the Waste Land and to free the Waters of Life, on a cosmic scale could alter the fate of the entire universe, and yet to accomplish that the quester may have little awareness of the enormity of his task. Only by progressing along the twin paths of self-awareness and super-awareness can the successful seeker learn that, if he fulfils his destiny, all the world will be changed and that he is responsible for that change. By becoming more self-aware through the ancient, seemingly unexciting, mystical states of meditation will the inner strength and insight be developed to cope with change, with mundane life, and with death itself. Awareness of the cosmic patterns.will teach how one small change in the settings of the stars may alter life on this planet forever. If the Grail turns out to be a new star in our sky, or an undiscovered planet, or a comet trailing good or evil in its luminous tail, its influence would be profound.

Those who seek the Grail or perhaps are its Guardians have often been outcasts. We may still have the people from the mystical city of Sarras among us today, and they are still generally unloved and mistrusted. The gypsy folk, descendants of Sarah, the one from whom Sarras is surely named, have always been wanderers, bringing both luck and misfortune. They have been persecuted, yet their traditional skills of reading the future, one of the Gifts of the Cauldron of Ceridwen, are sought after even now. Many are still healers, particularly of horses, and many preserve that ancient free spirit which marches to a drum which we city-bound and civilized people do not hear. They know the secrets of a hand's lines, they brought us the Tarot cards in their painted wagons (and the roots of that stolen wisdom have not yet been fully found!). They reverence the Oldest Gods, and in the circles about the camp fires it is the matriarch who holds sway. We would usually prefer them to settle into houses, obtain steady jobs and quell that inner spirit which longs to roam, that many of us secretly share, for they are different and their knowledge is not of books. What part in this ancient story do they hold in trust from the ages of ages?

Those who truly seek the Grail may well find themselves as outcasts, for their knowledge and work will be well away from that of the man in the street. It is hard for a magician to share his ideas and philosophy with others, even if they have studied in the same school, for the inner way is lonely. The path of the Grail seeker will set you apart from other people in your life. You cannot wholeheartedly take on the quest without allowing yourself to realize that the path to the Grail is often solitary and fraught with dangers. These things will be shown to you as soon as you take your first faltering steps along it. You will need courage and determination as well as calmness and patience. It is not an easy way for anyone to tread.

As an agent of change the Grail can alter everything which we take as normal. If a change of direction occurs on national, international or even cosmic scale then many people will be disconcerted, frightened and upset by the changes. To find the will of politicians making U-turns, to find worldwide attention focused on hunger, or the needs of the exploited lands taking precedence over the desires of the greedy, some people, often with great political power, will be angry and will fight back. Some wish to spread the Waste Lands, to reap harvests of death and human misery in order to satisfy corporate avarice. Some are so spiritually blind that they cannot perceive the anguish of the starving, the future disaster areas that will result from the exploitation of natural forests which can never be restored, the pollution of water and air, the destruction of the land's fertility by chemicals and overweight machinery. All these things can be avoided if wisdom and care are applied by people of farsight and knowledge. The will to change for good rather than evil is another gift of the Grail.

# Chapter Eight

## The Grail of Transformations

*I am a messenger only', the voice, if voice it were, uttered, 'but I am the precursor of the things that are to be. I am John and I am Galahad and I am Mary: I am the Bearer of the holy One, the Graal, and the keeper of the Graal. I have kept it always, whether I dwelt in the remote places of the world and kings rode after me or whether I removed it to the further parts of man's mind. All magic and all holiness is through me, and though men stole the Graal from me ages since I have been with it forever.*

*Charles Williams:* War in heaven

The Grail, it is clear, changes its form. Those who sought it, according to the various texts, did not necessarily have any idea what they were looking for, or where they might eventually find it. We who are the latest heirs to the quest may be just as uncertain what to look for or where to go and what might happen if we succeed as were our ancient forebears. This does not diminish our desire to seek a final solution to this age-old mystery, solve the riddle of our Celtic past and return the benefits of this most sacred symbol to our own world and time. Indeed, our need for wisdom about the future, for restoring the balance between mankind and the earth, for healing the ills of all aspects of Nature - the need for the Grail's magic -  grows ever greater. What better thing could we bequeath to our children?

We have many advantages in our time, and greater access to spiritualities of many kinds. We have the histories of the Grail to consult, we have maps and plans which might lead us through the maze of the material world to the Chapel in the Green. We also have the inner skills, the language of psychology to describe the innermost journeys leading to the Grail of the Heart, and the mystical and practical arts which may allow us to divine a clear path to our goal. We have the tales of the earlier seekers and information about the perils they faced, the dragons they slew, and the challenges to life and limb which many of them strove to conquer. The tests will be no less taxing, the journey, though better mapped, may be just as fraught with danger, even if it only be to venture within our individual consciousness.

As you will have seen, the different accounts of the Grail story give the Grail many separate physical forms. As well as the Grail itself, there are other sacred objects associated with it, or in some accounts, other versions of the Grail. These Grail Hallows usually consist of a Dish or Platter; a Spear or Lance from the point of which fall drops of blood; a stone or Green Jewel of Heavenly provenance; as well as the more common Cup, Chalice or Goblet, in which form, albeit veiled, the Arthurian knights saw the Grail carried mysteriously through the hall of Camelot. In the Welsh story of Culhwch and Olwen this collection of sacred and magical objects is further expanded to become the Thirteen Treasures of Britain, which not only includes the various versions of the Grail/ Cup etc. but also a Chariot, a Ring of Power, a Mantle of Invisibility, a Chessboard and a Horse's Bridle. All these items could be perceived as either magical objects in their own right, or as symbols which have an inner interpretation different from their obvious outer use: For example, the Chariot could be construed as a vehicle of change of either physical location or of inner-plane consciousness, and the Bridle might be used to steer a horse or else to control and direct the 'animal' part of the seeker.

Where the Grail itself has several forms it is necessary to decide for yourself if these are actually separate objects, inasmuch as the Grail actually transforms from a Cup to a Lance to a Stone and so on, or if they are individual sacred objects which exist separately in time. In the Welsh tale of Taliesin, in which the story of Ceridwen and her magical Cauldron are found, not only is the vessel itself changed by misuse, but the dregs of the potion (by which the boy Gwion is himself changed in shape from a child into a hare, and then a fish and then a bird and finally into a grain of wheat) change to poison. The goddess, Ceridwen also transformed herself to pursue Gwion, and in the shape of a black hen ate him as the grain of wheat, but later she bore him as a son.

Apart from the magical art of shape-shifting there are a number of interesting points about the changes Gwion chooses. A hare is a magical creature in its own right and was the form into which witches changed themselves when going to full-moon sabbats. It is taboo, seldom eaten, and has many strange attributes in folklore. The hare is an Earth creature, but next Gwion becomes a fish in the water. His third transformation is into a bird, flying in the air and his final change is into a sun-ripened grain of wheat. It is not difficult to tell that these changes relate to the elements of Earth, Water, Air and Fire. They are also stages in a personal initiation, and so, too, is the Grail Quest.

By perceiving that the Grail cannot only alter its form by its own magical power, but can also transform the seeker, those who seek will be changed by their Quest. This change should be seen as growth, and, as has been said before, those who found the Grail in the past often found that death was their prize, and this too must be accepted as a beneficial transformation. What is important above all is to discover your own way of seeing these varied forms, either as aspects of the Grail as a single though changeable object, or as a series of different things that may symbolically represent stages of the quest, degrees of initiation or magical elements.

Because the quest was never fully completed it is still important to find ways of imagining not only what form or forms the Grail may have in our age, but how this could change for the future. In each of the old stories patterns may be discerned which indicate the various stages of the quest as they unfolded in times gone by, and which might yet be discovered in the quest as it enters the

Aquarian Age. Anyone who is familiar with the magical symbolism
of the elements will see that the Grail in its earlier forms can be
considered in that way also. The Cup, the container of blood or
water is clearly a watery Grail. The Stone, even though it fell
from the crown of the Star of the Morning, is of the element Earth.
If the Lance is also a manifestation of the Grail some would see
this as the Air aspect, for though in some magical traditions the
Spear is a weapon of Fire, the Western Tradition attributes it to Air
and the intellect. The pagan Grail is the Cauldron which was
boiled for a year and a day and this has close connections with
Fire. The fifth, the most secret, transformation must be not only a
change of form and physical element but one of level of solidity
and plane of existence. The fifth element in magic is the realm of
the Spirit, so it seems likely that the new Grail will be a vessel of
spiritual value and form.

These are all matters to be considered from a personal
standpoint, both practical and metaphysical. Each must assess
the tales and bring back individual treasures from inner journeys
within the Grail landscapes, or as a result of conversations with
the characters of earlier seekers. Although there may be no
previous record of the kind of information which can be gleaned
from the inner worlds it must be judged for validity by the finder.
Much of our current knowledge actually originated from some
other realm, or in some other consciousness than our own. Usually
this material comes to us today in the form of books or some other
medium that seems quite natural, yet we also have individual
dreams, and, perhaps, visions. Many artists receive their inspiration
from a Muse or creative genius which is beyond their own inner
resources or artistic ability. This too would seem, at least in some
cases, to be a Gift of the Grail.

Because symbolism is the language of magic and of our dreams
and divination it is important to examine this and establish some
ideas about it for ourselves. When Dr Carl Jung was analysing his
patients' dreams he would ask them what the particular images
meant in their own experience. This is an important matter. A
symbol does not necessarily have a fixed and defined meaning. In
a different culture or age the value or interpretation of any shape,
colour, form, concept, character, object or archetype may be
different. Also, if you have had a personal experience involving

that symbol, its meaning to you will be changed. The language of symbols is both simple and direct. It talks to us in childlike (not childish) terms and conveys information not to the reasoning area of the brain but the intuitive level, which in children is still accessible and coherent.

Many recent books have taken the mistaken view that, for example, because a circle or square has a magical use or symbolic meaning, any such shape, in no matter what context, is therefore a magical symbol pointing to something. This is not true and falls into the same category of the statement 'If Plato is a philosopher and my dog is called Plato, then my dog is a philosopher'! To discover that certain hills, churches, gasworks or supermarkets when joined together form a recognizable (or nearly) symbolic shape does not mean that it actually exists, nor does it mean that it was deliberately put there by Atlanteans or extra-terrestrials - there really is such a thing as coincidence! Villages evolve in their particular location because such assets as fresh water, firewood, building material and so on are at hand, and because the chosen location is protected from natural disaster or external attack. If you are drawing lines on a map, you are dealing with a flat representation of a surface which is not only partially spherical but is also jagged or mountainous, and cut by river valleys, depending entirely upon the effects of millions of years of weather on the underlying geological structures. It would take some pretty powerful aliens to shape rock many miles thick in such a way that springs of water occur just where a village is intended to be built in the ages to come!

If you look at any map you will begin to see shapes formed by the contour lines, the placing of villages, the curves of rivers, and these might be recognizable to you as geometric shapes, but it does not mean they actually exist, or have been put there by some agency outside Nature. If the shape of a hill looks like a cow because the shading on the map makes it roughly so, and you happen to have read that the ancient Celts gave a magical meaning to the cow, that does not mean the ancient Celts carved out that particular hillside into that shape. If you looked at the real hillside, from a helicopter, say, rather than at the totally artificial picture of the map, you would be unlikely to see a cow or any other clear shape or symbol!

It is all very well studying the symbolic nature of magical objects and patterns within the Grail tradition, and it is possible by so doing that you will eventually uncover the answers to these age-old riddles, but the answers you get will be personal revelations. What you perceive will be the result of your own understanding, and the changes that the Grail might bring to your life will affect only your own world as you see it. Certainly, if the ultimate benefit of the Grail's restoration should come about then the world would be healed and changed for the better, but that involves the Grail for the World, rather than the inner Grail which is a goal more individuals are likely to achieve.

The Grail transforms itself and transforms things under its influence. You are also transformed by time and you can consider if there is any common pattern. Magic itself has a number of specific forms that are separate within the different Traditions. These varieties of magic are seldom written about in clear terms because understanding them is largely a matter of personal experience and intuition as your training progresses. They form a series of distinct stages that you will need to explore for yourself, if the theory is to have any validity for you. Very simply stated, there appear to be five levels of magic, just as there are Five Changes of the Grail. The pentagram is an ancient magical or religious symbol, and because it has five points it must fit into this scheme somewhere, but I don't know exactly where!

The oldest known forms of magic are those of the Earth - sympathetic acts which determine the outcome by miming it or acting it out. This is green magic, which uses the gifts of the Earth, the herbs for healing, the sources of roots and berries, fruits, nuts and leaves, and food, and fresh water to drink. It is the true heart of the old witches' magic, simply and directly related to the rocks and animals and plants as they exist in their natural state. In the Grail stories there is the form of the Green Stone which may be a memory of the potency of this most ancient collection of arts, and by its association with Lucifer, the Star of the Morning, it seems to fit the pagan pattern.

From studying the gifts of the Earth our ancestors must have looked up into the night sky and began to ponder about the strange and changing light that came later and later each night. In modern magic the Moon is associated with Mysteries of the Goddess, with the psyche and many aspects of intuition, feeling, emotion and inspiration. The metal of the moon is traditionally silver, so the silver cup (or perhaps its broader, flatter form of the platter) may be seen as the Moon-magic Grail, in which the enlightened mind can scry and discover the secrets of the future. Here, too, is the promise offered by Ceridwen's potion, 'the vision of the future state of the world'. In magical working it is usually found that your cup or chalice is a gift from someone who loves you, and so it should be, for the cup controls and shapes that which is within it, just as the trained will of the magician controls and directs his or her feelings. The magician will learn to trust his intuition, and accept the inspiration to write, to play music or to create from the gift of that goddess. Here, too, he may gain courage to venture into the inner dark realms of his own consciousness, the Otherworld that is eternally present within. Here the light of his personal Mirror of Truth will guide him safely back to the world above.

Above the Earth shines the Sun, and archaeological evidence now suggests that standing stones or circles were set out as markers of both the Sun and the Moon's seasonal rising positions. Today the Sun is generally associated with healing, with growth, with the expansion of knowledge, crafts and practical matters. Whereas the Earth and the Moon are usually seen as goddesses, in the West at least, the Sun is a god and life-giver. The rays of the sun, shining through a natural crystal, may have given mankind his first control over fire, and so allowed him to scare away wild animals which might take the kills from his hunting. The warmth of fire would offer a better chance of surviving the bitter winters, it would provide a way to cook meat, or break open tough nuts, and change herbs into a different form for other sorts of healing. Each year it appeared that the Sun God would fade away but in due time return, renewed. In many symbol systems the Sun God is associated with self-sacrifice, with death and rebirth.

As well as the changing phases of the Moon in the night sky, the people would have noticed the fixed and wandering stars. Here, too, is an ancient source of magic and power, for the stars can lead the traveller onward and then guide him home again. Star magic is that which takes us beyond the confines of Earth, to consider the depths of space and the wisdom concealed therein. Astrology grew up from these ancient observations, and great stores of knowledge have been drawn from stellar patterns, and even today, in the age of computer-horoscopes and instant interpretation, there is still a lot to be learned by studying your own birth chart. Magic is the art of controlling changes, and if you are aware of any forces for change working through your own life, as shown in your horoscope, you can benefit from them by being prepared and so taking the tide on the flood. Even the influence of the so-called 'malefics' can be used to clear out the debris of a long-cluttered life rather than allowing yourself to be swept away on an uncontrolled tide and so losing those things from the past that you treasure. Always try to reach the heights, in your chosen profession, in your relationships, and within the patterns of the world, so that others may find the path easier behind you.

The most subtle and distant form of magic is that of the Cosmos. It is the magic of the original creation, and its power is with us yet, as a force of change and transformation. Any form of true creativity takes of the nature of Cosmic magic. Its roots are far off in the outermost regions of the galaxies, and they began with the first act of creation. To understand the power of Cosmic magic requires you to be able to reach far beyond the limitations of Earth, beyond time and space. By transcending the spiritual gravity of the planet on which you have lived and had your being you may become free to work with the seeds of eternal transformation and by so doing alter the future of the world. Any form of magic has its own responsibility. When you dare to reach beyond the stars the weight of that burden is very heavy indeed, but daring souls who will risk all to bring about such great changes may be able to fulfil the quest, and bring back the gifts of the Grail Eternal.

You can see the Grail in many other, simpler magical forms. You might consider that, as a Grail yourself, you too are changing: from babyhood to childhood, to maturity, to old age and then to the transformation of death and rebirth. You can see it in terms of a great Tree of Life, whose roots are wrapped around the stone at the centre of the earth, the symbol of total stability. Above that reaches up the supporting trunk, the direct path from Earth to Heaven, the stem of the Grail cup. Above that the branches reach outwards, perhaps touching other trees, bearing leaves and flowers and fruit and threshing barren, all in their season. The Silver Branch of the magical apple tree of Avalon was the passport to a safe passage into the Otherworld, and a safe return from that inner journey. The fruit of the Apple is lodged deep in the symbolism of mystery, for not only is it said to be the Fruit of the Tree of Knowledge of Good and Evil in the Garden of Eden, but in the Celtic myth it is the source of Immortality. It was to the Isle of Apples that the mortally wounded Arthur was taken in the dark barge by the three queens, who must have returned to the sacred orchard to bring about his healing and repose.

At the top of the Tree where the branches brush the winter stars, the Air, the very breath of God, the first word of Creation, blows through them, creating and recreating the patterns of existence. Here is the source of the wisdom which unites the Earth and the Sky, and which, if brought back into true balance, will restore the patterns which cause the Waste Land to decay without rebirth, the winter of the bereaved soul which can only dream of spring.

There is no clear answer, no correct solution to these riddles that have been preserved within the mysteries. Each one who seeks the lonely rite of initiation of the heart and who walks the strange and eerie paths within his own consciousness will find his own treasure, in the unicorn- and dragon-haunted groves of the eternal within. Each one who overcomes the fear of entering the forbidden places, who sees through the mirror of illusion, who carries within him the flame of desire for the good of others, and the spirit of adventure will surely achieve the mystery of the Grail, and through his daring reunite the shattered fragments of Ceridwen's pagan Cauldron from which the poison of the land first flowed. If that task is completed then the beneficial drops of inspiration shall surely be released and the Waste Land made green again.

If the Christian seeker achieves his quest he will turn back time to the hour of the Crucifixion, withdraw the fatal Lance-Grail from the side of the Saviour, and from the Cup-Grail pour back the life-giving Blood and Water to restore the Ever-Living Christ. He shall redeem the Redeemer, and the waters shall flow in the desert places and light shall shine in the darkness, and the Prince of Peace will come into His kingdom. Mary, Mother of Sorrows, will rejoice, for the Queen of Heaven shall be reunited with the Son of Man.

If the spirits of the earlier Grail seekers should return and find the gates of the Fisher King's castle standing open they will enter and find the one who said 'I will make you fishers of men...' healed and restored to his land, the water that ran from his side will have been freed and the Waste Land will be no more. An answer will have been spoken to the Grail Question, 'Whom does the Grail serve?' and that service will have begun, and those who were in need will have been transformed by it.

You may find that you, too, are moving along the path of the Grail and so changing. Perhaps you are still on the first step, where your interest in the Grail legends is deepening but you have done little but read and think about the texts, watched the films or TV programmes, searched the internet for information, whilst seeing them as separate from you. You might have taken the next step, which is to learn to meditate, to enter the inner worlds where a deeper understanding of the symbolism within the surviving stories may be found. The third stage would be to begin to identify with some of the characters, to journey through their landscapes, share their adventures and trials, and also develop some of the magical skills of divination and controlled awareness of other planes of existence. Beyond this comes the next initiation, that of the seeker in two worlds, when not only have you been able to bring to life the reality of the quest from its ancient roots but also in the world today. You will have learned to heal and to bring forth some of the other Gifts of the Grail, of Inspiration and of Service. The final stage is that of Grail finder - one who has awoken all of the powers of the Grail within, the arts of magic and the communication with the other worlds. Here those few are willing to offer themselves as Grail Keepers, becoming priests forever in the service of the Light. This is the path of self-sacrifice and perpetual dedication.

# PART THREE: QUESTS

## Exercises, Meditations and Path-workings

# Chapter Nine

## Seven Paths to the Grail

Sink down, sink down, sink deeper and sink deep,
Into eternal and primordial sleep,
Sink down, be still, forget and draw apart...
Into the inner earth's most secret heart...
Drink of the waters of Persephone,
The secret well beside the sacred tree...
Then rise, made strong, with life and hope renewed,
Reborn from darkness and from solitude...

Dion Fortune: *Moon Magic*

We are now well upon the way of the quest. We have examined the texts, the landscapes they describe and the way in which those inner worlds are reflected in the outer. We have met and talked with the people of the Grail, those who guard its mysteries and interpret its secrets for those who know the way and the right questions to ask. And we have gone deeper, in the second part of this book, into the heart of the mystery that is the Grail; we have shown some of the ways in which it is related to our own world and our own time. Now it is time to take all we have learned and turn it into practical reality - whether inner or outer depends very much on what we want it to be. We have provided in this last section a series of graded meditations, designed to take the Grail seeker yet further and deeper. And have added sections on the correspondences that may be found in various other disciplines. Lastly we give two different ways of celebrating, either singly or in groups, the highest mysteries of all. The way of the

Grail seeker is open to all: as the quotation from Dion Fortune, herself no stranger to the quest, puts it: we must indeed 'sink deeper and sink deep' - what we find and how we find it is up to each one of us, individually.

What follows is really a series of seven linked and extended meditations. They should be performed slowly, taking plenty of time over each one, and above all not attempting to do all of them at once. The reasons for this are clear: we are dealing with living archetypes and too great an intake of such material is inadvisable, the result being psychic indigestion.

For the benefit of those who have not meditated before, or who are unfamiliar with the methods involved, the following instructions should be studied before continuing.

1: It is advisable to study the texts carefully before beginning. If you possess a tape-recorder it is a good idea to read them aloud into it so that you can play them back under more relaxed conditions and allow the images to rise naturally rather than having to see them while you are reading or immediately after. Some will be available on a tape produced by the authors, details of which will be found at the end of the book.

2: Whichever method you adopt, the important thing is to be there, within the scenes described, as totally as possible. This does require a good deal of concentration and may result in a mild headache to begin with; however, with practice you should be able to exclude your surroundings quite easily and bring before your inner vision the scenes described.

3: Remember that you are a part of these scenes, and that you should be experiencing them yourself, not watching them happen to an inner TV screen. If you want to test the validity of your experience try looking down at yourself with your eyes still closed. Can you see your hands and feet? What are you wearing? Extend this awareness outward, looking first at the floor beneath your feet, then outward still further at the walls or up at the sky and the scenery around you. Once you have established this inner reality and placed yourself firmly within it, you are ready to work upon the images and scenes described.

4: More than once you will be asked to 'build' these images. This means simply investing them with a strong sense of awareness, 'seeing' the stones of the castle wall, 'feeling' the breeze from the sea on your face or the grass beneath your feet, 'hearing' the music of the spheres. With a little practice you should be able to construct the scenes described in such a way that they possess tactile reality. Once this is achieved you can move easily from one reality to another.

5: Remember that you can always return to your own place and time by simply blanking out the images and reasserting the solidity of your usual surroundings. This is best done slowly, as a rather unpleasant sense of dislocation can otherwise result. The important thing to remember is that no actual harm can come to you in the inner realms and that you can return to them as many times as you choose.

6: Finally, always write down your impressions or realizations immediately after your inner journey. Sometimes these may not seem very relevant at the time, but as much as a year afterwards, or longer, you may find yourselves looking back on these records and discovering things you missed at the time.

A certain degree of repetition will be found throughout these meditations. This is in part to enhance the gradual building up of the images, and also because they are intended to be done one at a time, with at least weekly intervals in between. Thus it should not be necessary to refer back to earlier work, but simply to take with you the realizations gained from each succeeding journey.

## 1: First steps in pursuit of the Grail

*Find an upright, comfortable chair in a place and at a time when you won't be disturbed for at least half an hour. Study the text of the journey and, if possible record it on tape or cassette, reading slowly and allowing gaps for images or sensations to arise within your awareness. Relax and become very still, and try to remain poised throughout the exercise. It may take a few tries before anything much seems to happen, as path-working is a learning exercise, but persist and you will be amply rewarded.*

Here is the first journey. From the familiar things around you in the room, which have vanished as you close your eyes, you are going to make an inner journey to see, perhaps for the first time, the Grail landscapes which, if you continue, you will get to know very well. You will travel slowly, even though you might seem to cover large tracts of land. Before you is a well known road, and as you pass along it you come to a door or gate which you have never entered. On this occasion, this is the way through to another world. *PAUSE*

You open the door and step through. The door closes firmly behind you, and you see that the familiar has given way to a very different landscape. You find yourself standing, alone, on a high and windy ledge with a cliff of grey rock behind you, in which is the door by which you came here. You can feel a cool breeze on your face. You can hear the cries of birds and the rustle of the wind in the grass and bushes which cling to the cliff. You can sense beneath your feet the stability of the rock, and the softness of grass. The scents of wild flowers and the faint whiff of cooking or woodsmoke comes to mind. You reach out your hand, in your vision, and touch the rough surface of the rock behind you. You can feel and sense all these quite clearly if you allow yourself to do so. *PAUSE*

When you have sensed all around you you notice a smooth well-worn path leading along the foot of the cliff and you begin to walk along it. Although you are aware that you are somehow high up, you have no fear. Above you there is a clear and sunny sky, the air feels warm, the path comforting and your journey is relaxing. You have passed beyond the care of the mundane world. Below you the land is brightly lit in the sun. You continue walking along the path, becoming all the time more aware of the ground beneath your feet, the warm softness of the atmosphere, the 'realness' grows every moment. *PAUSE*

Soon you find you are on a curved platform-like surface, edged with solid rocks, which form a secure barrier between you and the steep drop below. You can see across a wide span of countryside to the blue shapes of mountains in one direction, and in another, where the horizon is flatter, the bright sparkle of the summer sea, glinting against the azure sky, in the misty distance. Looking directly down, where the tumble of boulders of the cliff's foot form a rugged rim to the land, you see a twisting path, pale against the darker greens of the plain below. Your vision is clear, the scents of flowers or hay drift up to you on the breeze. You hear birds, and the sound of the wind, the lowing of cattle and the far-off bark of a guardian dog. It feels very peaceful and calm, yet you sense adventure, and though you know that you do not need, on this first journey, to wander the path which lies below you, you can feel the spirit of adventure rising within you. For a while you continue to take in all the sights and sounds, the textures and the scents which come from your inner store of memory. *PAUSE*

In your mind's eye you begin to see more clearly the details of the land before you. There are tended fields of green crops, and ripening corn. There are orchards heavy with fruit, for this is a part of the Isle of Apples, in Avalon. There are deep green expanses of thick forest into which the path may lead, although you cannot see its exit. There are bright twisting threads of silver streams, and perhaps the sound of running water is carried to you on the wind, or the smell of earth-fresh springs reaches your nostrils. Here and there are copses of flowering trees, and great reaches of scrub-land, dotted with stunted willows and glossy alders, with beds of rushes at their feet. The pale blue of the sky is mirrored in a lake so still and calm that it looks like glass. Fields of mown and unmown hay make a chequered pattern of dark and light squares outlined by walls and hedges. *PAUSE*

You see too, buildings of various types, each becoming clearly focused as you look at it, with a more than life-like reality. Small, simple thatched cottages surrounded by multi-coloured gardens; a tiny chapel, roofed with moss and half buried in ivy; a fairy-tale castle, perched on a rocky spur of the distant mountains. Among all these winds a twisting path, here and there shaded by a mist which bars your sight, or it vanishes into the age-old woods and sacred groves which fill the middle distance. You know, as you look, that if you tread that path and face whatever is hidden in the mist, or what might lurk in the forest's dim shadow, you will go forward on your quest - but now it is time to return. *PAUSE*

You turn your back on the landscape below, and start to follow the broad path along the cliff, your guiding hand brushing the cool rock, your feet secure on the smooth path. You take your time to wander those few yards in inner space, to the gate to the world you know as real. Gently you feel it close behind you, cutting off that other vista, but not letting it fade from your awakening inner sight. The pictures and feelings will remain clear as you complete your gentle return to your own place. When you open your eyes, the after image, the subtle perception, the stirred memory will remain with you, if you make the effort, just as you can recall dreams if you wake up slowly.

*Allow yourself to become really still before you open your eyes to the familiar place, the ordinary world. Feel all the lingering inner sensations of shifted time, and 'other where': Permit yourself to respond to any emotion, the sense of freedom, the pang of a beautiful but unattainable world, the sadness of a missed opportunity. All these feelings may be caused by these mind's eye views of the Grail lands. To be moved by the images, to be gladdened by feelings, or even to be frightened, or touched by anything you encounter is an important part of the experience of using this method. It uses the image-making and storing part of your mind, but if you use it with skill it will also awaken feelings, emotions and awareness from which may come understanding and then wisdom.*

*The Grail lands are real - the experiences you may have are real experiences. Your delight or fear, your fascination or wonder are what can make these lands of legend come to life again. It takes time to be able to truly enter this inner space and become one with it, but there is no substitute for practice. If you can't sleep, wander in a peaceful landscape, counting the flowers, following a stream, drinking from a magic fountain, but when you awake remember your dreams. Record the experiences, whether on a simple path, or within the quest itself, for by looking back you will be able to chart your onward progress and fit into the Grail jigsaw the many pieces you discover on your travels in the mind fields of the inner lands. Be gentle with yourself, take these journeys seriously and venture with due care and preparation. Each is a key path, sharing potent symbols, charged images and magical scenes all designed to lead you further, deeper into the hidden world behind your closed eyelids. You may encounter dragons there, but they are your dragons, and they are in the place they are meant to be.*

*The next path is a harsher one, but it should explain how important the Grail Quest is, even in this age. Go forward surely, for the way is strewn with potent symbols, but know you will return safely, wiser but unharmed, for these secret paths are guarded, and all have been trodden before by the Way Showers, whose lantern always brings you home.*

## 11: The path to the Dark Tower

You are standing on a narrow, dark pathway, between high walls, and, as you begin to be aware of the darkness around you, you feel warm and steamy heat. You walk warily forward and begin to smell hot damp winds and you find that the walls have gone and you are now surrounded by great green trees, swathed with vines and clinging creepers. There is only a dim light, and the air is misty and dank. The path threads a twining way through the thick undergrowth. All about you the leaves are alive with the noise of birds, the rustle of larger creatures and perhaps the slither of snakes along the branches over your head. Things dimly seen in the green gloom brush your face and you dare not think whether they are poisonous spiders or merely the trailing roots of vines. Amid the sound of the wind in the leaves is the suspicion of voices, whispering, calling your name, urging you onwards...*PAUSE*

Gradually light dawns. Before you the track stretches onwards, ever unwinding within the dark jungle. Other tracks lead off into the distance, perhaps promising you success in life, power and money, and harsh bird voices seemingly make many similar offers. But you are becoming aware of the bright flowers among the greenery, butterflies dance before you and your way lies onward, to a greater light. Steadily you press onwards...*PAUSE*

Now you have come to the edge of the jungle - the air is drier, and it is much hotter. The steamy heat of the trees gives way to a sharp sweat, and there is no relief in the shimmering air. The low scrub is scorched and brown. Thorn trees rear jagged shapes against a blazing white sky, and offer no shade, only cruel spikes to those who would seek shelter in their armoured embrace. The ground is now dusty dun sand, drifted by some errant wind into sculpted dunes around red crags of scorched rock. You find you are in the bed of a river where no water has run for a long time. Here and there the faint outlines of buildings can be seen, long deserted by forgotten people. There is a well head filled with drifted sand and the bleached white skull of a perished beast. You are very thirsty, but there is no promise of coolness or of water. You have become one of the many lost people who dwell in the Waste Land and for whom little help comes. It is greed that has made this fertile land a desert, it is greed that has cut down the last sheltering tree to feed the fire, and allowed the well to fill with sand.

You search desperately for a way out of this scorching landscape, and looking up to the searing skyline of jagged hills you see the dark mass of clouds. Suddenly the blinding sun is hidden and a chill wind caresses your scorched face. Great drops of rain thud on the parched earth, silver streaks of water soak into the sandy soil, and in moments what was desert turns into a field of green as blades of grass thrust up. These are followed by flowers and through them leads a path you must follow, rising up a ridge. Here you see that the sky is still grey and lowering clouds reach across the landscape. The hills are green, but an evil smell hangs in the air and catches your throat. The rain on your skin burns and before you lie the ruins of factories, of houses and the charred remnants of fine trees. The path drops down to run beside a stagnant and polluted canal, where thick weeds and bright chemical scums make garish sheens over the rubbish; here all is decay. There is no life, no living thing is seen or heard here, no bird flies through the air or builds its nest among the pits and slagheaps of this ruined land. The Earth Mother is scarred and burned, her radiant face is hidden and her beautiful gown of finest rainbow silk is torn and encrusted with filth. We alone stand able to restore the balance of life and death. You turn your face away and hurry on, following the path at your feet, trying to avoid the rubbish that strews the way, heading for the shapes of buildings which seem to offer some comfort, some promise of familiar things.

You come to a city of grey buildings, shaped by an architect without a heart. Around you are grey, soulless people who murmur and gibber in a tongue you cannot understand. They drift like wraiths along the iron and concrete canyons, in mindless pursuit of nothing of value. You see a building which might be a church or cathedral. It, too, is grey, and the light inside it is grey. The walls are decked with grim scenes of both Christian and pagan stories. You see the deaths of the Old Gods and the torture of their followers; the Crucifixion of Jesus, the torments of the saints, but here is no hint of the Resurrection, no sign of redemption, no purification of the spirit. Some of those who haunt this once sacred place do wear brighter colours and begin to look more real. You try to speak to them and some reply, speaking haltingly as if they have forgotten the meaning of words. You feel soul-weary and long for peace.

You leave the grey city and strike out for the hills. It is now evening, and round a turn in the path you follow there comes the sound of a trickling spring. Over a small rise is a deep, clear pool, and a runnel of clean water drops over a ledge of white rock. You bathe your face and drink deeply. You cool yourself, and come forth feeling cleansed and refreshed. Ahead there lies a mountain path, steep and rugged but lit by the sparkling light of the stars, and a bright full moon rises to guide you onward, homeward, towards that source from which you can draw, to heal and restore the Waste Land, to wash the face of the Earth Mother. It will cleanse your spirit and refresh your will. You may return to that source at any time, so long as you are willing to see the dark side of human nature which has laid the lands waste, and despoiled the balance and beauty of our planet. You can restore the Waste Land, and make it blossom. Gently you return home, and open your eyes.

## III: The Chapel in the Forest

Imagine you are in a forest. See the tall trees rising above you on all sides. Listen to the rustle of leaves stirred by a light breeze. The sunlight slants down from far above, making a green twilight under the trees. If you wait for a moment to become accustomed to your new surroundings you will begin to sense a feeling of growth through the whole forest, every trunk and branch and leaf filled with life. There is a feeling, also, of anticipation, as though the forest has been awaiting your arrival as a harbinger of something long expected.

A wide pathway stretches before you and you set off along it.
The sun is already beginning to set, so you know it must be early
evening. It is shadowy now under the trees, and dark memories
of the scenes you experienced in the Waste Land return to you.
But the cooing of pigeons, the hammering of a woodpecker
somewhere off to one side, calms you. The ground is soft with
moss and long-fallen leaves beneath your feet, so that you move
without sound, and around you the wood is filled with echoing
quiet. Be aware of the forest stretching on all sides, try to feel it
breathing. It is not unfriendly, indeed it welcomes you to its green
and leafy ways.

Ahead now you see a clearing and come out almost immediately
into an open, sheltered place, filled with the sound of wood-pigeons
and the soft rustle of leaves. Dusk has now fallen, though it is still
possible to see that in front of you now is a long low building whose
steepled roof and pointed window arches show it to be a chapel of
some kind. As you approach you see that it has one door, heavy
and nail-studded, of the kind one might expect to find in a church
or cathedral. To one side is a window through which pilgrims may
watch what occurs within, and from it spills a soft golden radiance
which lights up the gathering darkness. You stand before the door
and hear sounds of chanting coming from within. Listen for a
moment to these sounds from the forest chapel.

Go forward now and push the door. It opens easily before you
and you step within. The chapel is small and sparsely furnished
with an altar bearing a simple cross and two tall candles from
which the light falls softly upon the scene. To either side of the
altar are two groups of people: on the left are five monks, and on
the right the same number of nuns. It is they whom you heard
chanting. Quietly you stand at the back of the chapel and watch
all that takes place.

In front of the altar a priest kneels in prayer. To his left stands a
child with a beautiful pale face. To the right stands a woman in a
blue gown with a wimple about her head which hides her face. As
you watch, the priest gets to his feet and approaches the altar to
begin saying Mass. The words are in Latin but you are able to
understand them and you listen as the great words resound in the

quite place. The woman takes the child upon her knees and sits with him in a great carved chair to the left of the altar. Her face is bent over the child's head and you clearly hear her say: 'Sire, you are my Father, and my Son, and my Lord, and my Guardian, and the Guardian of everyone.' As you hear these words you see that behind the altar is a tall window. A shaft of golden comes through it, illuminating the scene as brightly as day.

The priest begins to say Mass, and you stand quietly in contemplation for a few moments ... When the priest comes for the offertory you look towards the altar and see that the woman has risen and offers the living Child into the hands of the priest, who sets him upon the altar and begins the consecration. As you watch, see a change take place of a wondrous and mysterious kind. For the priest no longer holds a Child, but a wounded Man, bleeding from hands and feet and side. You watch in awe as the Mass continues ... *PAUSE*

Be aware again of the chapel in which you stand. There is no longer a body upon the altar, but you see again the beautiful, serious child standing at his mother's side. The priest turns to make the benediction upon all present, and in which you are included. You hear the words of blessing with bowed head and seem to hear a greater voice saying: 'Ite missa est'.

When you raise your eyes again the woman and the child are gone. The light that illumines the window has faded. The sun has set. The priest now comes forward, smiling a welcome. If you wish you may ask him one question, for he is a wise and holy hermit and knows much of your search. Listen carefully and remember all that he says . . . *PAUSE*

It is time now to depart. The old priest bids you farewell and you go outside again. Around you the forest stirs gently in the soft night wind. The moon has risen above the trees and you feel at peace.

Slowly let the scene begin to fade and gradually become aware of the room in which you are sitting. Take time to establish contact with your body again, feel the ground beneath your feet and the chair in which you are sitting. You are safely back where you began.

## IV: The Castle of the Grail

See before you a great wooden door made from massive, ancient timbers and studded with iron nails. It opens at a touch and you go through, passing into a short, wide tunnel which in turn issues onto open ground near the top of a hill. Rolling downland sweeps away on all sides under a grey sky, and you feel the wind on your face. Before you a grassy pathway leads downward towards a shallow valley carpeted by forest which stretches away into the distance. As you approach you see that the trees are tall and noble, and look as though they have stood there for all time. You pass beneath their branches and find yourself walking in a green twilight world. The trees become denser the further you go, and a green canopy of leaves is over your head. Your feet make no sound in the thick carpet of leaves and moss which lines the forest floor.

Patches of sunlight fall slanting onto the pathway before you, and you find that you have come to a place where the way divides in three. A broad, well-trodden path leads away to the right, and a narrow, less frequented one to the left. Between these runs a twisting, winding path that leads deeper into the tangled heart of the wood. As you stand for a moment, hesitating over which path to take, you become aware of a single great tree which stands to one side of the twisting path. In its topmost branches you see two naked children, about six or seven years old, one with dark hair and the other with fair hair. They are looking down at you from above and both seem sorrowful. When they see that you have noticed them, they both point silently to the narrow, twisting pathway, indicating that you should follow this way into the forest.

As you go on the air becomes still - there is an almost breathless feeling of expectation. Ahead of you the trees begin to open out and you see that you are coming to a wide grassy glade. As you approach, be aware of the sound of silvery bells, very faint and far off, somewhere in the air above you. They are like the bells worn by hunting hawks, which chime musically as they fly.

As you emerge into the clearing you see that the branches of the great encircling trees are hung with long palls of purple cloth, while tall slender beeches stand forth like pillars in a shadowy hall. In the centre of the clearing you see a great bed draped in hangings of red-gold. On it lies the figure of a man, dressed in mediaeval style. He is wounded in many places and his blood runs down and soaks into the earth. His eyes are closed as though in sleep, but he moves restlessly because of his wounds.

As you look at the wounded man, you become aware of a figure that has entered the clearing: a tall, dignified man dressed in a brown robe and carrying a hermit's staff. He beckons you to follow him and leads the way to a low hut set amid the trees at the edge of the clearing. Here he presents you with a magnificent black cloak embroidered with golden doves. These, he tells you, are the sign of the Grail, which you must seek if you wish to help the wounded man. No harm will come to you so long as you go forward under the protection of the doves of peace. Also he bids you listen for the sound of the bells which you heard as you entered the clearing. They will help you if you encounter any difficulty on the way. Then he leads you back to the edge of the clearing furthest away from where you entered, and directs you to follow the path before you.

Soon you find yourself leaving the woodland and entering a misty part of the valley with high steep cliffs rising far off on either side. Ahead you see a turbulent lake of water which bubbles and boils. Mists rise thickly from it, so that you can see nothing beyond. On the surface of the lake floats a small boat and in it sits a man fishing. He seems unperturbed by the heat and mist coming from the water. Seeing you, he points to a spot a short way along the bank, where you see a bridge which shows up dimly, its far end hidden from your sight. It looks perilously narrow, without rope or rail upon which to cling, but it is clear that you are meant to cross it.

As you hesitate, become aware of a figure approaching along the edge of the lake. It is a woman, tall and graceful and dressed in black. You cannot see her face as she has both hands pressed to it. You can hear that she is weeping bitterly. As she draws near you ask why she laments and hear her reply that it is because her lord, whom you saw in the forest clearing, is sorely wounded, and while he remains so the crops will not grow and all the land is wasted. As if scales have fallen from your eyes you look about you and see that the earth is barren on all sides of the valley. The grass grows sour and rank beneath your feet and the air is bitter with a tang like burning. You remember again the horror of the Waste Land you crossed before and are filled with a great longing to heal it. Look again at the dark-clad lady and see her face for the first time. She is ugly, with withered cheeks and furrowed brows. As you look at her you become aware that you must cross the narrow bridge if you are to help the wounded man, and remembering the words of the hermit, that you are safe so long as you go forward under the protection of the doves, you draw your black and gold cloak around you and prepare to attempt the crossing.

You cross slowly, inching your way across on hands and knees for safety. Feel the roughness of the stone beneath you and hear the water bubbling below . . .

At last you feel the firm earth under your feet again, and looking about see that the mist is much thinner here. You are on an island which rises slightly towards the centre, where stands a tall white castle. As you draw nearer you see that it is revolving.

Time and again you see the gateway turn past you, and as there seems to be no other way of getting in you are momentarily at a loss. Then you hear again the ringing of bells in the air above your head, though you cannot see from where or what it originates, and into your mind comes the thought that you must close your inner eyes and listen. When you hear the bells you can go forward, when they stop so must you. In this way, you may enter the revolving castle safely, but you must trust yourself to your guides.

With eyes firmly closed you await the ringing of the silvery bells and when they ring forth you leap forward to land safely. You open your eyes to find that you are in a great hall, the walls of which seem to be made of glass, though you can see nothing beyond them as the mist seems to have thickened around the castle. A weight of silence lies about you and there is scarcely a breath of wind.

At the centre of the hall is a great round table with chairs arranged about it. Standing to one side of this is the tall, regal figure of the hermit you first met in the woods. Smiling he bids you welcome, indicating that you should take your place at the table. As you approach you see that one of the chairs has your own name inscribed on its back. On the others you see many famous names, as well as those of friends or teachers that you personally know.

A wonderful feast is laid before you by the servants of the castle, and you will find that it consists of whatever food you like best. But it is spiritual food also, and makes you stronger in every way, so that you eat and drink you can feel new life flowing into your body.

Now become aware of a procession which passes through the hall. First comes a young man dressed in white and carrying a tall candelabra filled with candles that burn with a steady flame. Next comes a young woman who carries a tall Spear. It seems as though it would be too heavy for her, but she carries it easily. From its point run shining drops of blood, which fall and are lost in shadows close to the floor. Last of all comes another woman, slightly older than the others, and we see that she is carrying something covered by a white cloth. A soft radiance shines from within it, pulsing slowly like the beating of a heart.

When the procession has passed from view the hermit stands before you again and beckons you to follow him into another room. Here again you find the body of the wounded man, lying on a bed. The room is surrounded by tall tree-like columns, so that you seem to be once again in the forest clearing without ever having left the castle. Once again you hear the bells of the hawk peal out above you.

Standing around the bed are the people who passed you in the hall, and on a low stone altar are the objects they carried. The candles, which burn still with a steady flame; the Spear, laid slantwise across the altar; and the third object which, now uncovered, you can see is an ancient wooden Cup, black with age and cracked around the rim.

The hermit indicates that you may, if you so desire, take up the Cup and offer it to the wounded man to drink from. As you do so you must will with your whole heart and mind that he should be well again. The Grail alone can do nothing if it is not charged with love and compassion. So now you may go forward and take up the ancient Cup. The people of the procession support the wounded man so that he may drink. Will that with each sip he may grow stronger. *PAUSE*

When you have done what you came to do the hermit once again indicates that you should follow him. As you leave the room he tells you that you have helped the wounded man, and that you must depart now in the faith that he will be completely restored. He leads you to the gate of the castle - which no longer revolves - and as you depart you meet again the tall, graceful woman in black. But now she is no longer weeping, and looking into her face you see that she has lost the withered look she had before and has become beautiful and radiant. She thanks you with the words: 'Now the king is almost healed, and the land will bear fruit again'. She leads the way before you, and as you leave the island, crossing as you came by the slender bridge - which no longer seems unsafe - you see that it is dawn and that on all sides are the first signs of spring: green buds bursting open on the trees and bushes, fresh green grass soft beneath your feet.

As you pause for a moment you become aware of the extent of what you have achieved, for you are able to see the whole of the island laid out around you, and above it, vanishing into the blue reaches of the sky, are the pillars of a vast temple - empty as yet, but soon to be filled with a new and glorious light ... Then as you become aware again of the island, you hear again the chiming of bells far above.

The dark queen leads you through the woods until you find yourself back again in the forest clearing - where the hangings are now all of gold and where the king - as you now know him to be - lies on a great bed, but no longer seeming close to death. Then, as you watch, you see a hawk, the ringing of whose bells had guided you on your journey, descend in a flash of brown and white feathers onto the body of the king. But instead of tearing at him it merges with his body, and you understand that it is his soul. Now he is healed completely and leaps up from his bed to give you thanks for what you have done. The queen thanks you also and bids you remember all you have learned. You understand that in helping the king you have also helped those who work constantly for the healing of the wounds of this planet.

Now the hermit comes forward and bids you keep the embroidered cloak in token of your journey. It will be invisible to all but you in the outside world, but so long as you possess it you may return to the country of the Grail whenever you wish.

The hermit sets you upon the right road home, and you follow it back through the green woodland where birds now sing joyfully amid the trees.

On the way you pass again the great tree where the two children wave happily as you pass, and so you reach the green hillside and make your way up until you stand again before the great wooden door. It opens before you and you pass through, returning by way of the short passage to the place where you began your journey. Take time to open your eyes and re-establish contact with your surroundings, and remember all that you experienced in the realm of the Grail.

## V: The Vision of the Virgin

Build around you the walls and roof of the great hall within the Grail Castle. Above the Fisher King's chair hangs a silken banner embroidered with golden doves and a Grail surmounted by a sunburst. Around the walls are long purple hangings, and the scent of incense drifts on the air. You walk across the chequered floor and pass through a door to the left of the high chair, finding yourself in a small chapel, bare except for an altar on which stand two tall candlesticks and what seems at first to be a small casket.

As you stand before it you feel great power issuing from this object, and on looking more closely you see that it is intricately carved with scenes from the life of Christ. There are the miracles: the feeding of the five thousand, the casting out of demons, the raising of the dead - and finally there are the scenes of the Crucifixion in all their grim horror, followed by the great miracle of the Resurrection. All are carved in great detail and with such skill that they seem beyond the work of human craftsmen. You also notice that the casket is really a reliquary with two hinged wooden doors at the front, and as you watch they begin slowly to open . . .

A great light spills out into the chapel from within the casket and you fall back a step, going to your knees in wonder. Within the open box is a scene, and, while it must really be far away and tiny, it seems to you that it is full-sized and real as though it were happening in the room.

At the centre, standing upon a great silver globe, is the figure of a woman dressed in a glorious robe of stars and with a silver crown on her brows. In her arms she holds a radiant child and on either side of her hover angels with golden and scarlet wings who hold flaming swords in their hands.

Suddenly the earth beneath the crowned figure begins to crack open and there emerges, coil upon shining coil, a vast green and golden serpent which winds itself around and around the silver globe upon which she stands, finally resting its head at her feet. Yet it makes no move to harm either woman or child, and the guardian angels draw back from them ...

Now from right and left come more angels, issuing forth two by two. The first pair carries a great Spear, from the point of which blood flows, and four long cruel-looking Nails, stained red with blood. The second pair carry a wide, shallow dish and a seven-branched candelstick; the third pair hold between them a radiant Vessel covered in a cloth of silk. As these things pass before her the woman raises the child on high and great streams of light pour from him as he raises his hands in blessing ... Then the angels set out the Hallows upon the altar in the chapel: the Spear across the front and one of the Nails at each corner. The seven-branched candelstick is placed in the centre with the veiled object before it.

Then with a blaze of light and a noise like the slamming of a great door the angels, the woman and the child and the green and gold serpent are gone, and you are alone in the chapel with the awesome Hallows before you on the altar and a sound like distant music fading in your ears. The light issuing from the veiled object now seems less bright, but each of the things seem to shimmer with an otherworldly gleam.

You may spend some time in contemplation of these things until a bell sounds, at which point you must rise and depart the way you came, returning to the hall with its purple hangings and the great chair of the Fisher King, where he now sits smiling gravely at you and welcoming you to the Castle of the Grail. You recognize him as the wounded king whom you helped to heal in a previous visit to this place, and you may, if you so desire, ask him any question you wish concerning the events which transpired within the chapel. Listen carefully to his answers and remember them.

Finally it is time for you to depart, and as you take your leave slowly, gradually the scene fades and you return to your normal surroundings.

## VI: The Ship of Solomon

You are standing on the shore below the Castle of the Grail, which rises shining behind you, tower on tower towards the sky. Before you stretches the limitless ocean, blue and green beneath the summer sun, with a haze-like mist hanging above it. Out of this dazzle comes a ship, high at stern and prow, with a single sail upon which is the image of the Grail surmounted by a sunburst. In the prow of the ship stands a tall figure dressed in red, his fair hair streaming in the wind which fills the sail of the ship but does not reach the shore where you stand. Astern, in the middle of the ship, are two other figures, one in green and the other in blue. As the ship draws near the shore they greet you and invite you aboard.

As soon as you step onto the deck the ship begins to move swiftly away from the shore. You look back once to where the Grail Castle rises on its high cliff, gleaming like a star, then you look about you at the ship.

Towards the stern is a brilliant canopy embroidered with lilies and doves in silver and gold, and beneath it is a great bed with a scarlet coverlet. Upon this lies the body of a young woman, pale and still and beautiful, her lips set in a faint smile. There is a kind of radiance about her, and a sweet scent which lingers upon the air. She seems somehow familiar . . .

At her feet lies a great sword, half drawn from its sheath, upon which you can see faint golden letters which you cannot quite read, and a richly jewelled crown resting on a pillow. Turning now towards the prow of the ship you see that the figure in red has come to join his fellows, and that he holds before him a Cup, covered in a cloth of white. Its shape is outlined in bright light and as he holds it aloft the light falls upon his face. At first he seems like a fair and noble youth, but as you look his face changes to that of an older man with a silvery beard and bright, piercing eyes. For a moment he reminds you of the Fisher King, whom you last saw in the Castle of the Grail, then the likeness is gone and you seem to see another face, older still and more sternly beautiful, looking from behind the Grail . . .

Then as he lowers the Cup it is once more the face of a youth who looks out at you, smiling and joyful. The two other young men now come forward to stand at his side, and together the three turn to look forward past the bow of the ship towards a new shore that is fast approaching.

As you also look you see that a great city lies there, its tall towers and high walls glittering in the sun as though they were made of silver. The ship soon draws to the shore and you see a great crowd coming to meet you. Many faces amid the brightly clad throng you recognize: friends, relatives, those whom you would most like to see at such a time and in such a place . . .

Behind you a sudden clear bell-like note rings out and as you turn to look you see that the beautiful young woman has risen from her bed and comes forward with the sword in its sheath to fasten it around the waist of the fair-haired youth. Then taking up the crown upon its pillow she leads the way off the ship. The three knights and yourself follow her until a great procession begins to wind through the gates of the city and up towards a great basilica in the centre of the place.

Reaching this you pass within, into a scene filled with light and singing and the smoke of incense. As your eyes become accustomed to the change from outer to inner light you see before you a great circular concourse, crowded with people in rich robes. Many wear crowns or circlets of gold and silver and jewels, which flash and sparkle like stars. Behind and between them stand other figures, clad in plain robes of brown or green or white, some serious and stern, others with faces filled with laughter. And again, between them you see other figures, some of whom seem not quite human - laughing faces above, which are set small horns, or who wear wreaths of flowers about their brows.

Here, it seems, are gathered all the noble figures of the inner realms, from most ancient times to the present. All look towards a great throne which rises above them, and where sits a noble figure dressed in robes of blue and silver upon which all the constellations of Heaven seem to wheel and circle even as he sits. On his head is a triple crown, its three tiers of gold, silver and pearl, and in his hands is a great staff of ancient dark wood, carved and chased with silver.

His face is one that is known to you from your visits to the Grail Castle. As the Fisher King he has greeted you before, but now he seems different. From his eyes look out many other faces, so that, like the young knight who bears the Grail and whom he so much resembles, he seems to be many people within one form.

He greets all present in ringing tones, then the whole concourse of people falls silent as the young woman bears the crown to him. Taking it from her he places it upon the head of the scarlet-clad youth, then the other two knights come forward and lesser crowns are placed upon their heads also. The three, together with their companion, take their places in four chairs placed to the left and right of the great carved throne.

Now a great ringing of bells and blast upon blast of trumpets echo through the basilica, and, though no-one is there that you can see, the Grail is lifted and carried through that place, still veiled but blazing now even brighter beneath its covering.

Two great doors open before it at the Western end of the basilica and for a moment it flashes and sparkles before them. Then it is taken in and suddenly the place seems darker, as though the sun had been eclipsed by a cloud.

But now you find that the figure in the brown robe who led you, long ago, through the forest to the Castle of the Grail, stands before you. He bids you return on the morrow for the celebration which is to come. Then he smilingly takes leave of you, and the scene begins to fade, the last thing to go being the high and glorious music which seems to ring out continually in that place . . .

## VII: The Mass of the Grail

Once again you enter the great circular basilica in the high city of Sarras. The vast concourse is thronged, as before, with figures both human and otherworldly. You are shown to your place, which has been reserved for you, by the familiar hermit figure in his brown robe. You take your seat and look about you.

Above you the dome soars, and you see upon it pictures of the mighty angelic and archangelic hosts, and in the centre a great blaze of light which is almost too great to look at. At the western end of the basilica stands a high altar, with rank upon rank of mighty figures in robes of glory, and candles in their hundreds burning steady and still.

Now a hush falls over the throng and this is followed by a burst of sound and light too subtle to identify yet seeming to contain the threads of many kinds of music and song. Into the basilica comes a procession.

At the head comes Dindraine, clad in a robe of blue and bearing the veiled Cup before her. Next is Galahad, clad in red and with the Sword held before him, and behind Perceval, in green, with the great Spear from which drops of blood still endlessly well. They are followed by Bors with the deep curved Dish in which the Bread of Life is carried.

Slowly they process to the high altar and turn to face the gathering. Dindraine raises the Grail, and as light pours from it you see that it is no longer veiled. It will seem to you whatever aspect of the Grail to which you are most drawn: as Chalice or Cauldron or jewel, as Stone or Flower or Tree - it contains within its shape all the desires, fears, hopes and aspirations that have brought you upon this quest, and which centre in your being at this moment.

You and all the folk in the vast basilica bow your heads before the shining thing between the hands of Dindraine, and when you look again you see the real selves of the four Grail winners revealed in its light - nothing may now be hidden, either from yourself or from those about you: your own spirit stands naked before the most sacred things ...

In your own time, and in all humility, you may approach the altar and receive Communion in whatever form is most appropriate to you. Or you may remain where you are, and meditate for a while on all that has occurred and on all that it will mean to you in the weeks and months, indeed years, to come . . .   *PAUSE*

In due course become aware again of the scene before you. The three knights and their sister have set aside the objects they bore and have joined the throng before the altar. Now the Hallows are taken up by four other figures whom you are enabled to see by virtue of the Grail and of your realizations. They are bright figures, whose light is that of the glory of unveiled creation: to some they may seem archangelic beings, to others the gods and goddesses of their own tradition. See them together lift the four holy things and be aware of the joyful music and deep love that issues from all there, most especially from the high altar. Slowly let the light grow brighter until it seems as though you are walking into the heart of the sun and its light fills your whole being. The inner message of the Grail is addressed to you alone, as it is to everyone present at this high feast. Draw deeply upon its unending strength and reality, then without haste let the scene begin to fade, keeping the spark of divine fire which is planted within you burning brightly. Be always aware of that light from this moment. Become aware slowly of your surroundings, but keep the memory of what you have experienced - keep it always with you from this time . . .

# Chapter 10

## The Way of the Cauldron

Among the many versions of the Grail texts a large number are passed to us in their Christian form, but the Grail itself is far older, and so may be encountered in another form by those with pagan leanings. You will notice that the seeker has to go to the wild places, the forest, the jungle, the Waste Land, to an island in a lake or to a castle set in wide countryside or impenetrable woods. The Grail is always hidden within nature, for the Earth Mother, ultimately, is the Grail Keeper, just as we, being born of the substance of the Earth and of the Stars, are entitled to find it and use its magical powers. The Grail is seldom found inside a city or town, and the path to it has to lead the seeker through the wild and untamed places, which as well as being in the landscape he encounters are also always within him. Although we are still seeking, in a technological time, and in a man-made landscape, it is to the wild and empty places, of both the known world and of those vast unexplored regions within our own being, that our quest is bound to lead us. We cannot find this ancient symbol in our own domain, for if it were there the Waste Land of the world and of the inner spiritual realm would have no foundation. That Waste Land is very real, and in it is the ultimate objective of the quest. Unless the Waste Land, in its wild state, is restored, the free spirit of mankind is enslaved, earthbound and trapped within his own slime. His spirit is chained and cannot reach its true destination among the stars.

The Grail is the gift of liberty, of freedom of spirit, of which we, who live in cities, have been long deprived. The food from the

Grail restores the will, it clears the inner eye of the opaque lens of modern vision, which limits us, like a blinkered horse, to see only what is before us, in its material form. Our sight should show us the beauty of creation, and ways in which we can learn to create beauty also. The food of the Grail is wholesome - modern Western diets are being seen as unhealthy and the cause of many common sicknesses in the population. The Grail offers the blessing of spiritual peace, that calmness in which answers to the world's ills may be sought, and found, and applied, before it ultimately is too late. Like the other gifts, this has to be sought, it has to be earned by the sacrifice of time and effort. No one is denied the quest - it costs nothing, in a monetary sense, but a dedicated heart which has the vision that things can be restored, remade in a better mould.

The Stone Grail offers the gift of stability, a firm base on which to rebuild, an empty landscape to plant with trees of life, a building block to use as an altar to our own Gods, or as the hearth-stone of our future dwelling. We have the Emerald Stone of the Wisdom of the Oldest Gods, and in it, if we are daring, we can read what is to come, as did the sages of old.

We may take up the Spear of our own Destiny and cast it into the eye of the Sun, and receive back such power as we wish, to heal and to revive dying souls. Within the great Dish we may discover the waters of rebirth and offer ourselves as sacrifice to the living waters, be cleansed and rise up, shining, into a new day. All that is needed is the will to seek and the courage to follow the lonely path which takes us away from the main road which the dim-eyed masses follow. Each must become a hermit in a peopled land, and seek the wilderness which lies eternally within.

There are many ways to find that twisting path. The exercises in this book will all take you into those lost landscapes, the settings of dreams and visions, that the bards and troubadours have saved for us. The myth-makers are still with us, and they tell the same tales, setting them in the future, the distance of outer space, not within the vast inner realms of the unsullied mind. We are all potentially heroes or heroines, both on a local scale - as rescuers of the drowning child, the victim of a road accident, the trapped mother in the burning house - and as pioneers - in those inner toils, where dragons roam in untamed forests. From those depths of the human psyche may be brought forth great treasures which will bring healing, peace, and restored will to the many. It is the eternal promise of Communion, not for all, but for the many, and each one who treads that hidden path may, unawares, undergo the initiation of a true priest and so bring forth blessing upon others all through their lives.

We cannot seek the Grail without recognizing that to find it will cause great changes in our lives. We may encounter not a physical object, which tradition would tell us that the Grail is, but some spiritual gift which has to be shared in order to be made use of. This directs us to one of the other aspects of the Grail material, and the attribute that all who have sought in the past, and will seek in the future, have to face: the idea of service. The Question asked by the original finder was supposed to be 'Whom does the Grail serve?'. This is well worth a few sessions of meditation for it can mean a variety of things, just like the aphorism made famous, but by no means invented, by Aleister Crowley, 'Do what thou wilt shall be the whole of the Law'. Who is the 'thou' in the statement? What is Will, and how does that differ from want? The Grail question starts as many hares. It also ensures that the finder will not be the sole beneficiary of its power!

There are many Grails which we might encounter on our travels, and it will depend on our personal religious or spiritual points of view as to what we might recognize as a Grail if we saw it. Not only is the Grail capable of Five Changes, but so is the initiate/grail seeker, for that path of search leads us inevitably to our own source of initiation. This, certainly, is part of the mystery of Ceridwen's Cauldron. Here is a path towards it.

## VIII: The Cauldron of Rebirth

You are, as you will always be on this quest, on a path which leads through a forest. Here there is no obvious way, only faint deer tracks and rabbit paths that wind aimlessly among the tree boles of a very wild and ancient wood. Although the trees are familiar oak and ash and hazel underbrush, they have never been forested, and fallen trees make angular tunnels among the standing trunks. Honeysuckle and ivy bind the boles together with strong webs of leafy sweet-smelling fronds, and you have to clamber over fallen and rotting trees and scramble among thickets of bramble and

dense green undergrowth. You are not certain where you are
going, yet there is a strong impulse to go onward. This is not a
waste land, it is lush, but lush with the wildness that no hand has
tried to tame. It is rich with fruits and berries, nuts and herbs,
each in their season, yet the harvest is unused, except by the myriad
of wild creatures, the birds and insects whose unseen presence
you sense around you.

There is a dappled pattern of light when the high noon sun penetrates
the green canopy, and bright shafts illumine the verdant ground.
Ahead, well hidden in the stems of trees, you begin to make out a
golden-orangy colour, and the sound of trickling water comes to
your ears. A faint path shows to one side of your line of progress
and you force your way through the leafy maze to stand upon it. It
is not straight nor well trodden, but at least it offers an easier way
through the wilderness. You follow gladly, seeing more clearly the
place where a sparkle of sunlight has painted the face of a reddish
cliff of rock with umber and amber patterns. The path bends
against the spur of rock and winds along its foot, overhung with
clinging greenery, but starred with pale flowers along its borders.
Suddenly you become aware of the scent of woodsmoke, and the
trickle of water sounds more clearly in the quite shade. Turning a
corner of the high red cliff you see a rocky glade, lit by shafts of
sun, lying before you.

Sitting against the wall of the cliff is a blind man with a small harp
on his lap, and as you step into the bright light he turns his head
towards you, hearing your approach, and without a word begins to
play. It is not a tune as you would recognize it, but strange chords
and runs of notes which go right through you. You go towards
him, and sit on a smooth log with your back to the rock wall. You
close your eyes and become absorbed in the strange cadences
and harmonics of his playing. Although you do not directly hear
him speak, his voice, tinged with a Welsh accent, seems to tell you
a story. You learn that his name is Morda, and that he was wronged
by a great lady, but as a reward for his service he was repaid with
his uncanny musical ability by the Goddess of the Cauldron of
Inspiration, which he was once made to boil. When the potion had
spilled only Morda remained to put out the fire. As he groped
about to discover what his blind eyes could not tell him about the

fate of the Cauldron or the potion within, he found a few drops left in a broken part of the iron pot, and with great daring he tasted them. Immediately he was inspired with memory and with music. He could remember the scents of the many herbs which had gone into the brew of Inspiration, and with his wisdom and intuition he has remade the potion, leaving out those plants which poisoned the horses when the dregs had run into the stream from which they drank.

Morda tells you now that the potion is there, simmering on the fire which you see, wreathed in woodsmoke, across the clearing. Beside the small cauldron there is a dark wooden bowl. He says that if you have the daring you may drink. What you taste may seem to be the finest wine, or the richest soup, and no more. Or you may drink deep and feel filled with an inner nourishment which will strengthen your spirit and clear your intuitive sight. Or if you are most daring, you might dip in only one finger tip and from the few drops of the potion thereon receive the true knowledge of the Cauldron of Inspiration. For a few moments you pause, trying to decide. When you are ready, you go towards the cauldron, and dip the wooden dish into the seething pot, but the draught that you have in the bowl is no more than tepid when you set it to your lips. As you begin to tilt it to drink you hear again the strange sounds of that fairy harp echoing from the stiff red rock, humming through your whole frame and resonating within your head. Everything about you seems to shudder and change, and for a moment you feel totally dizzy and strange. The feeling quickly passes and you open your eyes. The scene before you has altered. You are low down and the tall grasses of the clearing loom above you. You try to reach out a hand, and a furry brown paw comes into your line of vision. You touch your face, and feel whiskers and long ears. A sound behind you makes you jump, and you literally leap forward in a great bound from powerful long hindlegs. You do not see what it is that menaces you from behind but you rush onward, under the spiky brambles, through the thickets of hazel and trailing ivy. Your heart is pounding like a drum when you finally stop, panting under the protection of a fallen tree. You are desperately thirsty, and by pricking and turning your large ears you are able to hear the trickle of a stream, and carefully, in case that which frightened you before is still about, you make your way to the bank of a clear, fast-running stream. The banks are steep, and below you the water runs swiftly over pale stones. You try to creep down the steep bank, using the long claws in your forefeet, but they cannot grip in the sandy soil, and helplessly you plunge headlong into the swirling cold waters, and sink like a stone.

You struggle and gasp for breath, again that wave of dizziness sweeps over you and then passes. Now you can breathe and you try to swim, reaching out with your arms to push you out of the watery world, but instead of going up you turn sharply in a circle and see a silvery tail fleetingly out of the corner of your eye. Again you try to kick with your legs, but movement works only sideways and you move swiftly towards the bank of the stream, almost bumping your nose, until you brake hard with your arms. Now, you are undoubtedly a fish, and for the first time can explore the underworld of the watery depths. You breath the cold water into your cold body and soon learn to swim and turn and fly in this new environment. Again your thirst for new knowledge is quenched.

After a while there is another shadow in the water behind you, and the vibrations of something large and fast coming after you. Plunging among roots and under weeds does not stem your pursuer, and you dart forward into deeper and then shallower water. Realising that you will be engulfed in the maw of the creature that is chasing you, you leap upwards, trying to resume your life above the water. Up and up you rise, again suddenly bewildered by the change of state.

Now your form has changed again. Your sight clears and you see that you are far above that green carpet that was the forest, with the winding silver thread of the stream which you have miraculously just left. Your arms are feathered with dark plumage, between your eyes is a golden yellow beak, and somehow you have already mastered the art of rowing through the air, spreading your finger-feathers to brake or turn, using your tail to help you remain stable in that invisible medium. Your vision has expanded and you can see across the great tract of the untamed forest. You can fly swiftly, and turn and sense the upwelling currents of supporting air in which you can swoop and circle, high above the familiar world. But yet again, the dark shadow, hiding the sun, hovers over you, and your fear causes you to dive among the trees, seeking protection from the unseen talons, the sharp hawk's beak, the whistle of wind over controlled feathers. Into the trees you drop, and somehow your instinct has guided you to the place of the rocky glen. The strange music floats up towards you, as the trees close in and your wings are lifted to stall for the landing. Unprepared, you crash to the ground, your head swimming and your sight dimmed. You curl into a ball and lie stunned for a few moments, regaining your breath and composure.

It is very quiet. There is the gentle touch of the wind on your cheek, the reflected light of the sun on leaves patterns the ground before your eyes as you lie upon the soft, leafy loam. You are quite alone. The only sounds are those of nature, the trickle of water, the sough of wind in trees, the chirrup of birds. You feel well, but are aware that something about you has changed.

Once again you are in your familiar form, and you rise to your feet and look about. You are in a glade among trees, now friendly and cultivated, and the sun shines brightly among them. The cliff of rock and the harper are gone, along with the wild tangle of jungle creepers. This is the tamed land, and the Old Gods have departed. Nothing seems to be left of the vision of the blind harper and his powerful potion, his hauntingly strange music, but somewhere within you is a subtle resonance which might be the faintest echo of his tune. As you are about to seek the safe road home, something in the long grass catches your eye. It is a wooden bowl, dark with age, perhaps a little charred by fire. You reach out your hand to touch it, but as your fingers close, there is again that inner swirling sensation and you find yourself drawn slowly, safely back into your familiar surroundings, your home. Gently you return fully to your ordinary awareness, enriched by this strange journey. Awaken fully, slowly, refilled with vitality and energy. You have drunk a little from the Cauldron of Inspiration, and by its magical charm you may well find yourself inspired with poetic muse, with music or song, with the concepts of a picture or a sculpture, a tapestry or a magical image.

*Allow yourself plenty of time to return from this journey with its many levels. Do have a snack to eat and a hot drink, for to travel this road to the place of the Oldest Gods is a long journey, even though you have not stirred from your chair. To sample any of the gifts of the Grail is a genuine experience, although you may not have fully appreciated it yet. Be gentle with yourself. These magical doors are being set ajar by techniques normally only taught within the confines of a lodge or school but now laid before you in the honest hope that students and seekers have the sense to travel with care and treat that which they encounter with respect and consideration. Don't rush. Each of these potent keys will work all the better for a little preparation, a firm decision to follow the strange path to its conclusion, in time and space.*

*These inner journeys' may have little obvious power upon the printed page, yet they have a great store of magical strength within them, and are all gifts from the Grail to you, the seeker. Each will resonate with aspects of your inner being and open doors for you to enter and explore. If you venture carefully, seeking all that may be encountered by turning each key one at a time, then the rewards will be enormous. If you are greedy for thrills, or rash in your entry to these doors, you may be in for a nasty surprise. I warn you, 'Here be dragons'!*

## IX: The Grail Communion

From the quiet room where you are sitting you begin another inner journey. Your path today takes you away from the forests to a wild moorland country, with heather and bracken, coloured with autumn tints, and against the clouded sky piles of boulders, like playthings of giants, form a rugged horizon. Your path winds its way across this lonely and deserted land, alongside rushing streams and around the time-worn outcrops of grey granite, speckled with shining mica and quartz crystals. Ahead of you is a great mound of these rocks, like the child of a mountain, spawned upon the barren and empty land. It seems huge in the distance, and as you draw nearer the vast size of the smoothed granite blocks tower over you, and you feel dwarfed by their sheer size and solidity.

The trodden way follows the steep face of the outcrop, curving beyond your sight round a polished slate-coloured boulder, the size of a house. Warily you walk round the curve and find that the path continues downwards into a cleft in the granite. The crack is triangular, meeting at a point above your head and only a yard across at the bottom. It is dark inside and you cannot tell what beast might have its lair within, yet your impulse is to enter this rock cavern, to continue along the path no matter how dangerous it might appear. The narrow cleft drops downwards but there is just enough room for you to squeeze inside. A faint glimmer of light comes from high above you, dimly illumining a paler path strewn with lumps of rock. Here and there white veins of quartz form ridges in the walls, and these form handrails on either side, guiding you surely ever deeper into the dark rocky cavern.

Down and down the passage winds, always narrow, always seeming to crush you under the sheer weight of dark stone, but you squeeze onward, into the heart of the earth, alone and in darkness. As you sink deeper into this rock tunnel you notice the colour is changing from dull grey to russet, and the pale streaks are becoming reddish. The walls are now more curved, making an almost complete circle, and they begin to narrow, but the light ahead is still bright and you are impelled onwards by a will that is beyond your own. There is a warmth and dampness in the air, and water oozes under your feet. The tunnel is lined with smooth stone now, in shades of pink and red and rust, and they close all round you in a stony embrace. It is an effort to push yourself through, but there is light ahead and a constant feeling of safety and comfort. The thud of your own pulse seems to echo in the narrow cleft, and the light dims in harmony. Suddenly, after a real squeeze, you are free, falling into a round chamber of glistening reddish stone, the glare of light for a moment blinds your sight, and the heartbeats throb within your ears.

You are in a cave, deep within the heart of the rock. You feel warm and strangely at peace. The walls are damp and glisten with the trickle of water, yet the floor is dry, made of soft terracotta-coloured sand. To one side the wall bulges outwards, and forms a ledge on which it is comfortable to rest after the toils of the journey through the rock passage. Opposite, you can dimly see a shape in the soft illumination whose source you cannot see. It may just be rough boulders, or a carving of a great sleeping figure lying on one side. As you stare, trying to make out the details, there is suddenly a movement, and a part of the cavern's wall bulges and surges away. You watch, fascinated, as the form of the sleeping figure stretches, slowly rolls over and finally becomes the figure of a great mature woman, towering above you, naked and rock-red - the Earth Mother herself. Before her you slide to your knees on the soft sand, and bow your head.

After a moment you look up again and see only her face, so calm and beautiful that you can hardly look. Her skin is smooth and tanned with the sun, but her eyes attract you most for they are dark and very bright. She is smiling, and without touching you she lifts you to your feet. You stand, bemused by this great apparition, not knowing what to do or say. Your mind is blank and you are bewildered. Slowly she reaches into her own body and offers you bread: 'Take, eat, this is grown from the body of the earth', a voice says to you. You reach out and take the bread and find it fresh and good and wholesome on your tongue. Again she reaches within and cups her hand, and offers you to drink. It is blood-red wine, and again the voice can be heard, although her lips are still: 'Drink, this is the wine of the spirit, distilled from the blood of the stars'. You drink deeply and feel the wine coursing through your veins like fire. For a third time she reaches within then brings forth her two hands cupped and closed, and as she opens them a great light shines forth, dazzling your sight and blinding your vision. For a last time that haunting voice speaks: 'Take the seeds of divine fire, nurture them in your heart, and kindle the spirit of the true light in the hearts of those you love'. Gradually your sight clears as the light is absorbed within you. You are alone in a dark, dim cavern kneeling on the damp sand.

For a few moments you pause, gathering your wits, and then start to look for the way you came in. To one side there is a narrow crack, so different from the round passage by which you recall entering, yet no other opening can you see. You edge round the wall of the cave, and slide into the cleft. It has no depth, but looking up there is a source of light, and there seem to be handholds cut into the glistening red rock. Carefully you reach up, place your foot upon a small ledge, and delicately start to edge your way upwards into the shaft. At each step hand and footholds are there for your use, and it is not long before you find the rock is again dull grey and seamed with white. Suddenly the gap widens and you can see that the chimney in the rock emerges onto the top of the moorland tor, in a dip of deep grass and soft heather. Above you the sun is shining, and skylarks hover in the blue, singing high anthems to their own gods. All round the purple-green moor reaches to the curved horizon, and you sense the loneliness and the loss of she who is part of the world below, and yet you can still taste the sweetness of the wine, the nutty flavour of that ancient bread, and feel the power of the light within you, knowing it will guide you on the road home.

After a rest you know that you must return to the world from which you came, and set off on a well-trodden path, winding gently down the side of the mound of grass grown rocks. Just as you are about to set foot on the plane below, something catches your eye. Embedded in the rock face is a nest of shining crystals, and when you reach out to touch them with your hand one of them, clear as a raindrop and sharp as a needle, sticks to your probing finger and you take it away, cupped in your palm. You know that it is both a symbol and a gift, and you will treasure it as you make the long journey home.

Gradually the moorland scene fades. The light dims and you rest in the dark silence. Gently you are able to drift back to the place you call home. Slowly you return to your relaxed form, merging and becoming one. Carefully you open your eyes to the familiar place, breathe deeply, and look around you. You have returned from the source of life, refreshed and renewed, and blessed by the power of the earthly Grail.

## X: The Chapel in the Green

*As you continue your Grail Quest you will have to make many journeys into the landscapes of the mind. Some have been clearly mapped by the singers of ancient songs and tellers of traditional lays; books describe them and pictures portray an artist's view of them. Other paths are harder to tread, more lonely, wilder and less well defined. This is one such path, and though many of the Grail stories speak of it none came back to draw its shape or sing of its wonders. You will have to find it for yourself, and what you will see there will depend on how clear your inner vision is, and how true your dedication to the Old Ways. It is never far away, but like so many of the Grail's hiding places, it lies deep within the Forest at the End of the World.*

Around you are many trees. Beneath your feet is a narrow path. About you are the signs and sounds of birds and wild creatures. The day is warm, the green canopy of the wood dappled with reddish light for the sun is setting somewhere ahead of you on this westward-leading path. Slowly you wander onwards, enjoying the peace and calm of this other timescape. Night is now falling and the colours fade from the greenwood, the flowers pale, but the rustles of wild creatures and the sleepy cooing of birds still surrounds you. There seems to be a continuing movement among the undergrowth on either side of the path you tread. There is no feeling of danger or of threat, but a steady and gentle urge to continue onwards through the duskfilled forest.

As the light fades the scents of the honeysuckle, the crushed grasses beneath your feet, the sharp smells of leaves and the dampness of dew tingle in your nostrils. Always the path runs smooth and level, and the overshadowing branches never touch your face. As your hearing becomes more acute you seem to hear a distant piping, perhaps the song of a late-singing bird. Quiet footfalls pad alongside you, advancing with you through the dreaming dark. Is that the antlered head of a stag caught against the evening sky? Is that russet form creeping at your feet a fox, the black-and-white splash in the undergrowth a passing badger? All around you the woods seems to be alive with birds and beasts, all going westward, to some unseen destiny.

Other larger creatures seem to be on the move, and you are almost pushed off the path as a shaggy pony and her foal shove their way onward. The next to urge you to make way is a large sow followed by an innumerable litter of pink piglets, all grunting with apparent pleasure as they travel the dark road. You quicken your pace, and find the path blocked before you by a piebald rump - as you draw near you make out the shape of a large cow, with wide spreading horns, who lumbers before you bellowing softly to the small black calf which runs at her side. The warm smell of the animals reaches you through the green scents of the woods as more and more moving shapes join the walk through the trees this mid-summer's eve. Ahead there seems to be more light, and you realize that the full moon is shining through the trunks of the tree, which now thin out before you. Eventually you emerge at the edge of a clearing and though the sky is not yet fully dark the stars sparkle high above. The ground is full of the scurrying of animals of all sorts, both domesticated and wild. The trees are ringing with sleepy bird calls, the hoot of owls and the scurrying of squirrels and martens. The white scut of a rabbit flashes past your foot, and the thump of its warning sound seems to echo across the clearing.

Gradually the comings and goings slow down and cease. There is no fear among the wild creatures, no fighting as both foe and food wait in the gathering crowd. Suddenly a horse which has come up behind you nudges you with its nose, and you step forward. A path is still clear through the glade, and you walk onwards between the rows of great and small creatures all drawn together for a special purpose. There seem to be clusters of fireflies dancing before you, lighting up the columns of tall grey beech trunks whose paler green leaves are still visible in the silvery moonlight. All around it is suddenly still, hushed in the star-light. Again the distant piping is heard - too faint to be close by, too musical to be a bird.

Looking ahead you see a paleness in the glade and sense movement and a feeling of power. The circle of the moon's face now edges between two trees and in her silver light you see an approaching figure, dressed and hooded in grass green. She seems to glow with her own light so that the colour of her cloak is clear. Before her she carries a great Dish of polished silver, as big and shining as the moon's orb above. Others have come with her, some as tall as she (for she stands well above your head), others of human stature, others of human shape but small as children. All her companions are clad in Nature's colours: greens and browns, and here and there the bright hues of summer flowers, the gold of sunlight, the silver of moon jewels. She seats herself upon a rock or log, and all

about her, people and animals, birds and beasts, bow down for a
moment, silent in prayer.

In that moment the piping is heard, coming always closer. A simple
tune, played in an archaic mode of falling notes. Out of the trees
and into the circle of sun-bright moonlight another figure comes.
He is tall, and his bare chest and shoulders gleam with muscles as
he lifts his pipes to play another verse of his ancient melody. The
light catches the small curving horns among his curly hair, and his
hairy thighs taper to neat dark hooves which tap gently on the soft
ground as the great God Pan dances and fills the Chapel in the
Green Wood with his wild music. All are hushed, for the birds and
creatures are his subjects, yet even he bows low before the seated
Lady with the Silver Dish. From the shadows all manner of other
beings come. Tree tall giants enter the moonlit arena, make their
bows and fade softly into the starlight and the woods. Unicorns
dance across the turf on delicate hooves, striking sparks of stars
with their shining horns. Dragons fly silently as moths, their scaly
skins shining in reds and golds, and the fire of their passing lights
the upturned faces in the glade. Dwarves come trudging by, each
bowing before the Sacred Vessel and its green-clad keeper. Elves
with starlit faces enter singing, clothed in the shades of English
flowers. Fairy folk, the Sidhe, come, and the Lords of the
Otherworld, bearing their silver branches of the tree of Avalon,
strung with the bells of falcons and tiercels. Heroes come in shining
armour, and the Oldest Gods, unnamed and long-forgotten in this
busy world, all make their silent vows anew.

On and on stream the many of the few, each making obeisance to
the most Holy Grail, pausing a moment to see reflected in its shining
bowl that inmost gift of love of Light. The knights come, one by
one, drawn from their resting places in Avalon, in Logres and from
Ys. The ladies, clad in shimmering silks, pass by and bow to she
whose burden all would gladly share. The Fisher King, restored,
salutes the keeper of that older Grail, and the shining Finders who
have gone before are earthbound for this sacred hour. Arthur is
there, and Guinevere; Morgan, pagan, bows before this Grail.
Bedivere, Kay, and all the Company of Camelot come by and
make their salutations to this Holy Dish.

In the dim light come all the beings of our earthly world, those of the underearth, the watery beasts, the free-flying birds and bats of the air all come and bow and then vanish in the forest's green. The shades of all the ones who went before, the spirits from forgotten realms, sunken cities, tide-worn towns. All who have been, and lived and loved the Light send messengers to do obeisance in the sacred grove, and see reflected what they may become when circling ages set them free. You too may make that gesture, if you choose, as representative of all your clan. Bow down before the Bowl of Light and join the company of this earth's paradise.

Last to come, when Pan's sweet pipes are still, is one who many seek yet few encounter on their road. He has gone down and dwelled within the dark, and risen singing when the sun was bright. All know his name, as god or hero, bard or prophet, teacher, healer, poet, priest or king. His knee is bowed, yet she who keeps this Grail has raised him up, and all around the light of their shared Sacrament blazes abroad, and with it all are blessed.

For one immortal hour all beings of this earth are still, and each from this source of blessing takes its share. The sacred gift, unseen but felt within, is carried forth to share with all their kind. In silence is this sanctifying moment held, yet in the air the sense of joy abounds. From land and sea, from myth and tale, from ages long forgotten to this world, from distant realms, the ancient peoples come to share this moment in the eye of time, to remake their vows to live in peace and strive to share their oldest light, that ageless wisdom, with the modern folk. It is not wine or bread from Heaven's sphere, nor light of lantern or of star, it is an inner blessing which all receive, in payment for the works they wrought, each creature serving for its kind the pattern of the first Creator's will.

Gradually the image fades. Silence falls. The scents of the greenwood and the crowding creatures drift away, but deep within you is a new sensation. You have been blessed, a light has grown within your heart, and even if you choose to tread another road, as is your right, some fragment of this holy rite will stay with you and offer benediction in your life. If you should choose to walk this path again, and call together all those scattered souls, they will rejoice to share this sacred benediction of the wild. No roof can shade the stars that shine on all true Walkers in the Ancient Ways, no house is room enough to hold the power, the Earth herself is merely a regent for that greater One that all who truly seek the Grail will find.

Return, return, slowly from the sacred land, where nothing fades and life will never die. Bring back the seeds of hope, the light of love, and share them in your Waste Land world that all may live and find the answers to the endless quest. You have the power to restore the lame, to heal the sick and make green the barren. Think hard about these many images, allow them gently to seep within the caverns of your mind and then return to the ordinary world. You will be changed, for this is a magical way. Soon you will discover how your gift has been received and learn to use it. Open your eyes, breathe deeply, and permit these images to sink into your inmost heart. They will not leave your mind, but they will vanish from your sight until you are ready to reawaken them at a later time. May peace be with you always.

# Chapter

# 11

# The Tarot of the Grail

We have already given some of the many correspondences between the Grail imagery and that of other systems such as the Tarot, the Qabalah and geomancy. What follows is merely *a suggested* table indicating some of the ways this might be worked with. Those already familiar with such systems will find their own identifications arising naturally as they penetrate deeper into the intricate maze of the Grail texts and characters.

| Path | Tarot Card | Character | Magical image |
|------|-----------|-----------|---------------|
| XI | 0 The Fool | Perceval | A Mirror |
| XII | 1 The Magician | Merlin | Serpent Egg |
| XIII | 2 High Priestess | Morgana/Ceridwen | Cauldron |
| XIV | 3 Empress | Igraine | Tower |
| XV | 4 Emperor | Uther | Rod |
| XVI | 5 Heirophant | Blaise/Prester John | Triple Crown |
| XVII | 6 Lovers | Lancelot and Guinevere | Winged Heart |
| XVIII | 7 Chariot | Taliesin | Maze |
| XIX | 8 Justice | Arthur | Siege Perilous |
| XX | 9 Hermit | Joseph of Arimathea | Flowering Staff |
| XXI | 10 Wheel | Round Table | Wheel of Fortune |
| XXII | 11 Strength | Bors | Sword in Stone |
| XXIII | 12 Hanged Man | Fisher King | Fish |
| XXIV | 13 Death | Green Knight | Waste Land |
| XXV | 14 Temperance | Galahad | Sword |
| XXVI | 15 Devil | Klingsor | Skull |
| XXVII | 16 Tower | Kundry | Thorn Tree |

| | | | |
|---|---|---|---|
| XXVIII | 17 Star | Dindraine | Blood Drops |
| XXIX | 18 Moon | Nimue | Spindle |
| XXX | 19 Sun | Gawain | Pentangle |
| XXXI | 20 Judgement | Avalon of the Stars | Tree |
| XXXII | 21 Universe | The Grail | Star |

When applied to the glyph of the Tree of Life these appear as the Five changes, on the next page.

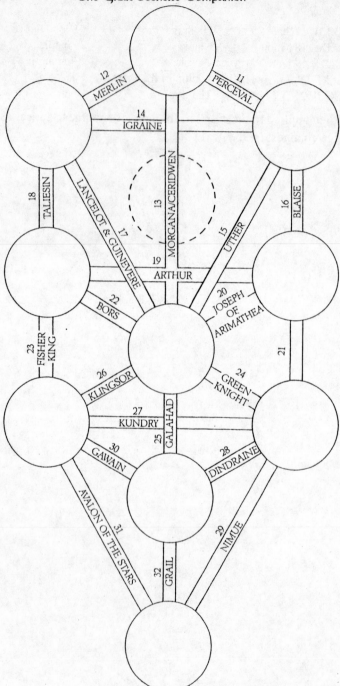

Fig. 4: The Tarot of the Grail

# Chapter

## 12

### The Five Changes

We have already written at length in the text about the Five Changes which the Grail is described as undergoing. But what can we say further about the nature of these changes, which are not described in the text? Their significance is obviously very great, and they clearly foreshadow the five inner mysteries of the Grail; but the Master Blihis, who wrote the *Perlesvaus,* disguised them in such a way that only through meditation or inner communication is it now possible to recover them.

Our own researches indicate that the changes were from Spear to Dish to Stone to Child to Cup. The Spear is that which pierced the side of Christ on the Tree; the Dish is that upon which the head of the Baptist or of Bran the Blessed is carried; the Stone is the *Lapis Exilis* or Philosopher's Stone which to the alchemists was the symbol of divine alteration; and the Child is the Divine Other, the living sacrifice which changes itself into the forms of Bread and Wine. The Cup is the vessel of offering from which all who truly seek may drink and partake of the higher mystery.

The actual sequence of the changes is thus: Spear - Cup - Child - Stone - Dish. Spear and Cup are the signs by which are showed forth the coming of the Divine Child, who will be sacrificed upon the Cubic Altar of the four elements, and whose body will afterwards be laid within the Dish. His blood flows down the Spear into the Cup and all begins again in endless cycle: the regeneration of the human soul into a divine being which it must one day become.

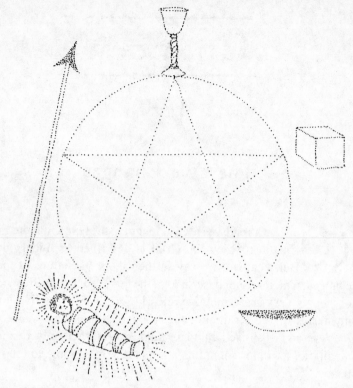

Fig. 5: The Pentagram of the Grail

Five is a significant number, and in the symbolism of the Grail it is reflected in the Rosary (five decades of beads for each mystery), in the five wounds of Christ, and in the five great knights and what *they* represent - Perceval (Youth), Gawain (Manhood), Bors (Maturity), Lancelot (Worldliness), and Galahad (Spirituality). Placed upon the pentagram, the five-pointed star, we see still further applications. Taking the Christian view, we have: at the top the Grail (Pure Spirit), to the left the Spear (Adam and Eve, the founders of the race), and facing/opposing them the Stone (Lucifer, the Lord of Light, from whose crown fell the Emerald Stone). Below, descending from the Spirit into the world, is the Child (Christ, the Divine Sacrifice) and the Dish, in which he is laid in token of sacrifice. Thus the inner harmonics of the seen and the unseen worlds resonate through the patterns of the Grail imagery, forming a nucleus from which the mystery of the quest is formed.

A further application of this symbology can be made which deepens the mystery still further. There are five 'houses' or castles in the Arthurian world: the Castle of Marvels, the Castle of Adventure, the Castle of Camelot, the Castle of Joyous Garde, and the Castle of Corbenic. In each of these rests one of the Hallows, the symbolic references of the Grail. One scenario in which some of this may be worked out is as follows:

| Castles | Hallows |
|---|---|
| 1. Marvels | Dish |
| 2. Adventure | Spear |
| 3. Camelot | Stone |
| 4. Joyous Garde | Cup |
| 5. Corbenic | Child |

In the Castle of Marvels the Holy Dish dispenses wider and deepening awareness which preludes the first mystery - that of the Spear, which must be sought in the Lands Adventurous. At Camelot lies the Stone, from which the Sword of the Spirit must be drawn. At Joyous Garde, the home of Lancelot, the feminine Cup of Love, human and divine, is kept hidden in a secret place beneath the altar in the chapel. At Corbenic the fruit of the marriage of Spear and Cup, the Child, Galahad himself as Christ, manifest in the womb of the Virgin Vessel, awaits the coming of the Acts of the Grail. Through these five houses, placed upon the pentagram, these acts are brought to birth. The glyph can be read from any direction, through any dimension. All ways lead to the Grail, and to the caves of initiation, where the deeper mysteries are revealed. Let us look closer . . .

The entrance is small and easily missed. Inside, the passage slopes steeply upwards inside the cliff, lit dimly by the light which enters by round windows cut in the living rock. By their light you see depicted scenes from the stories of the Grail Family. All are there, the Rich Fisher, the Wounded King, the Dark King of Castle Mortal (one of the qlipothic houses of the Grail). At the top of the first part of the seemingly endless stairway (it continues beyond our sight) the tunnel opens out suddenly into the heart of the rock. You find yourself in the First Cave - that of Mind. Here all dreams and visions are collected and stored in the very air itself, so that you breathe the stuff of your most secret hopes, fears and aspirations. Here you relive the experience of life itself, all its mysteries and manifestations, good and evil, joyous and sorrowful - for these too are the mysteries of the Grail.

From here you pass to the Second Cave - that of the Heart. Here are kept all the countless manifestations of love, those which we feel for each other every day: the love of man for woman, woman for man; of mother and father for their child and of child for its parents; the love of man for God and God for man. Here is every kind and quality of love - for these too are the mysteries of the Grail.

From here you pass to the Third Cave - that of the Spirit. Here is the consummation of all that has gone before. Here the mysteries of birth and death, love and hate, truth and falsehood, are transcended, collected into the great Cup which is given to each seeker to drink from. Here you await the entry of the procession and see the Hallows born before you: the pure youth who carries the Spear, the pure maidens who carry the Cup and the Dish. And these are placed on the Stone, the four-square altar of the elements upon which the sacrifice is made. For here it is that the greatest mystery of all is enacted, the Five Changes are laid out before your opened eyes and you perceive the divine order and rightness of them. The secret teachings of the Grail are made known to you, the hidden deep words which move forever in your heart and mind and soul.

    Here the seeker remains, lost to the outside world of men and time, until he hears the silver bell in the roof of the cave ring once to announce that another soul has joined the Company of the Grail. It is his own. Whereat the new Knight of the Hallows awakens and prepares to go out into the world, which for him, or her, will be changed, and where he, or she, will journey far, taking with them the message of the Grail.

* * *

It must be emphasised that the foregoing is merely a suggested pattern. Others will find completely different sets of correspondences, other attributions on the Tree and other meanings

Arthur

Gawain

Lancelot

Bors

Galahad

Perceval

Balin

Balan

Pellinore

Arms of
Joseph of Arimathea:
and the Grail Family.

The Arms of the Knights

to the five-fold Grail. It may well be that the Five Changes are not physical, but refer rather to different levels of understanding in a more abstract sense. As always with the Grail it is a matter for personal choice.

# Chapter
# 13

## The heroes and their houses

We suggested in Chapter 3 that one way of working practically with the materials of the Grail is to adopt a character or characters and take them as guide or companion on your inner journey. To this end we gave brief indications of the colours and arms of the knights. To extend this further we give here some of their armorial bearings as shields, and also their descent and relationship to each other. This last is important as there are several great 'houses' within the Arthurian world, each of which has a particular standing and function within the quest material. There is, of course, also the Grail 'Family' which shows the descent of kings and guardians from Joseph of Arimathea onwards. Reference to these family trees will be found to make the often complex interrelatedness of the characters more accessible, while meditation on their shields can reveal fresh insight into the individual knights' characteristic qualities.

There are many anomalies within the various houses, which though shown separately here often overlap and duplicate. Thus both the family of Pellinore and that of Lancelot are closely allied to the Grail Family, while Morgana, through marriage to Urien, also becomes part of the same house, back to Brons the Rich Fisher himself. It is probably not possible to set out the full relationship of many of the characters - though for any who wish to try it is a fascinating task. As it is, the interrelatedness of many of the great families shown here makes for interesting study.

The arms or armorial bearings of the Grail Knights and their kin are of considerable importance to those engaged upon the quest.

Heraldry is itself a deeply esoteric system of symbolism in which certain images became the badges of the knights who wore them, and where those images often reflected the inner character of the knight in an outward form. Thus Gawain, whose shield bears the five-pointed star, can be seen to both reflect and be reflected by the nature of the symbol. In the Middle English poem *Gawain and the Green Knight,* this simple device is interpreted thus:

> *That star is the same that Solomon once set*
> *As an emblem of truth by its own just claim and title;*
> *For that fair figure is framed upon five points,*
> *And every line overlaps and locks with another,*
> *And everywhere it is endless - thus Englishmen call it,*
> *In every dialect, 'the endless knot'.*
> *And therefore it suited this knight and his splendid arms,*
> *Five ways ever faithful on five different sides.*
>
> (trans. John Gardner)

As much and more than this can be found within every one of the shields given here. We have restricted ourselves to nine only of the many possible examples. A mediaeval manuscript, edited by Edouard Sandoz *(Speculum,* vol. XIX, no. 4, Oct. 1944) lists over 150 Knights of the Round Table and gives examples of their shields. These could all form the basis of meditation, especially if drawn and painted beforehand and studied carefully for their inner meanings.

## House of Pellinore

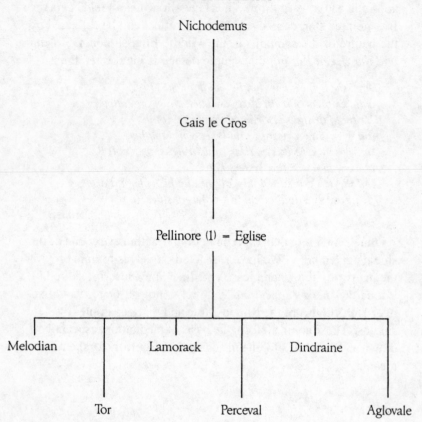

Nichodemus

Gais le Gros

Pellinore (1) = Eglise

Melodian     Lamorack     Dindraine

Tor     Perceval     Aglovale

# House of Corbyn

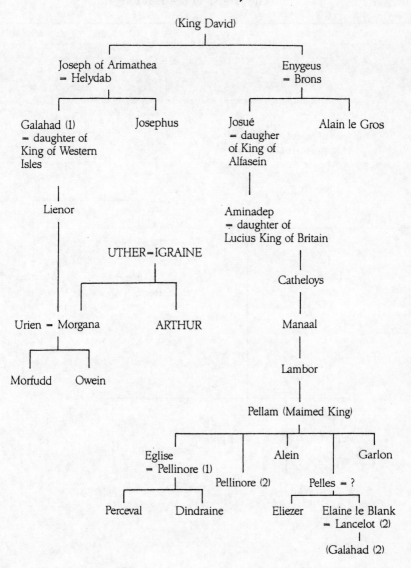

## The House of the Pendragon

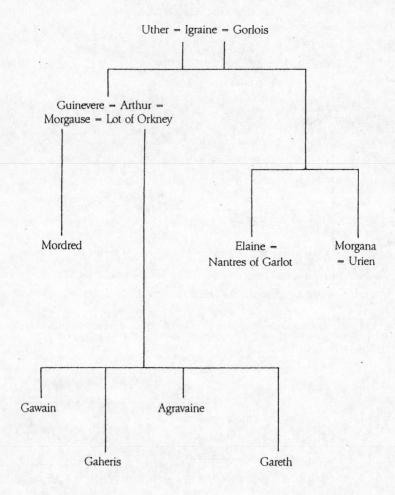

## House of Lancelot

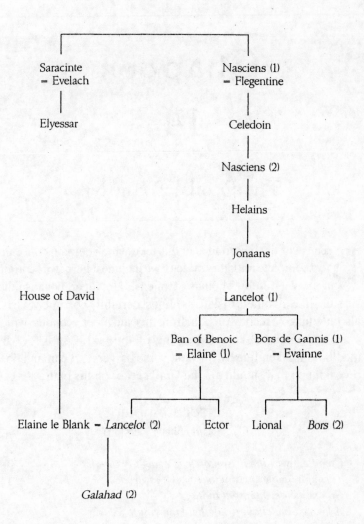

# Chapter 14

## The Spoils of Annwn

Because of the importance of this text, which contains the clues to a complete initiatory system, we include it here in its entirety in the version by Thomas Stephens. However, because that version, like all others to date, is almost certainly corrupt, we have also attempted a reconstruction, from this and other versions, which aims at making a sensible reading of the text. As a tool for meditation, taken line by line and verse by verse, it can and does reveal much that should aid the Grail seeker on his path.

### Preiddeu Annwn
(Thomas Stephens' version)

*Complete was the prison of Gweir in Caer Siddi,*
*Through the permission of Pwyll and Pryderi,*
*No one before him sent to it;*
*A heavy blue chain firmly held the youth,*
*And for the spoils of Annwn gloomily he sings,*
*And till doom shall he continue his lay.*
*Thrice the fullness of Pridwen we went into it,*
*Except seven, none returned from Caer Siddi.*

*Am I not a candidate for fame, to be heard in the song*
*In Caer Pedryvan four times revolving!*
*It will be my first words from the Cauldron it expresses;*
*By the breath of nine maidens it is gently warmed.*

*Is it not the Cauldron of the Head of Annwn in its fashion?*
*With a ridge around its edge of pearls!*
*It will not boil the food of a coward nor sworn.*
*A sword bright flashing to him will be brought,*
*And left in the hand of Llemynaug,*
*And before the portals of hell, the horns of light shall be burning.*
*And when we went with Arthur in his splendid labours,*
*Except seven, none returned from Caer Vedwid.*
*Am I not a candidate for fame, to be heard in the song,*
*In the four-cornered enclosure, in the island of the strong door.*
*Where the twilight and the jest of night moved together.*
*Bright wine was the beverage of the host,*
*Three times the fullness of Pridwen, we went on sea,*
*Except seven, none returned from Caer Rigor.*

*I will not have merit with the multitude in relating the hero's deeds,*
*Beyond Caer Wydr they beheld not the prowess of Arthur.*
*Three times twenty hundred men stood on the wall.*
*It was difficult to converse with their sentinel.*
*Three times the fullness of Pridwen, we went with Arthur,*
*Except seven, none returned from Caer Golur.*

*I will not have merit from the multitude with trailing shields,*
*They know not on what day, or who caused it,*
*Nor what the hour in the splendid day Cei was born,*
*Nor who prevented him from going to the meanders of Drevwy.*
*They know not the brindled ox, with his thick head-band,*
*The seven-score knobs in his collar,*
*And when we went with Arthur, of mournful memory,*
*Except seven, none returned from Caer Ochren.*

## Preiddeu Annwn Restored

*Perfect was the prison of Gweir in Caer Siddi*
*According to the testament of Pwyll and Pryderi;*
*No one before him was sent to it.*
*A heavy blue chain held the youth,*
*And before the spoiling of Annwn gloomily he sang:*
*Till released he continues his song.*
*Three times the fullness of Pridwen we went in –*
*Except seven, none returned from Caer Siddi.*

*In Caer Pedryvan, four times revolving,*
*We came upon the Cauldron of Annwn*

*With a ridge around its edge of pearls.*
*By the breath of nine muses was it warmed,*
*Nor will it boil the food of a coward.*
*Before Hell's portals lights were burning,*
*And when we went with Arthur, of splendid endeavour,*
*Except seven, none returned from Caer Veddwid.*
*In the four-cornered fortress, in the island of the strong door,*
*Where the twilight and the dark become one,*
*Bright wine was the drink of the host.*
*A bright flashing sword was placed In the hand of Llemynaug.*
*Three times the fullness of Pridwen we went upon the sea –*
*Except seven, none returned from Caer Rigor.*

*Beyond Caer Wydr they knew not the prowess of Arthur.*
*Six thousand men stood upon the walls.*
*It was hard to converse with their leader.*
*Three times the fullness of Pridwen we went with Arthur –*
*Except seven, none returned from Caer Golur.*

*The cowardly ones, with their trailing shields,*
*Know not the time of the bright one's birth,*
*Nor who prevented him from going*
*To the meadows of Drevwy.*
*They know not the meaning of the brindled ox*
*With the seven-score jewels on his collar.*
*And when we went with Arthur of mournful memory*
*Except seven, none returned from Caer Ochren.*

# Chapter
# 15

## The Table of the Grail

The image of the Round Table, where Arthur and his knights met to recount their adventures, is an enduring one which has deeper significance for all engaged upon the Quest of the Grail. Built by Merlin it was intended to echo the shape and symbolism of two earlier Tables: that at which Christ and his disciples sat to celebrate the Last Supper, which was in turn copied by Joseph of Arimathea in order to celebrate the mysteries of the Grail.

We have already seen (in Chapter 2) how the images of the zodiac may be related to the Table, but apart from this a valuable set of insights can be gained by constructing, either from wood or other suitable materials, a version of the Table at which either a group of people working with the matter of the Grail may meet - or, alternatively, at which the solitary seeker may sit and invite the archetypal figures from the stories to be present also. If the prospect of making a table seems too ambitious then it is equally possible to use an existing table or even to draw and paint one. Either way the object is to mark out the divisions to include as many places as you wish to occupy or have occupied. Once done, this can become a valuable tool for meditation purposes or more practical work with the archetypes.

Finally, if none of these options seem acceptable it is equally valid to build up an astral version of the Table, placing it in an appropriate setting, where you will take your seat along with the people of the Grail. The following is the kind of scenario you might wish to use.

Imagine that you are entering a huge hall by way of a solid oak-timbered door with a heavy metal ring for a handle. The light within is dim, but it is sufficient for you to see that the room is dominated by a great Circular Table with a number of high-backed chairs ranged about it. The hall is empty apart from yourself, and you take the opportunity to walk around the Table, looking at the seats and reading the names inscribed there. You see many that you recognize from your studies on the Quest for the Grail, and there are other names which are less familiar to you. At length you find your own name written there, and take your place in the chair with a sense of awe and humility. Glancing about you you see that the hall is set with twelve great long windows, like that you may have seen in a cathedral or certain larger churches. You examine their design with great attention and see there many scenes which you recognize, and again many that you do not. Above you the hall rises to a high domed roof, on which are painted many symbols from your work in the Grail Quest - the central one being a great multifoliate rose painted in gold and red. As you look up at this you may begin to see light radiating out from it and hear a strange unearthly music filling the air ... it may be, however, that it is not yet time to learn about these things, and instead you look towards the door by which you entered in time to see it open. In single file figures enter, knights and ladies and young men in squires' livery. One by one *they* take their places at the Table, until every place save one is filled. This chair remains empty until such time as you invite one to occupy it, which will not be until you have visited the hall many times and learned all there is to learn there of the quest upon which you are yourself now engaged. You may visit there as often as you wish and may invite others to sit in astral form at the Table with you, for it is one of its properties that there are always enough seats no matter how many are invited to sit there. Here you may see the visions of the high mystery of the Grail, or be invited to follow one of the knights or ladies upon an adventure. Many paths open out beyond the wooden door, though you have only to will it to take you back to your own world and your own place. Visit this place of the Grail with an open heart, for here all promises are kept and the highest ideals hold good. Use it wisely and always try to uphold the honour of the Knighthood of the Grail.

# Chapter 16

## Learning from the Grail

When you begin to work with the Grail symbolism you are certain to be instructed directly by one of the Grail Guardians, if you are willing to give them a chance to speak. As you will have discovered from the other exercises in this book, it is necessary to refocus your attention, away from the mundane affairs of the world, and listen to the voices of those inner instructions. There is no simple way of explaining how to go about this peculiar activity, except to say that it is a vital way of going forward on the spiritual quest. You will need space and time and silence so that you can tune your awareness to those subtle levels where direct inspiration, in a comprehensible form, can be received by you. This does take patience and the will to be instructed by the unseen in a sort of telepathic manner. It is a strange-seeming concept but it is the easiest way to go further on the quest. If you stop and listen it is likely that you will be taught all manner of interesting things about the process of questing and the stages you have to go through. Below is an example of what such a communication may be. You can read it as a piece of straight text, or use it ritually, with a companion; but meditation on both the questions and the answers is a valuable exercise and can provide startling insights.

### A Grail Catechism

Q: What is the quest?
A: To seek the Grail.
Q: What is the Grail?

A: It has many forms.

Q: How can I seek the unknown?

A: By following the path which will reveal itself to you.

Q: Where does such a path begin?

A: Here, at your very doorstep.

Q: How shall I know I am on it?

A: That which you seek will guide you.

Q: If I accomplish my quest, what shall I do?

A: You will return and create a garden.

Q: But what if the Grail has no physical form?

A: You will awaken the hearts of those around you.

Q: Will you come with me?

A: You will travel alone, but the Keeper of the
Grail will be near you.

Q: Is the quest easy?

A: Yes, but the path is long and the task heavy.

Q: Shall I accomplish this task?

A: All who go forth upon the quest achieve their true aim, but not
all have the wisdom to know this.

Q: Can you give me something to aid me?

A: I shall give you my blessing.

Q: When shall I set forth?

A: When the sun or the moon or the stars direct you.

Q: What should I take with me?

A: Your courage, your love and your dedication.

Q: Will I find companions on the journey?

A: The quest is always a lonely path, but you will not tread it
alone.

Q: How shall I bring back what I find?

A: In your heart or your soul you will bear it.

Q: What shall I tell those I meet?

A: That you seek the key to Paradise, that all people may return
there.

Q: And if they mock me?

A: Their laughter shall bear you up.

Q: But if people scorn and shun me?

A: Their sadness shall be a spur to you.

Q: In what place is the Grail hidden?

A: In the maze at the heart of the castle.

Q: Where does that castle stand?

A: In the Forest of Forgetting.

Q: How shall I recognise the castle?

A: By the voice of the Ever Running River.

Q: How shall I cross such a river?

A: On a boat of your dreams.

Q: What is the key to the maze?

A: The song that is in your heart.

Q: How shall I enter the castle?

A: The Gate Keeper shall direct you.

Q: With what shall I pay him?

A: With your memories of the outer world.

Q: How then shall I return?

A: By the path of moonbeams and forgotten dreams.

Q: Can you not speak to me more plainly?

A: I cannot explain to you things which are not of this world.

Q: It is my will to take up this quest. Will you give me your blessing?

A: Gladly:

Blessed are they who set out upon an Endless Quest.

Blessed are they who walk in the Darkness, seeking Light.

Blessed are they, who abandoning all worldly things, seek out the Gates of Paradise, That they may lead all beings to their rightful home.

Be Thy Ways Ever Blessed.

# Chapter
# 17

## Celebrating the Mass of the Grail

If you ake your studies of the Grail material seriously, and choose to follow the magical path beyond practising these various exercises in your mind alone, you may come to want to take up the task of priest of the Grail. Like any other undertaking in magic, it is not a light task, nor one to be taken up without a lot of prior thought and meditation. To some extent it is not really something you can expect to become, but rather something that the Inner worlds decide to lay upon you. There has to be rather more than a human desire for the priesthood, for it truly is 'of the Order of Melchisidek', not confined to any faith or Church, but a servant of the Creator. There is a kind of half-way house in this tradition though, a lay priest who serves his or her own altar, and who ministers only to the needs of family and friends. The following suggestions are aimed at them.

This is a 'real' ritual and you will need both a place in which to do it and a selection of items which you will need to collect to use for it. Like any other Mass you will need the elements of the Communion, some form of bread and salt and wine, things to serve these in and the symbols which seem most appropriate to you. If you are already on the path of ceremonial magic you may well have a robe and girdle, slippers and altar cloths etc., for these are the uniform of the initiate, just as the boiler suit or the laboratory overall is the working garb of employees in other jobs. If you are not yet familiar with the ideas of ritual apparel, look at any church prayerbook. There you will see the items of ecclesiastical attire described, and though most magical priests do not go in for albs and copes, many of them have both a basic plain working robe of a dark colour, and a stole or sash, and sometimes an over-robe without sleeves, or a cloak. These and the girdle often represent the stage they have reached in their training, or tie in with the colour of the festival which they are celebrating. Magical robes have an important psychological part to play, and doing real rituals without them imposes a considerable strain on the individual. A special garment does help the exchange of level of consciousness from that of everyday life to the magical true self. The best robes are made by the wearer, no matter how limited his or her skill at sewing.

You will also need representations of the Changes of the Grail. You can consider these as representatives of the Four Elements plus Spirit, if you wish, attributing them, perhaps, as follows: Stone/ Earth, Cup/Water, Cauldron/Fire and Spear/Air. There are plenty of alternative versions which will all work well, if you prefer them. Also, you may need to make or acquire the various Cups, Cauldrons and Dishes, as well as the Spear and the Stone, which latter ought to be larger than a pebble, and from somewhere you consider sacred or special - but this is not an excuse to go and prize lumps off an ancient monument or standing circle. There are plenty of magical beaches and holy sites where excavations are going on, and if you ask for a link with them no doubt the god or goddess of your choice will help you.

Being a priest, in modem terms, implies one who stands between the Deity and the worshippers. In the older sense it is a different task, and the priest is one who acts as a messenger, trying to become the voice of the Deity, speaking directly to the congregation. Now, with set services and formal ritual, this immediacy is lost and the voice of any god is unheard. To develop this form of direct mediation is again a magical art, taught only within the secrecy of the closed lodge or the training school. It also really only applies if you have a congregation, for the Grail priest/ess is more often alone, walking in these paths for his or her own reasons, rather than one who seeks to share and minister to the spiritual needs of others.

It is hard to explain how you will know when you are ready to take this definitive step in your Grail searches. Some may never wish to make the final dedication; others who have lived and walked the ways of the mysteries in earlier lives, may take up the burden quite easily and find the work natural. Undoubtedly there will be a need for those who will teach and lead and guide along the spiritual ways, not from a set text or Book of the Law, but from direct enlightenment, personally received. If you pursue these studies you will certainly be guided in such important matters by intuition. There is no kudos in being a priest who is guided directly from the inner - the rewards are far more likely to be internal than ones which will bring fame and fortune. All priests of the New Age are going to be servants of the Grail, just as the last true priesthood.

For the same reason, it is not possible to simply print the text of the Mass of the Grail, you will have to build upon the framework of tradition the prayers, the God names, the symbols, which you are impelled to use, so that it will become *your* Mass. There is a long tradition of the patterns of magical rituals, be they communions alone, or those rites which are used for individual healing, or when working for the greatest purposes known to humanity, under the direction of the angels. It is this pattern which follows, with suggestions only, which will help you build up the Mass so that you may celebrate it for yourself, or for a congregation of the chosen few, who are drawn to the Grail yet have not sought it for themselves. Just as you have had to find and obtain the various symbols for yourself and make your robes and regalia, so you may feel the need to acquire friends to share the ceremony, as you go along.

## Mass of the Grail

*This may be said alone or for a congregation, indoors or out of doors, by a priest or a priestess, here for convenience called the Celebrant. It requires a few actual symbolic objects which may take any form pleasing to you and suitable for their purpose. If you are already a magical initiate it is likely you will have many of them to hand. There ought to be an altar or table upon which the elements of the communion may be placed, together with your Grail-symbol and some lighted candles or lamps. An ideal arrangement for this celebration is that on a raised section at the back of the centre of the altar is the Grail symbol, veiled with an ornate cover. Either side is a single lighted candle, Below it is an ever-burning altar light, which may be a nightlight in a glass holder or a small oil lamp. Either side of that are the platter of bread, a chalice of wine or fruit juice or even spring water, and a small dish of salt. If you use incense or joss sticks these should be to one side where they will not get knocked over, or you could use a vase of scented flowers - roses or lilies are particularly relevant. The Celebrant may be robed or in ordinary dress, but some kind of ritual sash or pendant is a good idea as this acts as a focus of priestly power, and putting it on helps that inner force to surface so that the Communion is a magical as well as a mundane act. When all is prepared, and the congregation ready and still, and the Celebrant has become a true priest, a ritual along the following lines may commence:*

**Cele:** Let us now go to the Green Chapel. It has many forms. You may see it as a small stone building, dimly lit, within the midst of the Old Forest. Trees overshadow it, and climbing creepers enfold it. The light which enters the eastern window, above a simple altar, is also green from the foliage all about it. It feels very cool and peaceful. On the altar, made of grey stone with a white cover, The Grail stands, veiled from your sight. Some of you may see the older Chapel in the Green. Here amid the primal forest which once covered much of our landscape, you enter a small space of closely nibbled turf, where grey rocks make seats, and where vast, ancient oaks shade the sacred grove. Nearby the constant sound of a small stream, trickling over pebbles makes a background to the songs of wild birds, and the gentle stirring of leaves above your head. It feels a holy and blessed place of great power and your awareness sinks into its peace and sanctity.

We have each come here on our quest for the secret of life and the key to joy. We have come to partake, to share and to experience in our own way, the Communion of the Grail, which is, and was, and is yet to come.

Let us call upon the Guardians of the place that they may show us the Mystery, and bless our Communion.

I call upon Gabriel, Archangel of the Chalice, Healer and Messenger of Light - protect us now, and in our daily lives.

I call upon Bride, Goddess of Springs, and daughter of the Keeper of the Cauldron, to inspire and awaken our ancient wisdom within us, that this secret source may nourish our spirits.

Let us pause to meditate upon the Mystery of the Grail. Let us call upon its Keeper that in due time we may each perceive it in the form best suited to us, as we go forward on the path to enlightenment, that we may know it for what it truly is. PAUSE
Although we may not yet be ready to drink from the Holy Grail, we may share, in symbol, the wine of blessed inspiration and taste the gifts of the Eternal Creator.

Lady of Earth, bless this bread that it may awaken in us the links with the source of all creation, and strengthen our will to good. Lord of the Sky, bless this wine that in its symbolic sharing we may all join the Company of the Chosen Ones, to bring Light and Life and Joy into the world, for all the people. Great Spirit, bless this salt, whose pure grains echo the Mystery concealed in our world, yet known and acknowledged by the wise. Grant we may be of that number. So may this be.

Companions, please partake of these symbolic elements, for here is a Mystery.

*Each in turn comes forward and takes bread dipped into the salt and a sip of the wine, bows before the covered Grail-symbol, then says:*

**Communicant**: I HAVE PARTAKEN OF THE SYMBOLIC GIFTS OF THE GRAIL - MAY I ATTAIN THESE IN REALITY

*When all have partaken, the Celebrant empties the Chalice and upturns it on the platter. It is customary that a set of prayers for Peace in the World, for Healing of the Sick, for a Wider Understanding of the Mysteries, and for Plenty and Protection of the Earth should follow, according to your own tradition.*

**All**: Blessed are they that set out upon the Endless Quest,
Blessed are they who walk in Darkness, seeking the Light,
Blessed are they, who abandoning all earthly things, seek
out the Gates of Paradise,
That they may lead all beings to their rightful home.
Be our ways forever blessed - May blessing be.

**Cele**: Alone, we have partaken of the Gifts of the Grail, yet we shall seek to share the Light of the Mystery revealed to our world. From the place of the Grail there comes a Light:

*The Celebrant picks up the lamp and passes it clockwise around the Company.*

**Cele**: *I* give you this Light that you may find enlightenment.

**Each in turn**: *I* TAKE THE LIGHT BUT WOULD GLADLY SHARE IT.

**Cele**: From our small circle may the Light of the Grail spread throughout the whole world.
From the peace of the Chapel in the Green let us all gently return to our own place, and bring with us the Blessings of the Grail to around us.
There is a blessing on all who serve.

* * *

*This ceremony should be said slowly, and with plenty of time for thought and meditation. Suitable music can be recorded to accompany it or made during the ritual, and songs or chants may be used as you feel suit the purpose and atmosphere. From this very basic pattern a much more elaborate and magical ceremony could be developed, or it could be incorporated within any standard magical lodge working If any of the words of power or images distress you, change them to your own tradition - this could be far more Christian or pagan depending on your own feelings. Allow the inspiration of the Grail to teach you, so that you may build up a potent Mass to say alone, or with friends, as circumstances permit. Like most magical rituals, it is possible to incorporate a working for a specific healing of the sick; you may ask questions by some form of divination, before the Communion, so that your awakened senses may provide a true answer, and many other sorts of beneficial request maybe made, as need dictates. As your skill to enter these other realms develops, and your awareness of the power of the Grail in its many forms comes clearer, you will find greater ways to use that power for the good of all around you. That is part of the purpose of the quest.*

## WHOM DOES THE GRAIL SERVE?

### The Procession of the Grail

*This exercise is intended to be performed by at least five people, though as many as you wish maybe included as part of the Company of the Grail: A suitable quiet room, with a door that can be sealed, will be needed. Apart from this you will need: a table (preferably round); some chairs or cushions; a bell or similar; some wine and bread; a cup; a spear; a wide, shallow dish; and a candlestick. All those not acting as officers should carry either tapers or nightlights. You may wish to place a central light on the table before you begin. Robes may be worn, but this is not essential as it is the intention of the work which is important.*

*Begin by appointing someone in the room to read aloud the Composition of Place, which should be treated like any other meditation - listen to the words with eyes closed and allow the images to rise naturally before you. As the rest of the working proceeds those not actively involved may like to keep their eyes shut, listening and letting the words sink deeply within. The five officers wait outside the room until summoned by the ringing of the bell. The text is from Malory's timeless version.*

## Composition of Place

The king and all his followers went home unto Camelot, and so went to evensong in the great minster, and so after that to supper, and every knight sat in his own place ... Then anon they heard cracking and crying of thunder, and in the midst of this blast entered a sunbeam more clear by seven times than ever they saw day, and all there were alighted with the grace of the Holy Spirit. Then began every knight to behold other, by their seeming, fairer than ever they saw before, yet among them was no knight who might speak one word a great while, and so they looked every man on the other as though they had been dumb ... And there was all the place filled with good odours, and every knight had such meats and drinks as he best *loved* in this world, and then there entered into the hall the Holy Grail, and a Light borne before it, and a Spear behind, and lastly a fair goodly Dish with bread upon it ...

*Door Warden or person deputized rings the bell to show that the work is begun. The procession enters and circumnambulates the room three times. On the third circuit, each bearer of the Grail Hallows peels off to their place at the four quarters: Candle-bearer to the east, Spear-bearer to the south, Grail-bearer to the west, Dish-bearer to the north. Fisher King sits slightly outside the circle to the south-west. The door is sealed. A place is left vacant to represent the Siege Perilous.*

**Fisher King:**      What illumines the Waste Land?

(Pause for all to consider the answer in their hearts.)

**Candle-bearer:**      A light for all pilgrims.

**Fisher King:**    Why does the Spear drip with blood? *PAUSE*

**Spear-bearer:** In token of Sacrifice.

**Fisher King:** Whom does the Grail serve? *PAUSE*

**Grail-bearer:** The servants of Creation.

**Fisher King:** What is the Harvest of the Waste Land? *PAUSE*

**Dish-bearer:** Nourishment for all pilgrims.

*Dish-bearer then goes round the table/room clockwise, offering a piece of bread to everyone, stopping at the Siege Perilous in reverence for the One Who Will Come and leaving bread at this place. Grail-bearer circulates with Grail, giving to drink of the cup to all there. When all have partaken, the Grail is left at the Siege Perilous. The Spear-bearer circulates, passing the Spear over the heads of each person present. At conclusion he lays the Spear before the Siege Perilous. The Fisher King then goes forward to stand before the Grail and the Hallows, saying:*

**Fisher King:**      It is still dark as we pour this Cup *(pours a libation),* but Light dawns over Logres as we raise the Cup *(lifts Grail high)* against the day when we will commemorate the Deliverance of the Waste Land. We set this Cup aside as a sign of hope for the beginning of that redemption, awaiting the One Who Will Come *(sets Cup down).*

*Candle-bearer circulates, lighting everyone's taper from his own.*
*Fisher King returns to his place.*

**Fisher King:**      Let all those who sit this night at the Table of the Grail, who have eaten and drunk of its bounty and its love, raise their lights in token of redemption of the Waste Land *(All raise their lights).*

Send forth your thoughts to all those in need of healing and strength; to all those, far and near, who are with us in spirit; to the orders of Creation, creatures of sea, land, earth and air; to tree and spring; to hill and stone; to the earth and all which is in our keeping. *PAUSE*

Let us put out the light of the Grail in the knowledge that it burns still within us *(All douse tapers)*. There is a blessing upon all who serve.

*Doorwarden strikes bell once and unseals the door. The Grail Hallows bearers make three reverse circumnambulations, leading off with the Dishbearer. The remainder may wish to stay in silent contemplation for a while.*

# Endword

The quest can never be entirely completed, for like all acts of creation, until the world of that creation has become as dust swirling among the distant stars of outer space, the task is unfinished. Until each single seeker has found the Grail within and the Grail of their outer world, the Never-ending Quest cannot cease. The Grail, which is the container of Time, will not be emptied of its stored ages until Time ceases to be, and there is only the Grail Maker left, with the empty cup.

> And when Thyself, with shining foot shall pass
> Among the guests, star-scattered on the grass,
> And in Thy joyous errand reach the spot,
> Where I once was - turn down an empty glass...

(*Rubaiyat* of Omar Khayyam)

Now, Voyager, sail thou forth to seek and find...

(Walt Whitman)

# Contact Details

## John Matthews

*Hallowquest Newsletter* For details of forthcoming books and courses with Caitlín & John Matthews, send for their quarterly newsletter. Current subscription £8 (in UK) or $25 (outside UK). Send sterling cheque payable to Caitlín Matthews or US dollar bills (no foreign cheques) to Caitlín Matthews, BCM Hallowquest, London WC1N 3XX, U.K.
Website: www.Hallowquest.org.uk

## Marian Green
BCM-SCL Quest, London, WC1N 3XX. UK.

Foundation for Inspirational and Oracular Studies or FíOS founded by Caitlín & John Matthews and Felicity Wombwell is dedicated to shamanism and the oral and sacred arts. Each year the most inspiring exponents of living sacred traditions give practical courses. FíOS also offers an progressive programme of shamanic training world-wide. For more details of events and courses, write to Caitlín Matthews at BCM Hallowquest, London WC1N 3XX, United Kingdom. Membership of FíOS is currently (in 2003) £15 a year, giving members four issues of the Hallowquest newsletter and discounts on special events. Send a sterling cheque for £15 (within UK) payable to Felicity Wombwell to the address above: overseas subscribers, please send a sterling bank draft for £30.

# Bibliography

## List A: Texts

*Didot Perceval: The Romance of Perceval in Prose:* trans. D. Skeels
(Univ. Washington Press, 1966).

*Diu Crone (the Crown)* Heinrich von dem Tulin, trans by J.W.
Thomas (University of Nebraska, 1989)

*The Elucidation,* in *The Quest of the Holy Grail:* S. Evans (J. M. Dent,
1892).

*Joseph of Arimathea, Merlin and Perceval* by Robert de Boron.
Trans by N. Bryant as *Merlin & the Grail* (D.S. Brewer, 2001)

*Lancelot-Grail (formerly Vulgate Cycle) The Old French
Arrthguyrian Vulgate and Posdt Vukgate in Translation. Norris J.
Lacy General Editor (5 vols; Garland Publishing, 1993-1999)*

*Morte d'Arthur: Thomas Malory Ed. J. Matthews (Orion, 2000).*

*Parzival:* Wolfram von Eschenbach, trans. A. T. Heath (Penguin, 1980)

*Perceval: The Story of the Grail:* Chrétien de Troyes, trans. N. Briant -
including the *Three Continuations (D. S. Brewer, 1982).*

*Perlesvaus: The High Book of the Grail:* trans. N. Briant (D. S. Brewer,
1978).

*Peredur,* in the *Mabinogion:* trans. J. Gantz (Penguin, 1976).

*Preiddeu Annwn,* in *Taliesin, the Last Celtic Shaman,* John Matthews
(Inner Traditions, 2002).

*Quest of the Holy Grail (Queste del San Graal):* trans. P. M.
Matarasso (Penguin, 1969).

## List B: General Studies

Adams, H. : *Mont St. Michel et Chartres* (Bison /Hamlyn, 1980).

Allen, P M. (ed.): A *Christian Rosenkrantz Anthology* (RS Press, 1968)

Anderson, F : *The Ancient Secret* (Gollancz, 1953).

Ashe, G,: *King Arthurs Avalon* (Fontana, 1973).

Baigent, M.; Leigh, R. & Lincoln, H.: *The Holy Blood and the Holy
Grail* (Cape, 1983).

Barber, R.: *The Reign of Chivalry* (David and Charles, 1980).

Barto, P. S.: *Tannhauser and the Mountain of Venus (OUP,* 1916).

Beckett, M.: *The Pyramid and the Grail* (Lailoken Press, 1984).

Bond, F. Bligh: *The Company of Avalon* (Blackwell, 1924).

Brown, A. C. L.: *Origin of the Grail Legend* (Harvard University Press, 1943).

Cavendish, R.: *King Arthur and the Grail* (Weidenfeld & Nicholson, 1978).

Darcy, A.M. *Wisdom and the Grail* (Four Courts Press, 2000).

Durrell, Shelly *Healing the Fisher King* (Art Tao Press, 2002).

Evola, J.: *The Mystery of the Grail (* Inner Traditions, 1994).

Fairbairn, N.: *Kingdoms of Arthur* (Evans Bros, 1983).

Fisher, L.: *The Mystic Vision* (AMS Press, 1966).

Fortune, D.: *Avalon of the Heart* (Aquarian Press, 1971).

Gardner, Laurence: *Bloodline of the Holy Grail* (Element Books, 1996).

Gray, W. G.: *The Sangraal Sacrament* (Weiser, USA, 1985).

Griffin, J.E.: *The Holy Grail* (McFarland & Co, 2002).

Guest, Lady Charlotte: *The Mabinogion* (Everyman, 1906).

Green, Marian: *A Harvest of Festivals* (Longman, 1980).

Green, Marian: *Wild Witchcraft* (Thorsons, 2002).

Green, Marian: *The Path Through the Labyrinth* (Thoth, 1996).

Green, Marian: *The Gentle Arts of Natural Magic* (Thoth, 1996).

Graves, Tom: *Dowsing* (Aquarian Press, 1978).

Hall, M. P. : *Orders of the Quest* (Philosophical Research Soc., 1949).

Houghton, Rosemary: *Tales from Eternity* (Allen & Unwin, 1973).

Jaffray, R.: *King Arthur and the Holy Grail* (Putnam, 1928).

Jung, Emma and von Franz, M. L.: *The Grail Legend* (Hodder, 1972).

Kahane, Henry and Rene *The Krater and the Grail*.(University of Illinois Press, 1965).

Knight, Gareth: *The Secret Tradition in Arthurian Legend* (Aquarian Press, 1984).

Littleton, C. Scott & Linda A. Malcor *From Scythia to Camelot* (Garland Publishing, 1994).

Loomis, R. S.: *The Grail - from Celtic Myth to Christian Symbol* (Univ. of Wales, 1963).

Maltwood, K. *Enchantments of Britain* (James Clark, 1982).

Maltwood, K. *Glastonbury's Temple of the Stars* (James Clark, 1982).

Mann, William F. *The Labyrinth of the Grail* (Laughing Owl Publishing,1999).

Matchett, E. and Trevelyan, Sir G.: *Twelve Seats at the Round Table* (N.Spearman, 1971).

Matthews, C. and J. *The Western Way,* 2 vols. (Revised edition, Inner Traditions, 2003).

Matthews, C. and J. *The Arthurian Tarot* (Aquarian Press, 1990).

Matthews, C. *King Arthur and the Goddess of the Land* ( Inner Traditions, 2002).

Matthews, C. *Mabon and the Guardians of Celtic Britain* (Inner Traditions, 2002).

Matthews, J. King *Arthur and the Grail Quest* (Blandford, 1995).

Matthews, J. (ed.) : *At the Table of the Grail* (revised edition, Watkins Books, 2002).

Matthews, J. (ed) : *A Glastonbury Reader* (Aquarian Press, 1991).

Matthews, J. *Elements of the Grail Tradition* (Element Books, 1989).

Matthews, J. *The Grail: Quest for the Eternal* (Thames & Hudson, 1981).

Matthews, J. *Healing the Wounded King* (Element Books, 1999).

Matthews, J. (ed.) *Sources of the Grail* (Floris Books, 1996).

Matthews, J. *Taliesin, the Last Celtic Shaman* (Inner Traditions, 2001).

Merry, E. *I am - The Ascent of Mankind* (Rider, 1944).

Michell, M. *Tears and Threads of Enchantment* in *'The Green Book'*, No.5, 1981.

Moorman, C. *Arthurian Triptych* (Russell & Russell, 1960).

Morduch, A.: *The Sovereign Adventure* (James Clark, 1970).

Nutt, A.: *Studies on the Legend of the Holy Grail* (Cooper Sq., 1965).

Owen, D. D. R.: *The Evolution of the Grail Legend* (Oliver & Boyd, 1968).

Oldenbourg, Z.: *Massacre at Montsegur* (Weidenfeld, 1969).

Pratchett, Terry.: *Lords and Ladies (Corgi, 1993)*

Ralls-Macleod, K. & Ian Robertson.: *The Quest for the Celtic Key* (Luath Press, 2002)

Ravenscroft, T.: *The Spear of Destiny* (Neville Spearman, 1972).

Ravenscroft, T . *The Cup of Destiny)* (Rider 1981*)*.

Richardson, A.: *The Gate of Moon* (Aquarian Press, 1984).

Roberts, A. (ed.): *Glastonbury* (Rider, 1978).

Rowling, J.K.: *Harry Potter and the Goblet of Fire* (Bloomsbury, 2001).

Rolt-Wheeler, F.: *Mystic Gleams from the Holy Grail* (Rider, 1948).

Sansonetti, Paul-George: *Graal et alchemie* (Berg, 1985).

Saint-Hillaire, Paul: *Bruges - cite du Graal* (Rossel, 1978).

Schmidt, K.: *The Message of the Grail* (CSA Press, 1975).

Sinclair, Andrew: *The Secret Scroll* (Sinclair Stevenson, 2001).

Sinclair, Andrew: *The Sword and the Grail* (Crown, 1992)

Spence, Lewis: *The Mysteries of Britain* (McKay, USA, 1946).

Spiegelmann, J. M.: *The Quest* (Falcon Press, 1984).

Senior, M.: *Myths of Britain* (Orbis, 1983).

Steiner, Rudolf: *Christ and the Spiritual World* (R. Steiner Press, 1963).

Stewart, R. J.: *Advanced Magical Arts* (Thoth, 2004).

Stewart, R. J.: *Living Magical Arts* ( Thoth, 2004).

Stewart, R. J.: *The Underworld Initiation* (Aquarian Press, 1985).

Stewart, R. J.: *The Prophetic Visions of Merlin* (Arkana, 1985).

Waite, A. E.: *The Hidden Church of the Holy Grail* (Redman, 1909).

Weston, J. L.: *From Ritual to Romance* (Doubleday, 1957).

Weston, J. L.: *Legends of Sir Perceval,* 2 vols. (D. Nutt, 1906).

Westwood, J.: *Albion - Guide to Legendary Britain* (Granada, 1985).

Whitehead, J.: *Guardian of the Grail* (Jarrold, 1959).

Wyatt, I.: *From Round Table to Grail Castle* (Lantern Press, 1981).

Valiente, Doreen: *Natural Magic* (Hale, 1985).

## List C: Fiction and Poetry

There are literally hundreds of books of fiction concerning the Holy Grail, King Arthur and his Knights, quests and Celtic or Arthurian themes, some rewritten as science fiction or fantasy tales, including computer games, board games, cassette tapes of journeys and role playing adventures, all based on this material. New ones are constantly becoming available, and the list could be extended indefinitely. Here is a brief list of the most relevant works, many of which make excellent material for Grail meditations.

Ashley, M. (ed).: *The Chronicles of the Holy Grail* ( Carrol & Graf, 1996)

Attanasio, A. A.: *Kingdom of the Grail* (Harper Collins, 1997).

Canning, Victor.: *The Crimson Chalice* (Heinemann, 1976).

Chapman, Vera.: *The Three Damosels* (Methuen, 1978).

Clarke, Lindsay.: *Parzival and the Stone from Heaven* ( Harper Collins, 2001).

Cooper, Susan.: *The Dark is Rising* (Chatto, 1973).

Cornwell, Bernard.: *The Grail Quest 1: Harlequin, 2: Vagabond* (Harper Collins, 2000-2002).

Eliot, T. S.: *The Waste Land and other poems* (Faber, 1920).

Erskine, John.: *Galahad* (Nash & Grayson, 1926).

Garner, Alan.: *Elidor* (William Collins & Sons, 1965).

Greeley, Andrew M.: *The Magic Cup* (McGraw Hill, 1979).

Holdstock, Robert.: *The Iron Grail* (Simon & Schuster, 2002)

Hunter, Jim: *Perceval and the Presence of God* (Faber, 1978).

Jones, David: *The Anathamata* (Faber, 1952).

Lewis, C. S.: *That Hideous Strength* (Bodley Head, 1945).

Machen, Arthur: *The Secret Glory* (Secker & Warburg, 1922).

Mitchison, Naomi: *To the Chapel Perilous* (Green Knight Publishing, 2000).

Monarco, Richard: *Parsifal* (Macdonald, 1977).

Monarco, Richard: *The Grail War* (Sphere Books, 1981).

Monarco, Richard: *The Final Quest* (Sphere Books, 1982).

Monarco, Richard: *Blood and Dreams* (Berkeley, 1985).

Morland, Harold: *The Matter of Britain* (Graal Publications, 1985).

Powys, John Cowper: *A Glastonbury Romance* (Bodley Head, 1933).

Powys, John Cowper: *Porius* (Colgate University Press, 1998).

Steinbeck, John: *The Acts of King Arthur and his Noble Knights* (Pan, 1979).

Stewart, Mary: *The Hollow Hills* (Coronet, 1974).

Sutcliff, Rosemary: *Light Beyond the Forest* (Bodley Head, 1979).

Tarr, Judith.: *Kingdom of the Grail* (Roc, 2000)

Tennyson, Sir Alfred: *The Holy Grail* (Strahan & Co., 1870).

Toynbee, Philip.: *Tea with Mrs. Goodman* (Horizon, 1947).

Trevor, Meriol.: *The Sparrow Child* (Collins, 1958).

Williams, Charles.: *War in Heaven* (Gollancz, 1930).

Williams, Charles.: *Taliessin Through Logres and the Region of the Summer Stars.*

Zimmer-Bradley, Marion.: *The Mists of Avalon* (Knopf, USA, 1983).

## Tape

A Tape of the Meditations in this book is available, read by John & Caitlin Matthews, with an introduction by Marian Green, from BCM Hallowquest, London, WC1N 3XX.

# Index

# Other titles from Thoth Publications

## APPRENTICED TO MAGIC
*By W.E.Butler*

This volume is for the true aspirant after magical attainment. In his earlier books the author has defined the real magical art and described the training to be undergone by the serious student. Now he goes a step further, and has written a book which, if properly read, meditated upon, and followed up, will bring those who are ready to the doors of the Mysteries.

This book is not for those who seek sensation. It has been written by one who has himself followed the magical path as a sound and competent guide for all who seek initiation into the Western Mysteries.

Contents include:

Application Accepted
First Exercises
Postures and Breathing
Meditation
The Tree of Life
The Tree as an Indicator
The Contact of Power
Bring Through the Power
The Gates are Open

ISBN 1-870450-41-8

## PRINCIPLES OF HERMETIC PHILOSOPHY
*By* Dion Fortune and Gareth Knight

*Principles of Hermetic Philosophy* together with *The Esoteric Philosophy of Astrology* are the last known works written by Dion Fortune. They appeared in her Monthly letters to members and associates of the Society of the Inner Light between November 1942 and March 1944.

Her intention in these works is summed up in her own words: "The observations in these pages are an attempt to gather together the fragments of a forgotten wisdom and explain and expand them in the light of personal observation."

She was uniquely equipped to make highly significant personal observations in these matters as one of the leading practical occultists of her time. What is more, in these later works she feels less constrained by traditions of occult secrecy and takes an altogether more practical approach than in her earlier, well known textbooks.

Gareth Knight takes the opportunity to amplify her explanations and practical exercises with a series of full page illustrations, and provides a commentary on her work

ISBN 1-870450-34-5

\*       \*       \*       \*       \*

## THE STORY OF DION FORTUNE
As told to Charles Fielding and Carr Collins.

Dion Fortune and Aleister Crowley stand as the twentieth century's most influential leaders of the Western Esoteric Tradition. They were very different in their backgrounds, scholarship and style.

But, for many, Dion Fortune is the chosen exemplar of the Tradition - with no drugs, no homosexuality and no kinks. This book tells of her formative years and of her development.

At the end, she remains a complex and enigmatic figure, who can only be understood in the light of the system she evolved and worked to great effect.

There can be no definitive "Story of Dion Fortune". This book must remain incompete and full of errors. However, readers may find themselves led into an experience of initiation as envisaged by this fearless and dedicated woman.

ISBN 1-870450-33-7

# THE FORGOTTEN MAGE

The Magical Lectures of Colonel C.R.F. Seymour.
*Edited by Dolores Ashcroft-Nowicki*

Charles Seymour was a man of many talents and considerable occult skills. The friend and confidant of Dion Fortune, he worked with her and his magical partner, Christine Hartley, for many productive years.

As one of the Inner Circle of Dion Fortune's Society of the Inner Light, Seymour was a High Priest in every sense of the word, but he was also one of the finest teachers of the occult art to emerge this century.

In the past, little of Seymour's work has been widely available, but in this volume Dolores Ashcroft-Nowicki, Director of Studies of the Servants of the Light School of Occult Science, has gathered together a selection of the best of Seymour's work. His complex scholarship and broad background knowledge of the Pagan traditions shine through in articles which include: The Meaning of Initiation; Magic in the Ancient Mystery Religions; The Esoteric Aspect of Religion; Meditations for Temple Novices; The Old Gods; The Ancient Nature Worship and The Children of the Great Mother.

ISBN 1-870450-29-9

# PRACTICAL MAGIC AND THE WESTERN MYSTERY TRADITION

*Unpublished Essays and Articles by W. E. Butler.*

W. E. Butler, a devoted friend and colleague of the celebrated occultist Dion Fortune, was among those who helped build the Society of the Inner Light into the foremost Mystery School of its day. He then went on to found his own school, the Servants of the Light, which still continues under the guidance of Dolores Ashcroft-Nowicki, herself an occultist and author of note and the editor and compiler of this volume.

PRACTICAL MAGIC AND THE WESTERN TRADITION is a collection of previously unpublished articles, training papers, and lectures covering many aspects of practical magic in the context of western occultism that show W. E. Butler not only as a leading figure in the magical tradition of the West, but also as one of its greatest teachers.

Subjects covered include:

What makes an Occultist
Ritual Training
Inner Plane Contacts and Rays
The Witch Cult
Keys in Practical Magic
Telesmatic Images
Words of Power
An Explanation of Some Psychic Phenomena

ISBN 1-870450-32-9

## THE PATH THROUGH THE LABYRINTH
*by* Marian Green

The Quest for Initiation into the Western Mystery Tradition.

Underlying the evolving culture of the West there hides a complete strata of folk-lore, of traditional skills and wisdom, of ancient arts and festivals.

These are still emerging in myth and legend, in song and celebrations, each retaining aspects of a very great initiatory system rooted in the land and its magic.

Most available sources tell the reader about the how to of magic, but for the first time this book explores the way of magic, and the what happens when... of modern magical techniques.

In *The Path Through the Labyrinth*, Marian Green, a highly respected practitioner and teacher of the Western Tradition, examines these questions and guides the reader safely to the heart of the magical maze, and then out again.

ISBN 1-870450-15-9

*     *     *     *     *

## PRACTICAL TECHNIQUES OF MODERN MAGIC
*by* Marian Green

What is the essence of ritual magic?
How are the symbols used to create change?
Can I safely take steps in ritual on my own?
How does magic fit into the pattern of life in the modern world?
Will I be able to master the basic arts?

All these questions and many more are answered within the pages of this book.

ISBN 1-870450-14-0